AFTER THE ACT

After the Act describes the aftermath of the recent removal under LASPO of public funding from legal services in family matters other than in defined cases such as child protection and domestic abuse. Through analysis of the policy context, interviews with key players, observation of services provided by lawyers, students, lay support workers and the advice sector, the authors outline the work being done and the skills being used in a range of settings.

The book raises questions not only about access to family justice, but about the role of law in family matters in an increasingly post-legal society.

Fragmentation of the market in the new services offering information, initial advice, online or alternative dispute resolution – but rarely ongoing casework – raises questions about where costs fall and how quality can be assured. Many of these services are forms of private ordering, where outcomes are hard to assess.

If neither the state nor the individual can afford full legal services where the best interests of any child involved are of paramount importance, and lawyers negotiate to make best use of the resources available, perhaps it is time to consider using lawyers differently, with lay support, to solve problems before they become disputes.

After the Act

Access to Family Justice after LASPO

Mavis Maclean
and
John Eekelaar

•HART•
OXFORD • LONDON • NEW YORK • NEW DELHI • SYDNEY

HART PUBLISHING

Bloomsbury Publishing Plc

Kemp House, Chawley Park, Cumnor Hill, Oxford, OX2 9PH, UK

HART PUBLISHING, the Hart/Stag logo, BLOOMSBURY and the Diana logo are
trademarks of Bloomsbury Publishing Plc

First published in Great Britain 2019

A catalogue record for this book is available from the British Library.

Library of Congress Cataloging-in-Publication data

Names: Maclean, Mavis, author. | Eekelaar, John, author.

Title: After the act : access to family justice after LASPO / Mavis Maclean, John Eekelaar.

Description: Oxford, UK ; Portland, Oregon : Hart Publishing, 2019. |
Includes bibliographical references and index.

Identifiers: LCCN 2018053024 (print) | LCCN 2018056243 (ebook) |
ISBN 9781509920204 (EPub) | ISBN 9781509920198 (hardback)

Subjects: LCSH: Legal aid—England. | Domestic relations—England. |
Great Britain. Legal Aid, Sentencing and Punishment of Offenders Act 2012.

Classification: LCC KD512 (ebook) | LCC KD512 .M33 2019 (print) | DDC 346.4201/5—dc23

LC record available at https://lccn.loc.gov/2018053024

ISBN: HB: 978-1-50992-019-8
        ePDF: 978-1-50992-021-1
        ePub: 978-1-50992-020-4

Typeset by Compuscript Ltd, Shannon
Printed and bound in Great Britain by TJ International Ltd, Padstow, Cornwall

To find out more about our authors and books visit www.hartpublishing.co.uk.
Here you will find extracts, author information, details of forthcoming events
and the option to sign up for our newsletters.

PREFACE

The removal of most private law family matters from the scope of family legal aid under the Legal Aid Sentencing and Punishment of Offenders Act 2012 has had an unprecedented impact on access to legal help in family matters, despite the valiant attempts of courts and lawyers, students and volunteers, and the advisers of the Third Sector to mitigate this. As government began to prepare for reviewing the effects of implementation of the Act, we began to try to put together a picture of the various attempts being made to fill this 'LASPO Gap' in publicly supported legal help to family members, in order to inform the expected debate.

We felt it was necessary to set the present scene in its historical context, so this account starts with the historical and policy context of family legal aid, here and in some other jurisdictions. We have analysed existing data, and spent many hours talking with those involved throughout the country.

We cannot give more than a snapshot picture. We have, however, learned a great deal with the willing help of many of those concerned, despite the increased pressures they are experiencing. We would like to acknowledge this help, and repeat our thanks and appreciation. As always with this kind of research, many of those who spoke with us wish to remain anonymous. We therefore cannot thank them by name here, but have done so privately. They are aware of our gratitude.

We express our particular thanks to the former President of the Family Division, Sir James Munby, for helping us to contact the Designated Family Judges. We are most grateful to the members of the legal professions to whom we spoke, especially with regard to the Bar Pro Bono Unit, LawWorks, the Law Society, and CILEx. We were enabled to learn about and observe the involvement of students in Clinical Legal Education programmes, and to observe support in court provided by the Personal Support Unit and at the RCJ CAB at the Central Family Court. We were able to discuss the impact of Public Legal Education support to Law for Life who through the Legal Education Fund are providing the AdviceNow website and the work of major law firms, including DLA Piper, which have been sending young partners to run advice sessions in a number of settings. We are grateful for all the help we were given.

At the same time, the advice sector, which had little involvement in the field of family justice while legal aid provision was available, began to shoulder new burdens of demand for such help at a time of rising pressures on the resources of all voluntary agencies during the period of austerity which has followed the 2008 financial crisis. Citizens Advice has not only developed new expertise but also carried out research into practice, and has been involved in thinking about enhanced advice with lay advisers being given specific training in an area of law.

The Advice Services Alliance is addressing new ways of providing and quality assuring advice work, local advice agencies are developing family work in cooperation with local solicitors, as are Child Poverty Action Group and many more, while Gingerbread has developed secondary consultation whereby lay advisers are supported by practising lawyers. When we discussed their work with us, not only were our questions answered and discussed, but we were welcomed into a wide variety of clinics and centres. We thank them for that.

As this book goes to press in December 2018, the LASPO Review team are preparing to publish their report. We understand that resources are severely limited. And we are aware that current policy thinking must be about moving forward rather than looking back to the old days of legal aid. The focus is on new developments, particularly digital courts and processes, and on drawing on the work of the advice sector. There is growing interest in bringing together the various forms of information, advice and support into a more collaborative body of activity. Replacing lawyers with mediators is no longer the agreed panacea.

If we are to move forward safely after this period of crisis in access to family justice, and without further damage, we will need to develop a more nuanced understanding of the different ways in which law matters. It is more than dispute resolution. The rule of law is concerned with the development and awareness of social norms, and the mechanisms for encouraging and supporting them for everyone, not just those who can afford a lawyer. Legal help and support with legal issues already come, and will continue to come, not only from lawyers, but from a far wider group of providers.

We hope that this account of the struggle to provide information, advice and support to those with family legal problems may contribute to the debate which will follow the review process.

Mavis Maclean
John Eekelaar
Oxford, December 2018

CONTENTS

1

Family Legal Problems
and the Collapse of the Supportive State

I. Introduction

The Legal Aid, Sentencing and Punishment of Offenders Act (LASPO) 2012 removed private family law matters, with a few exceptions, from the scope of publicly funded legal help and representation. In 2017 its effects on all areas affected by the legal aid reforms (not just family) were closely examined in a Memorandum submitted by the Ministry of Justice to Parliament's Justice Committee as the first stage in the post-implementation review of the Act which began to collect information in March 2018.[1] In January 2015, the Ministry of Justice had been criticised in the Thirty-Sixth Report of the House of Commons Public Accounts Committee[2] over the lack of evidence about the effects of the legal aid changes. In March 2015 the House of Commons Justice Committee[3] reviewed the stated objectives for the reforms, namely: (1) to discourage unnecessary adversarial litigation; (2) to target legal aid at those most in need; (3) to make substantial savings in legal aid expenditure; and (4) to bring about better value for money for the taxpayer. It concluded that, while the reforms had succeeded in making significant savings in the cost of the scheme, they had not achieved the other three out of the four objectives and indeed had harmed access to justice for some litigants.

The Memorandum sought to assess the changes against the four declared objectives of the reforms. As regards objective (1), the Memorandum acknowledged the failure to divert family cases to mediation and to reduce family court proceedings. But it noted the difficulty in attributing this to LASPO,[4] as it did

---

[1] Ministry of Justice, *Legal Aid, Sentencing and Punishment of Offenders Act 2012: Post-Legislative Memorandum submitted to the Justice Select Committee*, October 2017 (Cm 9486): https://assets. publishing.service.gov.uk/government/uploads/system/uploads/attachment_data/file/655971/ LASPO-Act-2012-post-legislative-memorandum.pdf (last accessed 29 May 2018).
[2] https://www.parliament.uk/documents/commons-committees/public-accounts/HC%20808%20 civil%20aid%20final%20(web%20version)%20v2.pdf (last accessed 9 June 2018).
[3] House of Commons Justice Committee, *Impact of changes to civil legal aid under Part 1 of the Legal Aid, Sentencing and Punishment of Offenders Act 2012 Eighth Report of Session 2014–15 Report* (4 March 2015). https://publications.parliament.uk/pa/cm201415/cmselect/cmjust/311/311.pdf (last accessed 9 June 2018).
[4] Note 1, para 166.

the difficulty in evaluating the success of (2).[5] (3) had clearly been achieved,[6] but insofar as assessing (4) required looking at society as a whole, that would require considering the overall impact of the reforms 'on organisations such as charities, advice providers, individuals with justice problems and so on' which was a 'difficult task' requiring cost-benefit analysis.[7] However, in the Terms of Reference of the Evidence Gathering Exercise for the Review it is concluded that 'it is right that the government takes the time to assess the extent to which the objectives of the LASPO changes were achieved. In addition, this process of consultation and engagement with interested parties also represents an opportunity for the government to consider what the future should look like'.[8]

This book does not purport to undertake those difficult tasks. However, it does try to throw light on how those reforms have altered the forms of assistance that may be available to those experiencing what can generally be described as 'family' problems of a legal nature which do not involve the state (as in child protection cases) and who lack the resources to purchase such help. While we cannot supply any kind of sophisticated cost-benefit analysis, we are able to suggest how actual or incipient changes in professional roles might develop in response to the reforms, which have implications for public expenditure, the experience of citizens in need and the place of law in situations of family discord.

Much has been written about LASPO[9] and we will not spell out all the details, although we will provide a brief account of the background so the changes it has brought about can be seen in a wider perspective. We start by presenting data on the nature and scope of the issues with which we are concerned.

II. The Scope of the Problem

The problems or issues with which we are concerned might arise when a dispute or uncertainty arises over how parties in a family or family-type relationship should be required to behave towards each other. The words 'be required' suggest that the obligation is one that could reasonably be considered to be recognised by

---

[5] Note 1, para 187.

[6] Note 1, para 188.

[7] Note 1, para 209. On the problems of quantifying the overall economic effects of the reforms, see G Cookson, 'Analysing the Economic justification for the Reform to Social Welfare and Family Law Legal Aid' (2013) 34 *Journal of Social Welfare and Family Law* 21.

[8] https://assets.publishing.service.gov.uk/government/uploads/system/uploads/attachment_data/file/686576/pir-laspo-terms-of-reference.pdf (last accessed 29 May 2018).

[9] eg, A Paterson, *Lawyers and the Public Good: Democracy in Action?* (Cambridge University Press, 2012); Papers published in the *Journal of Social Welfare and Family Law, Special Issue*, vol 35, No 1 (2013); M Maclean, J Eekelaar and B Bastard (eds), *Delivering Family Justice in the 21st Century* (Hart Publishing, 2015); A Flynn and J Hodgson (eds), *Access to Justice and Legal Aid: Comparative Perspectives on Unmet Legal Need* (Hart Publishing, 2017); A Barlow, R Hunter, J Smithson and J Ewing, *Mapping Paths to Family Justice: Resolving Family Disputes in Neoliberal Times* (Palgrave, 2017).

the law, and is thus a legal problem, and it may be necessary to obtain advice as to whether it is so recognised. That itself is a legal question.

It is not easy to quantify the extent to which individuals experience the types of problem which could be legal problems as described above. Hazel Genn's pioneering study[10] aimed to elicit the extent to which people experienced a 'justiciable' problem over the period 1992–96 (five years) by asking specific questions in face-to-face interviews. The study covered a wide range of problems that people encounter, including those arising from family-type relationships. The questions included whether the respondent 'or your wife/partner' had been involved in divorce proceedings since January 1992, and if so, whether they had problems concerning division of money/property, payment of maintenance/child support, fostering or adopting a child, domestic violence, or inheritance;[11] or residence or contact regarding children under 18, child protection, abduction, 'or your child going to the school you want'.[12] These were reduced down to incidence figures for the whole sample of 4,125 respondents as 6 per cent having 'relationship' problems, 4 per cent divorce proceedings, and 3 per cent children problems.[13] There could be overlap between the categories, so the total incidence is probably 6 per cent or a little above. People across all income groups who experienced divorce or separation problems were more likely than people who experienced any other problem (eg, concerning faulty goods, employment difficulties, accidents or property issues) to seek advice, most often from a solicitor. They were the least likely to do nothing ('lump it').[14]

More recent information can be found in the English and Welsh Civil and Social Justice Surveys, based on face-to-face interviews of respondents from a survey of 10,537 adults drawn from a random selection of 6,234 household addresses across 390 postcode sectors in England and Wales. The survey published in 2010 gives figures given in Table 1 for surveys conducted in 2004 and 2006–09 of the percentages of respondents experiencing the listed 'civil justice problems' that had been 'difficult to resolve' in the preceding three years.[15] The survey published in 2013, also using face-to-face interviews, gives (for the period 2009–11) the information given in Table 2 for respondents who had experienced the stated 'problems' in the preceding 18 months (the words 'difficult to resolve' had been dropped). Wave 1 respondents were interviewed between June and October 2010; wave 2 respondents 18 months later.[16]

---

[10] H Genn, *Paths to Justice: What people do and think about going to law* (Hart Publishing, 1999).

[11] ibid, 303.

[12] ibid, 305.

[13] ibid, 23–4.

[14] ibid, 88–9.

[15] P Pleasence, N Balmer, A Patel and C Denvir, *English and Welsh Civil and Social Justice Survey* (Legal Services Commission 2010), Table 1.

[16] N Balmer, *English and Welsh Civil and Social Justice Panel Survey, Wave 2* (Legal Services Commission, 2013), Table 1.

Table 1 Respondents experiencing civil justice problems

	2004	2006–9
	N = 5015	N = 10537
	%	%
Divorce	2.1	2.0
Relationship b/d	1.6	1.8
Children	1.5	1.4
Domestic Violence	0.8	0.8
Totals	6.0	6.0

Table 2 Prevalence of civil justice problems

	Wave 1	Wave 2
	N = 3806	N = 3911
	%	%
Relationship breakdown	2.1	2.0
Divorce	1.1	1.2
Domestic violence	1.0	1.2
Care proceedings	0.2	0.2
Total	4.4	4.6

In 2016, Ipsos Mori published a large online survey of legal needs on behalf of the Law Society. 54 per cent of the 8,912 respondents had experienced 'issues or problems' over the past three years, and, of those, Table 3 gives the proportions who experienced problems on family-related issues.[17]

Table 3 Percentage of respondents experiencing issues or problems that were family-related

	%
	N = 4812
Relationship breakdown	10
Divorce/p'ship dissolution	6
Domestic violence	6
Children	3
Total	25

[17] Law Society and Legal Services Board, *Online survey of individuals' handling of legal issues in England and Wales 2015* (2016), para 4.1.1 and Table 4.1.

Since these proportions are of those who experienced some problem (about half of the total), the figures should be halved to represent proportions of the total. There will also be overlap between these categories, so the proportion experiencing problems associated with relationship breakdown would be 5 per cent or at most a little over. Finally, the Legal Problem and Resolution Survey (LPRS) 2014–15, published by the Ministry of Justice in 2017,[18] gives a figure of one per cent for an 18 month period across 2014–15 of those experiencing 'family problems' that 'people might encounter in everyday life' arising from relationship breakdown, such as division of property, financial arrangements and access to and care of children. It does not mention domestic violence. However, a further one per cent should be added for those who divorced, even though this did not represent a 'problem',[19] giving a total of two per cent. The survey was conducted by telephone with 10,058 respondents.

What can explain the differences in these results? One factor is the period over which respondents were asked to report their experiences. Genn's respondents reported experiences going back six years. The Law Society/Ipsos Mori reports, as well as those in the English and Welsh Civil and Social Justice Survey of 2010 covered three years, whilst the Wave 2 Survey and the LPRS respondents only reported on the last 18 months. One would expect respondents to report fewer experiences if reporting on a shorter time period. Still, it can perhaps be said that the problems with which we are concerned are probably experienced by somewhere between four and six per cent of the population[20] over a three year period, though of course a much larger portion of the population would experience this over a lifetime. It is also striking that people who *did* experience family problems as opposed to consumer or other problems were either the most likely or among the most likely to seek professional advice.[21]

In order better to understand how policies regarding the role of the legal system in these matters and the public support to be provided for its use have changed, we give a short account of the background to recent developments regarding legal aid in England and Wales.

[18] R Franklyn, T Budd, R Verrill and M Willoughby, *Legal Problem and Resolution Survey (LPRS) 2014–15* (Ministry of Justice, 2017), Figure 2.1.
[19] ibid, Appendix D.
[20] As the adult population of England and Wales is about 45 million, this amounts to some 2.25 million people. See Office for National Statistics, https://www.ons.gov.uk/aboutus/transparencyandgovernance/freedomofinformationfoi/populationbyagegenderandethnicity (last accessed 6 September 2017).
[21] P Pleasence, N Balmer, A Patel, A Cleary, T Huskinson and T Cotton, *Report of the 2006–9 English and Welsh Civil and Social Justice Survey* (Legal Services Commission and Ipsos Mori, 2011), Table 28; N Balmer, *The English and Welsh Civil and Social Justice Panel Survey, Wave 2* (LSC, 2013), Table 27; *Legal Needs Survey* (Law Society and Ipsos Mori, 2015), Figure 5.9 (above the average); *The Findings from the Legal Problem and Resolution Survey (LPRS) Survey 2014–15* (Ministry of Justice, 2017), Tables 4.1, 4.2 and 6.1 (much more likely to use both 'formal' legal processes or professional advice).

III. The Post-War Changes to Legal Aid

While it is now widely accepted that the state should support an individual's access to the law when they come into conflict with the state, this view is of relatively recent origin. Provision for legal assistance for poor prisoners has historically been abysmal, if only because of their restricted rights during trial. Only after 1836[22] could lawyers address the court on behalf of the defendant in a jury trial, if the defendant could afford it, unless he could take advantage of the bizarre custom of the 'dock brief', allowing a defendant in the dock to select a barrister who happened to be in court and gowned to act for him. Statutes in 1903 and 1930 allowed courts (including magistrates' courts) to grant legal aid in 'grave cases' if they pleaded not guilty and disclosed their defence[23] and in 1930 this was extended to those pleading guilty. Payment would be from local funds at a fixed rate.

The Rushcliffe Committee Report, published in May 1945,[24] laid the foundations for the post-war legal aid system. Tamara Goriely has pointed out that its publication, a month after the German surrender in World War II,[25] reflected a time when confidence in state institutions, and the role of the state, was high, and there was determination to build a fairer society after military victory. Reviewing the report in The Modern Law Review in 1946, EJ Cohn concluded that 'its acceptance will result in a considerable portion of all Court business being financed by the State' and added: 'That the citizen of the modern State has a right to receive legal aid seems to have become a principle upon which, happily, all are agreed'.[26] This sentiment was echoed by TH Marshall in a lecture given in Cambridge in 1948 in which he argued that such funding was a necessary condition of citizenship legitimising democracy.[27]

As regards criminal cases, Rushcliffe built on the existing system, but with important improvements. The criterion for granting legal aid for counsel and a solicitor would be 'the interests of justice'. Solicitors were to be given four days to prepare. Payment would be according to taxed bills of costs, and would fall on the state rather than the local community. This was brought into effect only in 1960 (taxed costs) and 1963 ('interests of justice').[28] In respect to civil cases,

---

[22] Trials for Felony Act 1836.

[23] Poor Prisoners Defence Act 1930.

[24] Rushcliffe Report, *Report of the Committee on Legal Aid and Advice* (1945, Cmd 6641). For a detailed account of the background to the Rushcliffe Report, see RI Morgan, 'The Introduction of Civil Legal Aid in England and Wales, 1914–1949' (1994) 5 *Twentieth Century British History* 38–76.

[25] T Goriely, 'Rushcliffe Fifty Years On: The Changing Role of Civil Legal Aid Within the Welfare State' (1994) 21 *Journal of Law & Society* 545.

[26] EJ Cohn, 'Legal Aid to the Poor and the Rushcliffe Report' (1946) 9 *Modern Law Review* 58, 66.

[27] 'Citizenship and Social Class' in TH Marshall, *Sociology at the Crossroads and other Essays* (Routledge, 1963). See also the views expressed in Parliament, cited by F Kaganas in 'Justifying the LASPO Act: authenticity, necessity, suitability, responsibility and autonomy' (2017) 39 *Journal of Social Welfare and Family Law* 168, 170–3.

[28] See T Goriely, 'The Development of Criminal Legal Aid in England and Wales' in R Young and D Wall (eds), *Access to Criminal Justice: Legal Aid, Lawyers and the Defence of Liberty* (Blackstone, 1996) 412–44; A Paterson (note 9) 65.

prior to the twentieth century, assistance for poor persons had been through the *in forma pauperis* procedure, available only to plaintiffs in the High Court, and dependent on the willingness of a barrister to apply to the court and take on the case without charge. The Rules of the Supreme Court (Poor Persons) 1914 established Prescribed Officers of the High Court to identify solicitors who would assess whether the client had a case and was financially eligible, and, if the court granted a certificate, the Prescribed Officer would refer the case to a volunteer solicitor or barrister to conduct it without payment. However, as Richard Morgan observed: 'There were ... very real limits to the "charitable" impulses of solicitors and counsel'[29] and it proved difficult to find sufficient volunteer solicitors. The highly legalistic structure of the divorce law at the time meant that a very high proportion of poor persons' cases were in matrimonial matters, but Colin Gibson reports that 'Less than a tenth of the 790 London solicitors undertaking divorce work in 1918 had handled a Poor Persons case.'[30] Barristers proved less difficult to find, apparently because their role involved much less 'unpleasant' work than that of solicitors.

To try to overcome this, appeals were made to the lawyers' moral instincts. The Second Lawrence Committee (1925) enunciated that there existed 'a moral obligation on the part of the profession in relation to the monopoly in the practice of the law which it enjoys to render gratuitous legal assistance, provided that no undue burden is thereby cast on any individual member of the profession'[31] and the Law Society reiterated the message.[32] But in order to distribute the 'burden', the granting of certificates was removed from the High Court and transferred to local committees of the Law Society, populated solely by solicitors, who would decide whether an applicant qualified. Government funding was confined to administrative costs. Effectively, the Poor Persons Procedure was decentralised. But while provision was improved, difficulties in recruiting solicitors remained,[33] with the Welsh Law Society refusing to operate it at all after 1939.

Ironically, in view of the fate of family law in the current legal aid reforms, the immediate goal of the post-war legal aid scheme was to deal with the 'divorce crisis' caused by service personnel returning after the war to broken marriages.[34] Dissolving a marriage at that time required a good deal of legal preparation for presentation of a petition in court, and the Rushcliffe Committee envisaged a comprehensive network of area committees, with paid administrative staff,

---

[29] Morgan (n 24) 38, 43.

[30] C Gibson, *Dissolving Wedlock* (Routledge, 1994) 87.

[31] *Report of the Poor Persons Rules Committee* (Second Lawrence Committee) (1925) Cmd 2358, para 12.

[32] See the Law Society Annual Report (1927), 30: 'Poor's work is one of the duties undertaken by the legal profession in return for its privileges .... So long as the burden is equitably distributed we think that no real hardship is involved', cited in A Paterson, 'Professionalism and the legal services market' (1996) 3 *International Journal of the Legal Profession* 137–68, n 29.

[33] Morgan (n 24) 51.

[34] See Goriely (n 25) 550.

overseeing local offices serviced by full-time or part-time paid solicitors who would assess cases for eligibility, issue legal aid certificates, using the National Assistance Board to assess means, and assign appropriate cases to solicitors or barristers from a panel of volunteers. Crucially, the eligibility levels were to be raised, with contributions to be paid on a graduated scale, extending the scheme beyond those 'normally classed as poor',[35] and no longer confined to the High Court. Apart from a proposed extension to the wartime Services Divorce Division whose employees would cover all civilian divorces of people who could not afford to contribute more than £10 to the costs, the report rejects the idea of a salaried professional service in favour of a 'judicare' model, using lawyers in private practice and entitled to remuneration for their work at 85 per cent of their taxed costs.

The scheme would be financed by a block grant from the Treasury, which would cover not only administrative costs, but also professional fees. Accepting that this would be the more expensive model, EJ Cohn commented in 1946 that the savings made if a salaried service was used 'would have been made at the expense of depriving the independent profession of practically all connection with legal aid (and) introduced an official and bureaucratic element which is fortunately utterly alien to the traditions of the English legal profession'.[36] The report was largely translated into law by the Legal Aid and Advice Act 1949, but with some major practical limitations. A few actions were placed out of scope (libel, slander, breach of promise of marriage, seduction, enticement and relator actions); proceedings before tribunals were excluded, and extension to those before County and Magistrates' Courts postponed. But family law matters were very much included.

As regards legal advice alone (not accompanied by representation), the Rushcliffe Committee also both built on, and transformed, the earlier position, whereby unpaid advice had been supplied on a voluntary basis by social activists through a few 'law centres' originating in a movement (Poor Man's Lawyers) started at Toynbee Hall in London. They tended to be concentrated in a few cities, especially London, and were poorly regulated, with some lawyers using them for profit (eg, by taking a portion of moneys they helped to recover[37]). A suggestion that they might receive state funding was rejected by the Second Finlay Committee in 1928.[38] There was some expansion both in London and beyond during the war, aided by the newly established Citizens Advice Bureau and the National Council for Social Service under arrangements in which in some cases solicitors agreed to act for reduced fees. Under the Rushcliffe proposals, the area committees were to provide advice directly, employing solicitors for the purpose, for payment

---

[35] Rushcliffe (n 24) para 127(2).

[36] Cohn (n 26) 65.

[37] See the account of such an office in London in 1938 in *The Spectator*: http://archive.spectator.co.uk/article/15th-july-1938/14/the-poor-mans-lawyer (last accessed 16 February 2017).

[38] *Final Report of the Committee on Legal Aid for the Poor* (1928) Cmd 3016.

of 2s 6d if possible unless it was thought the person could pay the ordinary fee. Morgan writes that 'while it might seem to indicate support for a salaried, state-financed advice services, it should be noted that the nature of the service to be offered was limited'. For example, it did not extend to negotiation (though it might involve the solicitor writing a letter).[39] To obtain help for that, the applicant would need to apply for a legal aid certificate.

The proposals were enacted in the Legal Aid and Advice Act 1949. Advice was limited to oral advice, although a written note could be made of it.[40] However, the financial crisis of the late 1940s meant that the whole section on advice was put on hold as it would have involved substantial salaried staff. It was estimated that the salaried divorce department and advice provision would have consumed 44 per cent of the legal aid budget.[41] So when the advice scheme was implemented in 1959, the envisaged structure of local committees providing advice directly was abandoned; instead lawyers would deal with cases individually under the 'judi-care' model. The Services Divorce Department was closed in 1961.[42] However, fearing the loss of fee-paying clients, the profession forced down the eligibility levels. Even so, when the scheme started, it covered 80 per cent of the population.[43] But the scheme was still limited by the restriction to oral advice, and exclusion of further work unless it was covered by a legal aid certificate that contemplated litigation.

The 1970s saw some consolidation of public legal assistance. In April 1973 the Green Form Scheme, which allowed £25 worth of written advice and other assistance for eligible clients by the simple submission of a form and its acceptance by a solicitor (a certificate from the legal aid authorities was required for further work) was introduced.[44] By 1981/82 matrimonial and family work accounted for 49 per cent of Green Form work.[45] In addition, the 1970s saw the growth of community law centres, supported by funds from both local and central government: there were 55 of them by 1986, and 63 at their height in 2005.[46] At the same time non-lawyer advice services, such as Citizens Advice Bureaux, flourished.[47]

IV. Family Law: a Victim of its Own Success?

As observed above, one reason for the post-war divorce 'crisis' was the highly legalised nature of the divorce law at the time, which was then based on fault,

---

[39] Morgan (n 24) 70.
[40] Legal Aid and Advice Act 1949, s 7.
[41] Goriely (n 25) 548.
[42] ibid, 551–52.
[43] ibid, 547.
[44] See HL Deb vol 332, cols 502–31 (23 June 1972).
[45] Legal Action Group, *A Strategy for Justice* (LAG, 1992), 33.
[46] Law Centres Network, *Funding for Law Centres* (25 November 2014) 3.
[47] ibid, 9–10.

involving extensive documentation and proofs, which required presentation by 'a competent and experienced legal team'.[48] After the reform in the divorce law in 1971, the process of acquiring a divorce became much simpler: almost an administrative process. But the numbers of divorces rose from 47,421 in 1970, to a peak of 165,018 in 1993, gradually falling back to 119,389 in 2010.[49] Although obtaining the decree became simpler, the simultaneous expansion of the courts' jurisdiction to make financial and property orders, which worked especially in favour of women, coupled with an increase in home ownership,[50] raised the importance and complexity of financial and property settlements between divorcing parties, which would often require legal advice and even a court order to resolve.

But while the number of divorces has risen from the 1970s, the number of marriages in England and Wales has fallen steadily from a recent high of 426,000 in 1972 to a low of 232,000 in 2007, recovering slightly to 247,000 in 2014.[51] The number of opposite-sex people 'cohabiting' rose from about 1.5 million in 1996 to around 3.2 million in 2016.[52] It might be thought that the decline in marriage would result in fewer legal issues arising on separation, because unmarried partners can separate without legal formality. This does not mean that legal issues cannot arise when unmarried people separate, though the absence of specific financial remedies means that they probably seldom resort to legal solutions on those matters when they separate.

However, disputes about children could certainly lead to legal intervention. Prior to the Children Act 1989, court orders dealing with arrangements for children after divorce, where made at all, were usually in the form of 'custody' to one parent (usually the mother) and 'access' (or 'reasonable access') to the other. A study of court files in the 1970s showed that 'access' by the non-resident parent was probably exercised regularly in only 44 per cent of cases, and probably not exercised at all in 30 per cent, and that only 3.5 per cent of husbands had apparently challenged the award of 'custody' to the wife.[53] The 1989 Act clarified that both married parents possessed 'parental responsibility' which continued despite divorce, and allowed the courts to give a more refined 'residence' and 'contact'

---

[48] S Cretney, *Family Law in the Twentieth Century: A History* (Oxford University Press, 2003) 253.

[49] Office for National Statistics, *Statistical Bulletin, Divorces in England and Wales 2012* (February 2014), http://webarchive.nationalarchives.gov.uk/20160105160709/http://www.ons.gov.uk/ons/dcp171778_351693.pdf (last accessed 31 May 2017).

[50] In 1971 the proportion of home owners to renters reached 50% for the first time, thereafter raising to 69% in 2001, but dropping back slightly to 64% in 2011: Office for National Statistics, *Home Ownership and Renting in England and Wales (full story)* (19 April 2013), http://webarchive.nationalarchives.gov.uk/20160105160709/http://www.ons.gov.uk/ons/rel/census/2011-census-analysis/a-century-of-home-ownership-and-renting-in-england-and-wales/short-story-on-housing.html (last accessed 31 May 2017).

[51] Office for National Statistics, *Marriage in England and Wales 2014* (March 2017), www.ons.gov.uk/peoplepopulationandcommunity/birthsdeathsandmarriages/marriagecohabitationandcivilpartnerships/bulletins/marriagesinenglandandwalesprovisional/2014 (last accessed 31 May 2017).

[52] House of Commons, *Briefing Paper 03372* (March 2017) 5.

[53] J Eekelaar and E Clive, *Custody after Divorce* (SSRC Centre for Socio-Legal Studies, 1977).

orders in disputes between separating parents, married or unmarried. In 1997 it appeared that 69 per cent of a representative sample of formerly married parents who were living apart and the child was living with one of the parents maintained contact between the child and the other parent,[54] suggesting a growing degree to which such contact was being exercised, and greater pressure by fathers to exercise it, and even to share living arrangements with the child.[55] This has proved fertile ground for dispute.[56] So, for example, the number of applications for custody orders (which would have included any order for access) stood at 82,081 in 1988.[57] In 1993/4, two years after the implementation of the Children Act 1989, there were 108,201 applications for equivalent orders,[58] an increase of 32 per cent.

All this had an impact on legal aid expenditure. From the early 1990s, governments began to express alarm at what they saw as the rising costs of legal aid in family matters. By 1981/2 matrimonial and family work accounted for 49 per cent of Green Form work (that is, advice provided by solicitors).[59] By 1996/7, 48.5 per cent of the whole civil legal aid budget was spent on matrimonial and family cases.[60] Indeed, the legal aid scheme was becoming, as Stephen Cretney said, 'a victim of its own success'.[61] So in 1995 the government launched the idea that all people wanting to divorce should attend an 'information meeting' that would explain the 'advantages' of mediation and so keep them away from lawyers.[62] Using lawyers was presented as equivalent to litigating in court. But the government's efforts to persuade people to use mediators suffered a setback when a pilot study showed that 39 per cent of the people who attended the information meetings wished to consult a lawyer compared to only 7 per cent who were persuaded to go to mediation.[63] So the scheme was abandoned. But there still remained a requirement introduced in 1996 that anyone seeking legal aid in a family matter should meet a mediator: a system which subsequent research showed probably simply added to costs because it resulted in mediation in only one in three to four cases.[64]

---

[54] M Maclean and J Eekelaar, *The Parental Obligation: A study of parenthood across households* (Hart Publishing, 2007) Table 7.14.

[55] See J Eekelaar and M Maclean, *Family Justice: The Work of Family Judges in Uncertain Times* (Hart, 2013) 164–75.

[56] See S Maclean, 'Public Involvement in Private Problems: Legal aid and the family justice system' (2000) 22 *Journal of Social Welfare and Family Law* 145, 147–48.

[57] *Civil Judicial Statistics 1988*, Cm 745, Table 5.10.

[58] *Judicial Statistics 1993–4*, Cm 2623.

[59] Legal Action Group (n 45) 33.

[60] Legal Aid Board, Annual Reports 1996/7, 2.

[61] Cretney (n 48) 318.

[62] Family Law Act 1996, ss 7–9.

[63] J Collier, 'The Dashing of as "Liberal Dream": the Information Meeting, the "New Family" and the Limits of Law' (1999) 11 *Child & Family Law Quarterly* 257.

[64] G Davis, 'Reflections in the aftermath of the family mediation pilot' (2011) 13 *Child & Family Law Quarterly* 371.

Another strategy was the introduction of more market forces by allowing lawyers to advertise, and from 2004 gradually allowing barristers to deal directly with clients rather than through a solicitor, and removing some protected areas which previously only lawyers could perform, such as conveyancing. But even at that time, there was no requirement to have a legal qualification in order to provide 'general legal advice'[65] (eg, in family matters), a situation which, as will be seen at various points in this book, seems still to be insufficiently appreciated. The exceptions concern a narrowly defined list of 'reserved legal activities',[66] the most important of which in our context is the exercise of the right of audience in court and the conduct of litigation. Only *authorised or exempt* persons may carry them out. Under the Solicitors' Regulation Authority (SRA) Rules 8.1 and 9.1 solicitors are so authorised if they are 'involved in legal practice' and practising as a solicitor (ie, and hold a practising certificate, or are exempted from doing so). Rights of audience, previously confined to barristers, were extended to authorised solicitors and even in some cases to non-lawyers. Non-lawyers could be authorised to manage firms providing legal services (Alternative Business Structures: such as the Co-Operative Legal Services).

Whereas under the post-war system lawyers could submit their bills for approved payments for work for eligible clients, under the Access to Justice Act 1999 legal aid monies, which were now subject to a 'cap', would be paid under block grants to providers, who would be chosen as a result of competitive tendering, and payments would be according to fixed or graduated fees for categories of work, rather than according to the time taken. The result was that far fewer firms could carry out legal aid work, and such work became much less attractive to barristers. More stringent eligibility tests were introduced.[67] Further significant constraints on the system were the introduction of payment of 'prescribed rates' including for family work in 1994 and the introduction in 2000 of a system of contracting for funding for legal aid work under a strict 'Funding Code' operated by the Legal Services Commission, which controlled the nature of and time spent on legally aided work, and was intended to concentrate work in large firms on the grounds of efficiency and value for money. A 'market-based' approach to granting legal aid contracts recommended in 2006[68] began to be implemented over the next few years through the use (among other things) of fixed fees in social welfare, family and immigration cases.[69] This reduced the number of firms doing such work, the number of family contracts being almost halved in the

---

[65] See Sir David Clementi, *Review of the Regulatory Framework for Legal Services in England and Wales, Final Report* (December 2004) 92–3.

[66] See now Legal Services Act 2007, ss 12, 13. Other reserved activities relate to matters of conveyancing or probate, and are not usually relevant to family issues.

[67] Legal Action Group (n 45) 24–26 and Appendix 1.

[68] Lord Carter of Coles, *Legal aid: a market-based approach to reform* (2006).

[69] See Ministry of Justice, *Proposals for the Reform of Legal Aid in England and Wales* (Ministry of Justice) Cm 7967 (November 2010) para 3.6.

2010 tendering round[70] and, because law centres relied heavily on legal aid monies, their numbers fell from the peak of 63 in 2005 to 54 in 2011 and 45 in 2014.[71]

The restrictions on legal aid most strongly affected firms doing criminal and family work. Between 2007 and 2011, 32 per cent of all solicitors' firms in a survey of solicitors' firms reported an increase in turnover, but 41 per cent reported a decrease. Some areas of family law practice remained unaffected: for example commercial and international firms, or niche firms specialising in limited areas, like international child abduction. Medium sized firms with a strong family department were finding it challenging, while smaller firms were struggling. The smaller firms had more problems coping with the new legal aid provisions, and these were often firms dealing with family cases. The firms were responding in various ways: cutting staff, reducing office space, using IT more, outsourcing aspects of their work, forming networks to share administrative costs, and offering 'unbundled' legal services, where, instead of taking a client through a whole process, offering the kind of support described above (sometimes called the 'full legal', 'end-to-end' service), the client is given advice on only a part of the matter (which can lead to problems if not carefully defined in advance).

The Access to Justice Act 1999 introduced another policy aimed to deliver legal advice in a different way, in order to respond to the evidence that social problems tended to arise in clusters, requiring intervention on a holistic basis, which would be more cost effective.[72] A Community Legal Service (CLS) was to develop services to this end to be delivered by partnerships between members of the legal profession, Citizens Advice Bureaux and Law Centres[73] in entities known as Community Legal Advice Centres (CLACs) and Community Legal Advice Networks (CLANs). Since these can be seen as precursors to developments following LASPO we will describe this initiative in more detail later.[74]

V. Legal Aid in Family Matters After 2013

But worse was to come, especially for family law, when the LASPO 2012 became effective from April 2013 the Legal Services Commission, which had succeeded the Legal Aid Board, and operated at arms-length from ministerial control, was abolished[75] and replaced by the Legal Aid Agency within the Ministry of Justice

---

[70] See Paterson (n 9) 94–96.

[71] Law Centres Network (n 46) 3.

[72] See P Pleasence, A Buck, NJ Balmer, A O'Grady, and H Genn, 'Multiple Justiciable Problems: Common Clusters and their Social and Demographic Indicators' (2004) 1(1) *Journal of Empirical Legal Studies* 301.

[73] Lord Chancellor's Department, *Community Legal Services Consultation* (25 May 1999): http://webarchive.nationalarchives.gov.uk/+/http:/www.dca.gov.uk/consult/access/mjch2.htm; (last accessed 29 May 2018).

[74] pp 29–30.

[75] LASPO, s 38.

(MoJ). The government had stated the reasons for this as being to 'transfer all relevant functions and responsibilities for the administration of legal aid to the Lord Chancellor. It aims to tighten financial control of the legal aid budget (funded through the MoJ), improve accountability for policy decisions, as well as linking legal aid policy-making in the context of wider justice policy issues, and reduce organisational barriers. Whilst offering clear lines of ministerial accountability and ensuring strict controls are in place to manage the cost of the scheme, the policy also aims to ensure that case-by-case funding decisions remain at arm's length from ministers. The intended effect is to set up a structure which will foster more joined up working between the MoJ and the new agency, whilst considering wider organisational budgetary demands such as to achieve greater utilisation of shared corporate services'.[76]

In a Consultation Paper in 2010 setting out its priorities for legal aid funding, the Lord Chancellor stated that 'cases which can very often result from a litigant's own decisions in their personal life' were less likely to be considered as 'issues of the highest importance'.[77] So, instead of defining excluded matters, the only matters within scope are those expressly designated as such by LASPO. Schedule 1 sets out where legal aid might be available to eligible claimants in 'civil' matters. It includes what are usually called 'public law' proceedings, such as where local authorities seek care, supervision, or emergency protection orders regarding children, or place children for adoption or the matter concerns contact with children who have been subject to such proceedings.[78] Also included are a variety of issues which relate to especially vulnerable children or adults. As a result, legal aid for 'private' family law issues which do not fit those categories was completely withdrawn apart from limited exceptions, such as where 'there has been, or is a risk of, domestic violence',[79] or the occupation of the home was at stake, or the matter had an international dimension, or when human rights were concerned or the case was deemed 'exceptional'.

The attempt to identify specific circumstances where legal aid might be provided only to parties to family disputes who 'deserved' it, is clearly part of a strategy to reduce public expenditure, but may also indicate a flawed understanding of the nature of such disputes. This is demonstrated by the measures taken to implement the exception for domestic violence. This required the complainant to produce evidence of a certain kind from a formidable list of acceptable sources,

---

[76] Abolition of the Legal Services Commission (a Non-Department Public Body) and the establishment of a new Executive Agency within the Ministry of Justice (20 May 2011): https://www.justice.gov.uk/downloads/legislation/bills-acts/legal-aid-sentencing/ia-abolition-lsc.pdf (last accessed 25 July 2018).

[77] Ministry of Justice, *Proposals for the Reform of Legal Aid in England and Wales*, CP 12.10, Cm 7967; see J Eekelaar, '"Not of the Highest Importance: Family Justice under Threat' (2011) 33 *Journal of Social Welfare and Family Law* 311.

[78] Cases where children were placed for adoption outside such proceedings were not covered. In 2017 the government promised to cover this 'gap': http://www.communitycare.co.uk/2017/03/01/government-tackle-legal-aid-gap-parents-challenging-adoptions/.

[79] LASPO, s 9(1) and Sch 1, Pt 1, cl 12(1)(a).

which needed to show that the matter had come to their attention within the previous two years. In 2016 the Court of Appeal held that this restriction frustrated the purpose of the Act to make legal aid available to the great majority of sufferers of domestic violence.[80] The requirements also rendered it effectively impossible to establish financial abuse. The Ministry of Justice subsequently extended the time limit from two to five years,[81] and in 2018 the time limit was removed altogether.[82]

But the problem goes deeper than that. In its original version, LASPO defined domestic violence as meaning 'any incident of threatening behaviour, violence or abuse (whether psychological, physical, sexual, financial or emotional) between individuals who are associated with each other'.[83] This was soon seen to be too narrow, and in 2013 was broadened to cover 'any incident, or pattern of incidents, of controlling, coercive or threatening behaviour, violence or abuse (whether psychological, physical, sexual, financial or emotional) between individuals who are associated with each other'.[84] Yet, as Adrienne Barnett has argued,[85] the conception that coercion can always be established by demonstrable evidence of individual 'incidents' can miss the more hidden, but nonetheless real, nature of controlling behaviour. Hence she argues for less emphasis on fact-finding and more on an assessment of risk, based on a holistic examination of the circumstances. While this is feasible for judicial proceedings, it would be hard to apply at the stage of application for legal aid. The evidential requirements needed to qualify a case for legal aid can be such as to cause concern for adults and children in conflicted situations regarding child arrangements between separated parents. One could therefore go further than Barnett and maintain that degrees of power imbalance are present in most relationships, that it is a primary role of the law to redress these imbalances, and therefore that any attempt to separate out cases that are particularly 'deserving' of legal aid, or at least some form of public assistance where a person lacks the means to secure it, is futile, and that the law should be accessible in all cases of conflict on relationship breakdown. We revert to this issue at the conclusion of this book.

VI. The Renewed Push for Mediation

The government once more looked to mediation as a means to divert people from court, and indeed from lawyers in general. While public funding for legal advice

---

[80] *R (Rights of Women) v Secretary of State for Justice* [2016] EWCA Civ 91.

[81] The Civil Legal Aid (Procedure) (Amendment) Regulations 2016 (SI 2016/516).

[82] The Civil Legal Aid (Procedure) (Amendment) (No 2) Regulations 2017 (SI 2017/1237).

[83] LASPO, s 9(1) and Sch 1, Pt 1, cl 12(9).

[84] The Legal Aid, Sentencing and Punishment of Offenders Act 2012 (Amendment of Schedule 1) Order 2013 (SI 2013/748), arts 1, 4(1).

[85] A Barnett, '"Greater than the mere sum of its parts": coercive control and the question of proof' (2017) 29 *Child & Family Law Quarterly* 379.

and representation in family matters suffered drastic reduction in April 2013, help remained for mediation, with small additions for legal advice during or after mediation, but not before it.[86] To further encourage its use, a Practice Direction from the President of the Family Division in 2011[87] had stated the 'expectation' that applicants in most family proceedings will have first contacted a mediator, and now the Children and Families Act 2014 stipulated that a party intending to bring such a proceeding needed first to attend a Mediation Information and Assessment Meeting (MIAM),[88] which is often used as an occasion to try to 'sell' mediation.[89] As an inducement for the other party to attend mediation, where the applicant was eligible for public funding for the mediation, in 2014 the government allowed the other party to be publicly funded too without a means test for the first mediation session.[90]

Yet this has failed to draw more people into mediation. The number of publicly funded MIAMs dropped from 31,336 to 13,348 between 2011/2 and 2015/6 (a fall of 54.4 per cent). Perhaps more strikingly, while a higher proportion of those meetings that were held led to mediation starting in 2015/6 than in 2011/2 (66 per cent against 49 per cent), more of the mediations that were held failed to reach agreement (37.9 per cent against 31.4 per cent).[91] The drop in the number of MIAMs of course partly reflected a drop in actual court applications as a result of LASPO: financial applications dropped from about 42,950 in 2012 to 37,657 (12.3 per cent) in 2014, and private law applications regarding children dropped from 52,062 in 2012 to 42,114 (19.1 per cent) in 2014.[92] But it also indicates that people were seeing solicitors less often, so referrals by solicitors for mediation fell sharply. Very few claims were made for legal aid in support of mediation.[93] What is certainly clear is that mediation was not *replacing* the role previously performed either by courts or solicitors. There also seems to have been a reduction in privately funded mediation: formal referrals to National Family Mediation dropped by 31 per cent between 2012/3 and 2014/15.[94] We have calculated that the average number of mediations (whether publicly or privately funded) carried out by all accredited mediators a year over the period 2006–14 was 7.2.[95]

---

[86] LASPO, s 9(1) and Schedule 1, Part 1, clause 14.

[87] Practice Direction 3A, *Pre-Action Protocol for Mediation Information and Assessment*.

[88] Children and Families Act 2014, s 10(1).

[89] See M Maclean and J Eekelaar, *Lawyers and Mediators: The Brave New World of Services for Separating Families* (Oxford, Hart Publishing, 2016) 76; Barlow et al (n 9) 77.

[90] See Ministry of Justice (n 1) para 123.

[91] *Legal Aid Statistics England and Wales December 2016*, Tables 7.1 and 7.2. Ministry of Justice (n 87) para 161. For fuller discussion see R Hunter, 'Inducing Demand for Family Mediation – before and after LASPO' (2017) 39 *Journal of Social Welfare and Family Law* 189.

[92] Ministry of Justice, *Family Court Statistics Quarterly, England and Wales, Annual 2016, October to December 2016* (2017) Table 1.

[93] See E Hitchings and J Miles, 'Mediation, financial remedies, information provision and legal advice: the post-LASPO conundrum' (2016) 38 *Journal of Social Welfare and Family Law* 175.

[94] Maclean and Eekelaar (n 89) 18.

[95] ibid, 73.

Government has tended to attribute public coolness to mediation to a lack of awareness or understanding.[96] Yet Anne Barlow and her colleagues, reporting on research conducted in 2011 and 2012, showed that both among the public generally and people who underwent divorce or separation, there was higher awareness of mediation than of solicitor negotiation as a means for resolving disputes.[97] Despite that awareness, people were much more likely to take up lawyer negotiation than mediation, although of course one reason for not taking up mediation could be that both parties must be willing to do it. But there were other reasons for rejecting it, such as belief that communication was so poor it would serve no purpose, feelings of pressure, lack of emotional readiness and concerns over violence.[98]

While mediation remains an important element in the legal system's, and the community's, response to people experiencing family problems, it is only one part of it, and one which does not suit everyone. For example, in their survey population, Barlow et al found higher rates of satisfaction both of the process and the outcome among those who used solicitors than those who resorted to mediation.[99] In 1988 Gwynn Davis, reporting on interviews with divorced parties, referred to solicitors as being 'more than just a partisan', but as providing advice, counselling and emotional support to clients in conflicted cases.[100] We have remarked on that as well, and have drawn attention to the fact that, in its promotion of mediation, government documents frequently contrast mediation with 'going to court', ignoring the fact that consulting a solicitor rarely leads to court action. The 'settlement' culture among solicitors has been frequently commented on.[101]

In our earlier study of the work of lawyers and mediators,[102] we acknowledged the usefulness of mediation in some cases, but also drew attention to disparities between approaches and codes of practice (for example in the extent to which 'steering' participants towards certain outcomes was considered appropriate), and between mediators who were legally trained and those who were not. It also appeared that mediation, which is premised on the resolution of disputes, was not well adapted to providing the kind of advice that separating individuals or couples were often looking for. Indeed, this function was theoretically beyond its remit, which included providing information but excluded giving advice. However, we found examples where this distinction was unrealistic, and therefore made a proposal that this restriction should be removed and that it should become

---

[96] eg, Ministry of Justice, *Report of the Family Mediation Task Force* (2014) paras 27, 28.

[97] Barlow et al (n 9) 70.

[98] ibid, 85, 90–92.

[99] ibid, 112, 122, 156. Slightly different results were yielded in their 'party interviews', but these interviewees were not drawn from a representative population: see ibid, 60, 156.

[100] G Davis, *Partisans and Mediators*, (Oxford University Press, 1988) 89–90.

[101] J Eekelaar, M Maclean and S Beinart, *Family Lawyers: The Divorce Work of Solicitors* (Hart 2000) 13–18; see also Barlow et al (n 9) (their Omnibus Survey found 74% who used solicitor negotiation settled on some or all issues compared to 48% of those who used mediation: 154): G Davis, SM Cretney and JG Collins, *Simple Quarrels* (Oxford University Press, 1994) 40.

[102] See n 89.

possible for legally trained mediators to provide legal advice to a couple in a mediation context ('legally assisted mediation').[103] The more recent observations by Barlow et al,[104] who remark on the fact that many women 'felt empowered' by the advice they received from their solicitor (although some chose to ignore it for reasons of 'guilt, pragmatism or sacrifice') are entirely consistent with this evidence.

VII. Paucity of Legal Provision

Since 2016/7, total legal aid expenditure had fallen by 38 per cent compared to 2010, and civil legal aid by 45 per cent,[105] although as a proportion of the Ministry of Justice budget, it fell only from 24 per cent to 23 per cent.[106] The consequences of this policy for legal provision are described by Natalie Byrom as having 'reduced the absolute number of providers available: they have affected the geographical distribution of legal aid funded civil law advice across England and Wales, creating "advice deserts"; they have altered the nature of the service provided by moving the focus away from early intervention and complex casework, on to one-off pieces of advice provided once a situation has already escalated. The cuts have led to an overall reduction in the number of providers of legal advice that are funded by legal aid by nearly 50 per cent since 2007–8.'[107] Changes in eligibility levels for clients seeking legal aid and lower payments to legal aid practitioners contributed to this decline.[108]

Private law family matters have been almost completely removed from the scheme, surviving only in the specially designated areas which indicated some serious crisis (domestic violence, forced marriage, home rights, occupation orders and non-molestation orders, international abduction and proceedings related to certain international instruments).[109] In 2016–17 the Legal Aid Agency agreed funding for legal help (ie, advice) in 74 per cent fewer family cases than in the year before the reform, and for legal representation in 29 per cent fewer.[110] The total number of family law cases started in April–June 2014 was 41 per cent

---

[103] Maclean and Eekelaar (n 89). See also Hitchings and Miles (n 93), observing that the absence of legal aid for lawyers is likely to push mediators towards a more 'evaluative' form of mediation, which borders closely on giving legal advice.

[104] Barlow et al (n 9) 196–97.

[105] See Ministry of Justice (n 1) Figure 11.

[106] ibid, Figure 11.

[107] N Byrom, 'Cuts to Civil Legal Aid and the Identity Crisis in Lawyering: Lessons from the Experience of England and Wales' in Flynn and Hodgson (n 9) 223.

[108] Maclean and Eekelaar (n 89) 16–20. National Audit Office, Ministry of Justice and Legal Aid Agency, *Implementing Reforms to Civil Legal Aid* (2014).

[109] LASPO 2012, Sch 1, Pt 1, paras 10–13. For the definition of violence, see text associated with n 84.

[110] Ministry of Justice (n 1), Figure 6. See also Ministry of Justice and Legal Aid Agency, *Legal Aid Statistics in England and Wales, January to March 2015* (2015), Figure 15.

lower than between April–June 2013.[111] Financial applications dropped from about 42,950 in 2012 to 37,657 in 2014, but recovered to around 41,507 in 2016. Private law children applications dropped dramatically from 52,062 in 2012 to 42,114 in 2014, recovering to 48,244 in 2016.[112] This shows that, after the initial shock, use of the courts in those matters continued at much the same level, but the significant factor was that private family law cases where neither party was legally represented rose from 16 per cent in 2013 to 34 per cent in 2016, and cases where both were represented fell from 38 per cent to 21 per cent over the same period.[113] People were accessing the courts, but many were having to do so without legal assistance or advice.

This debasement of public concern for the legal regulation of these matters stands in sharp contrast to attitudes that prevailed in the years immediately following World War II. The statement in the government Consultation Paper of 2010 preceding LASPO that, since its inception in 1949, the scope of the scheme had been extended 'far beyond' its original intentions[114] is hard to accept, given the breadth of the Rushcliffe proposals, as observed by EJ Cohn cited earlier. One might summarise the post-LASPO conception of the provision of legal aid as being something like an emergency service, where justice in itself is not seen as a public entitlement, and help is confined to those circumstances where its denial could have consequential effects highly detrimental to the individual and others in a material way, namely, domestic violence, threatening public safety, or child protection where a vulnerable third party is threatened.

Consistently with this, central government failed to maintain and resource community legal services which could have played a part in preventing family crises from arising.[115] This is a very different approach from that taken in Scotland, where the funding emphasis lies on early intervention and preventative action to enable matters to be resolved without litigation: for example, where early advice on payment of housing costs can avoid actions to evict or dispossess.[116] This point was strongly made in two reports published in 2017. One, the Bach Report published by the Fabian Society, called not only for the restoration of legal aid for representation in private law cases involving children, but for legal help in all family cases at an early stage so that later conflicts could be avoided.[117] The other,

---

[111] Ministry of Justice, *Court Statistics Quarterly April–June 2014* (2014) 13.

[112] Ministry of Justice, *Family Court Statistics Quarterly, England and Wales, Annual 2016, October to December 2016* (2017) Table 1.

[113] Ministry of Justice, *Family Court Statistics Quarterly, England and Wales, Annual 2016* (2016), Figures 1 and 8; Ministry of Justice (n 1) paras 166–67.

[114] Ministry of Justice (n 74) para 2.7. See also Paterson (n 9) 64–65.

[115] See the discussion of the Community Legal Services, pp. 28–32 below.

[116] See Paterson (n 9) 80–114; M Evans, *Re-thinking Legal Aid: An Independent Strategic Review (of Legal Aid in Scotland)* (February 2018).

[117] Bach Commission, *The Right to Justice: Final Report of the Bach Commission* (The Fabian Society, September 2017).

by the Law Society, was a further analysis by Ipsos Mori of the data mentioned earlier,[118] in order to compare the time taken to resolve issues in cases where early legal advice had been given and where it had not.[119] This showed that within three to four months of receiving it, a quarter of those given legal advice had resolved the issue, whereas it took nine months for a quarter of those without the advice to resolve it. The latter group were also 20 per cent less likely than the former to resolve the issue at a particular point in time. Most of the issues concerned debt and homelessness or its threat, but also included family issues. Similar results of the apparent effect of other forms of advice in hastening resolution have been reported.[120]

VIII. Child Support

Prior to LASPO, the government had pursued another means for removing private law family cases from the courts, those where a parent (usually a mother) was seeking child support payments from the (usually non-resident) father. In this case, an alternative structure was set up which it was believed would be more efficient than the courts, and particularly that it would reduce public expenditure overall by replenishing the social security budget from the (hoped-for) child support payments made by fathers. However it serves as an example of the difficulties that can arise by moving an issue that can involve a family dispute away from the courts, and eventually how such issues were largely left to private resolution with online assistance and residual state involvement.

During the 1980s government had become concerned about the increasing number of single mothers who were claiming social security benefits, and the inefficiency of the method of recouping some of it from 'absent' fathers. Therefore from 1993 the Child Support Act 1991 instituted an administrative process for child support through a statutory Child Support Agency (CSA), virtually removing from the courts the power to make child maintenance orders, except with the consent of both parties. There were exceptions. Courts could make orders in favour of children with disabilities, to pay school fees, and for payment of capital sums, though these could be overridden by CSA orders. The government estimated that the administrative costs of the previous system, which used the courts, was £50.8 million per annum. It is however difficult to know how much, if any, legal aid savings were made. In fact, legal aid expenditure on civil and family matters rose from £448 million 1991–92 to £752 million in 1994–95 (remaining at around that figure during the 1990s).

In the event, the new child support system was beset with difficulties, due mainly to the cooperation of the Lord Chancellor's Department with the

---

[118] See n 17.

[119] Ipsos Mori, *Analysis of the potential; effects of early legal advice/intervention* (November 2017).

[120] See below p 171.

Department for Social Security resulting in the development of a structure which failed to recognise that child support was part of a dispute between two parents. It approached (and was perceived as approaching) the task as a revenue raising rather than child support measure because of the requirement that welfare claimants needed to seek a child support order against the absent parent (which was later strengthened by treating any claim for welfare benefits as automatically an application for child support); the absence of any 'disregard', so that unless the support payments exceeded the totality of the welfare benefits, they would all be diverted to the state; excessive severity of the extraction rate; a complex system of exemptions and lack of flexibility, such as failure to take sufficient account of the debtor's newly acquired family responsibilities; retrospective operation; failure to integrate with the court system; failure to appreciate that procedures designed for paying benefits were unsuited to extracting payments; and serious administrative and processing shortcomings. Despite desperate attempts in 2003 to simplify the calculation of the amount owed and the introduction of a new computer system, by July 2006 the CSA had a backlog of 300,000 cases and it was calculated that it cost 70p for every £1 collected (compared to 1.4p for every £1 of taxation).

This resulted in a complete reversal of policy. The requirement that welfare claimants needed to seek a child support order against the absent parent was removed for new applicants after July 2008 and from April 2010 a full disregard was introduced, so that welfare claimants could keep both the welfare benefit and the child support payments in full, thus abandoning a policy going back to the Poor Laws of attempting to claw back some welfare expenditure from a liable parent. This seems to have resulted in an increase in single parents on benefit who receive maintenance from 24 per cent (in 2007) to 36 per cent (in 2012).

Furthermore, the CSA was replaced by, first, the Child Maintenance and Enforcement Commission, and then in 2012 by the Child Maintenance Service (CMS) within the Department for Work and Pensions. This demands that potential users first attempt to reach a 'Family-Based Arrangement' using on-line calculators, an approach which has been said to force some people into difficult confrontations. A charge of £20 is made for an application for CMS assistance in setting the maintenance due unless the applicant is a victim of domestic violence, under 19 years of age or in Northern Ireland. The CMS can access the debtor's tax records and calculate maintenance liability, but will then leave it to the parties to arrange for the payments to be made (Direct Pay). It is possible to appeal against the initial assessment, after a mandatory process of reconsideration, to the Social Security and Child Support Appeals Tribunal. There were 565 appeals to the Tribunal from December 2015 to November 2016 of which 160 (28.3 per cent) were successful. There is no legal aid for tribunal appeals.

Should a recipient be dissatisfied with compliance, he or she may make a further application that the CMS use its powers of enforcement, which is primarily through making Deduction of Earnings Orders or orders against bank accounts (Collect and Pay) against which there is appeal to the courts, or by the CMS applying to a court for a 'liability order' which may result in various measures against a defaulter, including distress against goods, and even committal to prison. However, there are collection fees for use of this service: paying parents must pay the CMS a sum equal to 20 per cent of the child maintenance amount payable and receiving parents a sum equal to 4 per cent of that amount, plus a range of enforcement charges for paying parents who don't pay child maintenance in full and on time. A person using the CMS can appoint a representative to deal with the Service on their behalf (for example, a friend, family member or professional).

It seems that about 70 per cent of payments are made by Direct Pay and 30 per cent by Collect and Pay. The Department for Work and Pensions claims that 89 per cent of the amount due under the 2012 scheme was paid in the quarter June–September 2016 and that the total arrears under that scheme run at 13 per cent of total maintenance liability.[121] However, this assumes that the sums owed which are paid directly (ie, 70 per cent of the total) are paid in full. The Department justifies this claim by saying that if there is a default the creditor can come back to CMS for a recalculation or use of the Collect and Pay Service. But that seems optimistic. The House of Commons Work and Pensions Committee heard evidence that recipient parents were often reluctant to confront the deterrent effects of the Collect and Pay Service, or were even discouraged from doing so by CMS staff, even where payments under Direct Pay were low or inconsistent. Such recipients cannot take direct action in the courts for enforcement (even assuming they could afford it): they have to use the CMS.[122]

There is evidence that a very low proportion of single parents who are receiving benefit are also paid child support. A 2012 study of 760 single parents who were receiving benefits found that, in 2007, only 24 per cent of the total sample had an arrangement that produced any maintenance payments at all for them, though by 2012, the proportion receiving maintenance had risen from 24 per cent to 36 per cent.[123] The increase was almost certainly due to the introduction of the disregard in 2010 so that the recipient could now keep both the benefit and the entire maintenance payment. Nevertheless, it remains that 64 per cent of all single parents on benefit in 2012 did not receive any maintenance payments at all. Of the one-third who did, about half did so through the Child Support mechanism and half through a private arrangement. Where it was paid, it could be important for some, pulling just over half (57 per cent) of those receiving it (the 36 per cent) out of poverty.

As an alternative to courts, this attempt to establish an administrative system to deal with a disputed personal obligation has little to commend it. It might be noted, however, that as a way of bringing to public attention the need for all

---

[121] Department of Work and Pensions, *Child Maintenance Service 2012 Scheme – Experimental Statistics August 2013–May 2016.*

[122] Work and Pension Committee 14th Report: *Child Maintenance Service* (HC 587) (2 May 2017).

[123] C Bryson, A Skipp, J Albeson, E Poole, E Ireland and V Marsh, *Kids aren't free: The child maintenance arrangements of single parents on benefit 2012* (Nuffield Foundation).

parents not living with their children whether married, separated or never having lived together to provide financial support, did have some impact. As a form of public legal education rather than dispute resolution or child poverty reduction some progress was made.

IX. Are These Purely Private Matters?

Some commentators have ascribed the present state of legal aid provision in England and Wales, and elsewhere, to 'neoliberal' policies that grew from the 1980s. There have been many characterisations of neoliberalism. This one is typical: 'Neo-liberalists believe that leaving matters to private enterprise is far more efficient than collective action, and consequentially seek to replace the state with private enterprise, and notions of social justice and the public good with profit-making and self-interest'.[124] Hilary Sommerlad proclaims: 'It is common ground that the attacks of the last three decades on post-war social citizenship in the UK – fundamental to which was access to justice – are attributable to neoliberalism'.[125] She continues: 'In this instance, this entails, first, practical policies ... of stigmatising and penalising the poor and excluding them from state-sponsored dispute resolution in the courts ...'.[126] The same rhetoric was employed in the government's arguments for withdrawal of legal aid from most private family law disputes in England and Wales. Barlow et al see the encouragement of the use of mediation as part of the neoliberal project to 'redirect behaviour' towards people 'tak(ing) responsibility for resolving their own disputes, without the involvement of courts, solicitors or the law'.[127]

However it is labelled, a feature of this period has been a growth in wealth inequality, marginalisation of those unable or less able to live their lives successfully, and unwillingness to use state mechanisms to support such people. The decline of state support for institutions that provide such support can suddenly leave them fragile and close to collapse, so that eventually they virtually disappear. The policy was particularly marked after the economic crisis of 2008, with attempts to restore capitalism by retrenchment (austerity) and increased privatisation.[128] The process had been promoted by injecting management structures into those remaining public institutions designed to bring about a 'business-like' ethic in the

---

[124] D Nicolson, 'Legal Education, ethics and access to justice: forging warriors for justice in a neo-liberal world' (2105) 22 *International Journal of the Legal Profession* 51–69, 52.

[125] H Somerlad, 'Access to Justice in Hard Times and the Deconstruction of Democratic Citizenship' in M Maclean, J Eekelaar and B Bastard (eds), *Delivering Family Justice in the 21st Century* (Oxford, Hart Publishing, 2015), ch 1, 243. See also Kaganas (n 27), 178–79.

[126] ibid, 245.

[127] Barlow et al (n 9) 13.

[128] W Streeck, 'Markets and Peoples: Democratic Capitalism and European Integration' (2012) 73 *New Left Review* 63–71.

name of efficiency. This sometimes resulted in complete, or partial, privatisation (transport, telecommunications, energy and water suppliers) and in the health services new management structures 'subjected the NHS to a particular form of managerialism that in turn led directly to the introduction of a quasi-market in health care centred around competition and choice'.[129]

As regards social care, an intercountry study, centred on the UK, found that 'the experience of many countries has been neoliberal implementation through the rhetoric of public service modernization and a drive for greater resource efficiency. Other changes have been the discourse or ideas of social work "clients" and "citizens" recast as that of "consumers", whilst at the same time public organisations are remoulded as replicas of the business world'.[130] The management style that developed has been termed the 'New Public Management', and its devices have been described as including breaking down 'monolithic' units by disaggregating functions (or products), decentralisation and diversity to enhance 'choice', top-down management directives, discipline and frugality of resource usage, efficiency savings targets, flexible hiring, short-term contracts and use of public relations (PR) techniques.[131]

In the family context, the focus is upon encouraging individual responsibility and therefore confining public support to circumstances where individuals are perceived to be especially disabled from 'looking after themselves' so that, unless individuals can pay for the service, the legal system will operate something like an Accident and Emergency Department of a hospital. Where the state does not become directly involved, as, for example, it does in child protection matters, it might be thought that, as these issues arise within what are usually considered peoples' private or intimate lives, if they choose to utilise a public resource, like the law, to resolve them, the cost should fall on them. This was the position taken by the UK Coalition Government in 2010 when, in its proposals to limit legal aid funding, it referred to such instances as 'cases which can very often result from a litigant's own decisions in their personal life' and which therefore the government was 'less likely to consider (to) concern issues of the highest importance'.[132] Although expressed as a matter of prioritisation, this verdict signalled a withdrawal of 'public' interest in assisting any person who wished to bring about compliance with legal norms with respect to the kinds of issues mentioned earlier.

---

[129] A Scott-Samuel, C Bambra, C Collins, DJ Hunter, G McCartney and K Smith, 'Neoliberalism in Health Care: the Impact of Thatcherism on Health and Wellbeing in Britain' (2014) 44 *International Journal of Health Services* 53–71, 61.

[130] G Spolander, L Engelbrecht, L Martin, M Strydom, I Perovova, P Marjanen, P Toni, A Sicora and F Adaikalam, 'The implications of neoliberalism for social work: Reflections from a six-country research collaboration' (2014) 57 *International Social Work* 301–12, 306.

[131] See eg, C Hood, 'The New Public Management in the 1980s: Variations on a Theme' (1995) 20 *Accounting, Organizations and Society* 93–109; N Hyndman and I Lapsley, 'New Public Management: The Story Continues' (2016) 32 *Financial Accounting and Management* 385–408.

[132] Ministry of Justice (n 77) and Eekelaar (n 77).

Only limited exceptions were recognised, such as where a person's health or safety was threatened by violence, or the matter had an international dimension. Otherwise the provision of such protection was to be left to the market: those with the requisite means could purchase it, otherwise they had either to attempt to secure it without assistance, or 'lump it'.

Whatever force may lie in the argument from ideology, it remains true that, as Alan Paterson remarked in 2012: 'Part of the ever-present pressure for cost-cutting emanates from the figures that show that over the years the real cost of legal aid not infrequently rose faster than inflation, productivity or GDP.'[133] Over the period 1988–89 to 2003–04, the total cost of legal aid rose by 160 per cent in real terms.[134] It was concerns such as these that immediately prompted the controls placed on legal aid work, including family law work, by the Access to Justice Act 1999 and the recommendations for introducing competitive tendering for legal aid contracts with the Legal Services Commission, referred to earlier.[135] Restrictions on the provision of legal aid may therefore have been driven as much by reasonable concerns about the control of public expenditure as by political ideology. If that is so, it becomes important to try to identify the causes of this pressure on legal aid funding.

Various causes have been suggested. One was 'supplier-induced demand', to which a judicare system which guarantees payment for work undertaken by private professionals is susceptible.[136] However, the more likely reason lies in growth in the scope and complexity of the law. For example, it has been estimated that between 1997 and 2010 approximately 3,000 new criminal offences were created. During this period there were also rises in cases disposed of by Crown Courts, in the prison population and in expenditure on policing.[137] We have referred earlier to the increasing legal complexity of family law matters. Despite this, the government's claims that legal aid expenditure in the UK greatly exceeded that in other countries, while true, ignored total expenditure on the justice system, so that when expenditure on courts (including the judiciary) and prosecution is added, the total spend for England and Wales was not significantly out of line with that of selected European countries.[138] Furthermore, in Scotland, where per capita spend of legal aid is similar to that in England and Wales, there has not been a comparable reduction in scope and eligibility.[139]

---

[133] A Paterson (n 9) 74.
[134] Ministry of Justice (n 77) para 3.37.
[135] See p. 12.
[136] E Cape and R Moorhead, *Demand Induced supply? Report to the Legal Services Commission* (LSC 2005); Paterson (n 9) 75–76.
[137] See T Smith and E Cape, 'The rise and decline of criminal legal aid in England and Wales' in A Flynn and J Hodgson (eds), *Access to Justice and Legal Aid: Comparative Perspectives on Unmet Legal Need* (Oxford, Hart Publishing, 2017) 69.
[138] See Eekelaar (n 77) 316–17.
[139] See Evans (n 116) 16.

X. Conclusions, Methodology and What Follows

This significant expansion in legal regulation in family matters was not designed to exert state control over people's behaviour, but to redress power imbalances and promote justice. But it may not be surprising that the costs of delivering this through lawyers and the legal system has caused concern and that government has looked to achieving these goals in different ways. Debates about the prioritisation of spending public moneys belong in the political sphere. Our task here is only to observe the change that has occurred in the degree of public provision for services that formerly were thought to warrant such provision and to consider what, if anything, may be done to make up for shortfalls in such provision.

The reasons for that change seem to lie partly in the ideologies that underpin neoliberalism, but also in the difficulty of responding to pressures put upon the previous system by legal and social change. But whatever they were, we now need to explore what, if any, forms of assistance have developed to replace that now absent provision to see whether some coherent pattern is emerging which will fulfil the need for people of limited means to receive the support necessary to receive the protection to which as members of the community they are entitled from the community's laws. Such an investigation over the impact of legal aid cuts on social welfare law in issues such as debt, employment, housing, immigration and welfare benefits to help people cope with the problems of everyday life was carried out by the Low Commission in 2012. The Commission was concerned that legal support would be lost in situations such as: getting a landlord to undertake repairs; a nurse working for 20 years in the NHS unable to rent because immigration status not regularised; anxiety about losing a home because of debt; unfair dismissal; loss of disability benefit because of wrong assessment.[140] The Commission did not, however, include issues covered by family law.

This book is an attempt to assemble a picture of the varied and fragmented contexts in which those who previously might have been assisted through legal aid, but for whom such assistance is no longer available, might find some support. It is by its nature exploratory, and aims to investigate the *nature* of the different kinds of assistance that exist. Although we cannot produce quantifiable data, our conversations with key participants and use of various data sources allow us to give some indication of the extent of availability of some of the sources. As in our previous studies we have also observed how these new kinds of help are provided and used in practice, and how they differ from traditional full legal service, both in and out of court, but again these are provided by way of illustration rather than the result of systematic acquisition through a representative sample. Our focus, as

---

[140] Low Commission, *Tackling the Advice Deficit: A strategy for access to advice and legal support on social welfare law in England and Wales* (Legal Action Group 2014) vii.

in the earlier studies, is on who is doing what, what skills are used and what tasks are performed; for example, how much of the available help is procedural, how much more strategic? And how far can non-lawyers provide help with legal issues, including information, advice and support ?

In what follows we first consider the instances where government is involved in, and commits resources towards, assisting parties experiencing family issues as understood above, including through the development of digital resources. We then look at the response of the legal profession and of the judiciary to the need for affordable legal help with family matters, the development of help provided by students through the expansion of Clinical Legal Education, and the work of the advice sector. We end by looking at the approach aiming to develop greater public legal capability through Public Legal Education and the potential contribution of legal expertise which may be provided not necessarily by lawyers.

2

Government Activity After LASPO

LASPO did not mean that government involvement in regard to help with family issues of the kinds referred to in the previous chapter totally ceased. The policy focus on alternatives to widespread use of courts and lawyers continues, and, as will be described, a number of ways in which this might be achieved have developed. These include increasing the use of digital technology in both modernising access to court and developing alternative digital pathways to conflict resolution. These were preceded just before LASPO by attempts to promote cooperation between legal aid services provided through lawyers and community-based advice services which it was hoped would provide a more holistic approach to the clusters of problems often experienced by those in need. Although these attempts were ultimately unsuccessful, we will look first at this pre-LASPO plan to encourage community legal services before considering the various ways in which government support has continued after the Act.

I. Community Legal Services

Even though the activity of legal aid solicitors in family matters was geared to resolving issues without seeking resolution by a court, this had been insufficiently recognised by government, and, as explained earlier,[1] prior to LASPO, concerns over legal aid expenditure had led to significant regulation of legal aid work by solicitors and a reduction in its availability. But the government had not abandoned a policy of attempting other forms of more holistic community-based intervention in family problems. One of its aims was to prevent more extensive legal problems arising later which would require the assistance of court. This lay behind the promotion of mediation during the 1990s, but, as we saw in the previous chapter,[2] mediation has not provided this. The 1997 Labour Government's concerns about the dominance and cost of the legal profession in the legal aid system and a new understanding of how families often experience 'clusters' of legal problems and require interlinked complementary support with benefits, housing and employment as traditionally offered in the independent advice sector,

---

[1] See pp 11–13.
[2] See p 16.

prompted fresh thinking about early intervention.[3] The Access to Justice Act 1999 tasked a newly formed non-departmental public body, the Legal Services Commission (LSC) 'to establish, maintain and develop a service known as the Community Legal Service (CLS) for the purpose of promoting the availability to individuals of (specified) services'. The specified services included 'the provision of general information about the law and legal system'; 'the provision of help by the giving of legal advice as to how the law applies in particular cases'; and 'the provision of help in preventing, or settling, or otherwise resolving disputes about legal rights and duties'.[4] This holistic CLS was to be contracted by the LSC and delivered by local partnerships between members of the legal profession, Citizens Advice Bureaux and Law Centres.[5]

Despite this emphasis on prevention, the strict budgeting and franchising requirements of the CLS and competitive tendering in fact reduced the overall provision of legal advice by law firms and made it *more* difficult for the advice sector providers to take part in a collaborative venture. Furthermore, few individual firms held contracts for a sufficiently wide range of legal issues, so clients experiencing a 'cluster' of issues needed to be referred to other providers. In 2005 the LSC proposed a new initiative in an attempt to provide a seamless and integrated service through Community Legal Advice Centres (CLACs) where the various sources of help would be co-located, and Community Legal Advice Networks (CLANs) where service providers would work together from different locations, to be funded as single entities.[6] John Flood gives the examples of the Gateshead Community Legal Advice Centre (CLAC), 'formed of the Gateshead Citizens Advice Bureau and additionally, as subcontractors, three private law firms that provide specialist advice, and is funded by the Gateshead local authority and the LSC' and 'another CLAC in Derby … run by Access2Law, a community interest company that subcontracts to a citizens advice and law centre, Derbyshire Housing Aid (voluntary sector), and two solicitors' firms. The centre is jointly funded by Derby City Council and the Legal Services Commission.'[7]

Initial advice was covered by the Citizens Advice Bureau (CAB), which also met further costs not covered by legal aid. The service provided a 15 minute assessment followed by 30 minutes advice from a CAB adviser or paralegal, with

---

[3] H Genn, *Paths to Justice: What people do and think about going to law* (Oxford, Hart Publishing, 1999) 31–36. For an overview, see P Pleasance, NJ Balmer and C Denvir, *How people understand and interact with the Law* (Cambridge, PPSR, 2015).

[4] Access to Justice Act 1999, s 4.

[5] Lord Chancellor's Department, *Community Legal Services Consultation* (25 May 1999): http://webarchive.nationalarchives.gov.uk/+/http:/www.dca.gov.uk/consult/access/mjch2.htm (last accessed 30 May 2018).

[6] See Legal Services Commission, *Annual Report 2006/7*, 2: https://assets.publishing.service.gov.uk/government/uploads/system/uploads/attachment_data/file/250788/0716.pdf (last accessed 30 May 2018).

[7] J Flood, *The transformation of access to law and justice in England and Wales*, https://www.ces.uc.pt/projectos/mutacoes/media/pdf/THE_TRANSFORMATION_OF_ACCESS_TO_LAW_AND_JUSTICE_IN_ENGLAND_AND_WALES_2.pdf (last accessed 27 Septeember 2018).

referral to a specialist solicitor where necessary.[8] However it proved difficult, and costly, to bring disparate providers (such as law firms and local authorities) together in a joint commissioning process, and the emergence of a single larger entity could disrupt the functioning of local networks of smaller interdependent advice agencies. When these schemes were evaluated[9] shortly before the plans for LASPO were announced, it was found that they were taking a long time to establish. Each contract tendered for took over a year to complete, even with an LSC policy person working on it. By 2010 there were still only eight CLACs and two CLANs. This failure coincided with the reduction in both legal aid and local authority funding and a decline in the number of Law Centres affected by this, and, as legal aid rates for payment fell further behind private rates, the work became less attractive to local practitioners. The LSC's aim to work to 'prevent legal problems from arising' proved too costly in money and time, though pressure to increase case volume had continued to mount.

Despite this, government has provided some assistance to the advice sector by contributing £33 million to the Advice Services Transition Fund set up by the National Lottery for this purpose over the first two years following LASPO.[10] The role of the advice sector in family matters will be considered in chapter nine. Public funding for such a holistic and preventive approach was and remains evident in some other jurisdictions. For example, in Scotland, where the Legal Profession and Legal Aid (Scotland) Act 2007 permitted grant funding projects with the third sector, the Scottish Legal Aid Board has been working with local authorities to deliver an integrated advice service in outlying parts of the country.[11] In Scotland, with this approach they have been able to avoid any reduction in the scope of civil legal aid, or caps on amounts to be paid out, and 70 per cent of the population have been able to remain eligible for legal aid funding.[12] This is in strong contrast to the position in England and Wales and may have been made possible because in Scotland legal aid is administered through the more independent Scottish Legal Aid Board, whereas in England and Wales this was brought under direct ministerial control when, as described in chapter one, LASPO set

[8] A Buck, J Sidaway and L Scanlan, *Piecing it together: exploring one stop shop legal service delivery in CLACS* (Legal Services Commission, 2010).

[9] C Fox, R Moorhead, M Sefton and K Wong, 'Community legal advice centres and networks: process evaluation' (2011) *Civil Justice Quarterly* 91; A Paterson, *Lawyers and the Public Good: Democracy in Action* (Cambridge University Press, 2012) 81–5.

[10] See https://assets.publishing.service.gov.uk/government/uploads/system/uploads/attachment_data/file/80217/not-for-profit-advice-services-england.pdf (last accessed 10 June 2018). Or adviceservicestransition.org.uk.

[11] A Paterson, *Lawyers and the Public Good: Democracy in Action?* (Cambridge UP, 2012) 85.

[12] M Evans, *Re-thinking Legal Aid: An Independent Strategic Review (of Legal Aid in Scotland)* (February 2018). Alan Paterson has described the creative use of legal aid funds, eg through the Highlands Project, whereby the SLAB funds 5 salaried lawyers in Inverness who will take legal aid cases which the 37 contract holders in local firms cannot handle. A Paterson, *Paper to the Access to Justice Workshop*, University of Leeds, 1 May 2017.

up the Legal Aid Agency which now sits within the Ministry of Justice under an internal Director with a largely internal Board.[13]

In Australia the 2009 Strategic Framework for Access to Justice (civil)[14] states that 'in many situations early action (which includes triage and ADR) can resolve a matter or identify the best course of action … failure to address legal problems has been shown to lead to entrenched disadvantage'. The State Legal Aid Commissions remained the largest providers, with salaried lawyers and pro bono practitioners.[15] But, following a successful campaign to halt funding cuts in 2017,[16] the Community Legal Centres (CLCs) have been able to develop a more holistic approach, combining legal with non-legal services. CLC lawyers take part in community legal education and law reform as well as traditional legal advice and representation. A new initiative for a Health Justice Partnership (HJCs) is trying to train health professionals to identify people who are experiencing legal issues. The key words are 'co-location', 'outreach' and 'multidisciplinary settings'.

In Europe, despite concerns to control public expenditure, public legal intervention is widely seen as part of the primary function of the state in implementing legislation. In the Netherlands, where approximately 36 per cent of the public are currently eligible for legal aid,[17] the government has remained committed to the active pursuit of access to justice for all those with limited resources through a range of interventions including duty lawyers, community legal clinics, law shops and direct payment of lawyers by the state. It is famous for its Legal Service Counters (*lokets*), the one-stop shops which give legal information and advice, or refer clients to a private lawyer or mediator, who act as the secondary line of legal aid, or to other forms of professional help or support. These counters see over 2,700 cases a year, and offer services which are specialised and reach the disadvantaged. When costs were reviewed in 2011 and a loan system as used in Germany was proposed, the Dutch Legal Aid Board responded by suggesting simplifying the legislation instead. In Belgium there has been discussion of a service linking law with social work, to respond to the increasing legalisation of social relationships, in order to support social citizenship and to uphold fundamental social rights. The Belgian Public Social Welfare Office (OCMW) provides general universal

[13] A Paterson, 'Does independence matter for Legal Aid Boards', Paper given at the Research Committee on Sociology of Law Working Group, Andorra July 2018.

[14] A Strategic Framework for Access to Justice in the Federal Civil Justice System Australian Government Attorney General's Department (September 2009) 9: https://www.ag.gov.au/LegalSystem/Documents/A%20Strategic%20Framework%20for%20Access%20to%20Justice%20in%20the%20Federal%20Civil%20Justice%20System.pdf (last accessed 27 September 2018).

[15] Yu Shan Chang, *The Mechanisms and Rationale for Integrated Publicly Funded Legal Services: a comparative study of England and Wales, Australia and Taiwan* (Doctoral Thesis, University College, London, 2016).

[16] M Riboldi, '#FundEqualJustice – increasing public funds for legal assistance', Paper given at the Access to Justice and Legal Services Conference, University College, London, June 2018.

[17] See Report by the Raad voor Rechtsbijstand, *Legal Aid in the Netherlands* (2015). http://www.rvr.org/binaries/content/assets/rvrorg/informatie-over-de-raad/brochure-legalaid_juni2013_webversie.pdf (last accessed 30 May 2018).

social services including help with debt and the general welfare Centre for the Vulnerable, but the Law Shop makes a charge for their service.[18]

II. Assisting Litigants

While in England and Wales the overall aim of reducing the role of courts and lawyers in private family matters does not appear to have been furthered by the attempt to substitute mediation or early holistic local intervention, government has revealed plans to speed up the court process, minimise the need for attendance and develop a digital Out of Court Alternative Pathway to dispute resolution in family matters. So there is government activity after LASPO, but it is less visible, less accessible, less generous, and less comprehensive than before. Access to justice is no longer seen in terms of provision of professional legal help but instead as *including* developing personal responsibility and self help through the use of web-based procedures. In addition to investing in these new developments, government has also been obliged to extend a degree of assistance in the traditional procedures through the Litigants in Person Support Strategy (LiPSS) to support the rapidly expanding population of litigants in person (LiPs) now going to court without professional help, and also by supporting public legal education activity and promoting high quality accessible information. We deal with public legal education separately in chapter ten. Here we consider government activities primarily directed at supporting those people who do use the court system. Other sources of help for these people are described at various points in later chapters.

A. Modernising the Courts

Following the Family Justice Review of 2011[19] the government accepted and has largely put into effect the recommendation to make the family court system clearer and more transparent.[20] Since then, the Ministry of Justice (MoJ) has committed to a £1 billion programme of court reform, £700 million for civil justice and £270 million for criminal justice.[21] The focus will be on interagency work, on signposting to ADR, fewer adversarial hearings, faster completion rates, more virtual working and an improved service for business citizens and the vulnerable. The three core principles build on existing strengths: the system must be just, proportionate

---

[18] B Hubeau and A Terlouw, *Legal Aid in the Low Countries* (Intersentia, 2014), Foreword by J van Houtte.

[19] Ministry of Justice, *Family Justice Review* (November 2011).

[20] Mr Justice Ryder, *Judicial Proposals for the Modernisation of Family Justice* (The Judiciary, London, 2012); Children and Families Act 2014.

[21] The Lord Chancellor, the Lord Chief Justice and the Senior President of Tribunals, *Transforming Our Justice System* (Ministry of Justice, September 2016).

and accessible. For straightforward cases, the aim is to make procedure simple and easy to use, with a choice of approaches enabling the judge and litigants to decide on what is the most appropriate. There will be innovation, introducing new and less combative methods for disputes to be resolved, with case officers to handle basic case management and case progression, allowing the judiciary to focus where their time and expertise is really needed. Implementation is still in progress, but a press release[22] from HMCTS (HM Courts and Tribunals Service) on 6 April 2018 described the successful progress of the Civil Money Claims Pilot for online processing of claims under £10,000 which went live in August 2017, and was described as a success by the Justice Minister, Lucy Frazer MP, and also by the PSU (a charity supporting people who represent themselves in the civil and family justice system, whose work is described further below). The same announcement described how fare evasions are being handled without paper at Lavender Hill Magistrates Court, and how tax appeals can now be submitted online.

In family matters, online divorce applications moved from the pilot stage to full scale provision in April 2018.[23] The new service allows applicants to complete their divorce application, upload their documents, pay and submit online. There is 'light touch' assistance over the telephone, and more intensive face-to-face support for users who are completely digitally excluded. Earlier findings from Liz Trinder's study of 11 regional divorce centres in England where trained staff (not judges) worked through 30 to 40 files of papers submitted to initiate the divorce process in a morning showed that this was resulting in over one-third of the papers being sent back, largely for clerical reasons (eg, ticking the wrong box, failure to sign).[24] The government announcement of the full launch of the online system[25] stated that the online version had resulted in a 95 per cent drop in the number of applications being returned because of mistakes, when compared with the paper forms. Only 0.6 per cent of online forms had been returned between January and May.

Of course this process assumes the application is not contested, and covers only the initial application, not later procedural stages (although it is planned to extend the service to the completion of the process), and covers only the grant of the divorce, not 'ancillary' matters that may need to be settled or resolved. The priority for the family courts remains the welfare of children. There is an overall commitment to provide digital assistance in the civil courts of over £5 million a year, based on the assumption that 85 per cent of court users will have basic online skills (for example, social media use, buying online and online banking). Total revenue raised by sales of courts so far amounts to £45 million.[26]

---

[22] See https://www.gov.uk/government/news/quicker-way-to-resolve-claim-disputes-launched-online (last accessed 26 June 2018).

[23] https://www.gov.uk/apply-for-divorce (last accessed 26 June 2018).

[24] L Trinder, 'Losing the particulars? Digital divorce and the potential for harm reduction' (2017) 47 *Family Law* 17.

[25] See n 21.

[26] C Denvir, 'Online Courts and Access to Justice: Providing Support for the Digitally Defaulted' Paper given at the Access to Justice and Legal Services Conference (University College, London, June 2018).

B. Digital Out of Court Pathway

While the court modernisation initiative uses the new technology to facilitate and speed up existing court processes, the new Digital Unit at the MoJ will take the digital revolution further, not by looking at how to make courts work better, and making it easier to use them, but at how their use can be avoided by at least a substantial group of those currently making applications. A digital Out of Court Pathway is being developed by government, aiming not only to ameliorate the position after LASPO but also to find better outcomes for children and families by encouraging a shift to 'self service' and reducing court appearances, particularly repeat court appearances. The team has studied developments in other jurisdictions, and while wanting to learn from the Australian holistic experience, acknowledges that this jurisdiction at present lacks the resources to follow the same path. Australian policy has long needed to respond to the needs of the indigenous population often in remote areas, and this may have added to their recognition of supporting access to justice in a number of ways, including a very effective telephone helpline in New South Wales.[27]

The Ministry of Justice is not the only department seeking to develop digital service provision. A government website entitled 'Assisted Digital Support Service Manual'[28] sets out the digital standard for all departments, the criteria for defining users who need help, how it can be provided and how to assess costs and effectiveness. There is a new (2017) requirement that when taking a service out of face-to-face or telephone access into digital there must be a contract for services to support its use. In the case of the MoJ, this contract is with the Good Things Foundation. In the context of family justice however, there is a marked contrast between the position in England and Wales, characterised by the aim of reducing court appearances, and the policy landscape in other jurisdictions, which is characterised by greater acceptance of public responsibility for legal services and interest in improving access to justice and linking legal help for the vulnerable to other welfare provisions.

The Digital team described their approach to participants in a Show Case event in August 2016 after a six month developmental stage which included consultation with experts, parties and practitioners. The group is aware that at separation parties are often in conflict and emotionally upset, and this may affect their decision-making ability. The idea is that each party will be required to input their details, and will then be given a personalised action plan. Parties will be assessed by a Family Court Assessor as to whether they may proceed to court, probably taking into account whether they have taken reasonable steps to engage with other alternative ways of dealing with the problem. There will be a fast route

---

[27] See https://www.legalaid.nsw.gov.au/get-legal-help/legal-helpline (last accessed 30 May 2018).
[28] See https://www.gov.uk/service-manual/helping-people-to-use-your-service/assisted-digital-support-introduction (last accessed 30 May 2018).

to court for those in need, for example as a result of domestic abuse. And there will be assistance for those who find the digital process difficult. There is mention of the need for information from the right person in the right place at the right time, and to consider user preference. But while there is considerable technical expertise, there is as yet no detail about the content of the assessment exercise or the action plan. In civil justice, there is also little interest in the management of digital interaction, such as preparing a witness to talk to a camera.[29]

The inspiration for the undertaking comes from the Dutch interactive website for family legal problems known as the '*Rechtwijzer*' (Law Guidepost), which was designed to take two people through their divorce process and deal with finance and arrangements for children. The website identified a conflict domain, used a dynamic questioning agenda, taking into account the degree of urgency in the matter and giving links to other sources of help and aids to self help. The divorce and parenting plan[30] listed issues, supports communication between the parties, and offered objective criteria and a calculations tool leading to the now mandatory parenting plan which must be submitted in the Netherlands before a divorce can be granted.[31] The project was developed as a dispute resolution process by The Hague Institute for Innovation of Law (HiiL), a not-for-profit organisation, with considerable financial support from the Dutch legal aid budget in the hope that it would provide a quick and low-cost alternative to the traditional legal aid counter services for family matters in the Netherlands. The cost to those not eligible for public funding was low, 300–400 euros, depending on how much additional legal advice was requested during the process. At a later stage a 'decision' button was added for parties to receive a decision on a particular issue from a 'decision maker', usually a lawyer, though not necessarily a specialist family lawyer. The process was supported with software by the large firm, Modria, which provides consumer dispute resolution services internationally.

The lawyers involved in the publicly funded aspect of the work were paid the hourly market rate, but not always for the full number of hours of work done. They began to express increasing concerns about the fairness of some of the agreements reached, and to be less willing to continue to review agreements reached for viability in court. The project was not as successful as hoped, and was suddenly suspended in April 2017.[32] The UK charity, Relate, which had entered into an

---

[29] Unlike in the area of criminal justice: see P Gibbs, 'Defendants on Video – Conveyer Belt Justice or Revolution in Access' Paper given at the Access to Justice and Legal Services Conference (University College, London, June 2018).

[30] https://translate.google.co.uk/translate?hl=en&sl=nl&u=https://www.rvr.org/nieuws/2010/maart/echtscheidings--en-ouderschapsplan-online.html&prev=search (last accessed 3 October 2018).

[31] For an assessment of the effectiveness of these plans, see S de Bruijn, A-R Poortman and T van der Lippe 'Do Parenting Plans work? The Effect of Parenting Plans on Procedural, Family and Child Outcomes' (2018) 32(3) *International Journal of Law, Policy and the Family* 394.

[32] See D Bindman, 'Pioneering ODR platform to rein in ambitions after commercial setback' Legal Futures Blog 3 April 2017: https://www.legalfutures.co.uk/latest-news/pioneering-odr-platform-to-rein-in-ambitions-after-commercial-setback (last accessed 19 June 2018); R Smith, 'The decline

agreement to buy into the service, put the project on hold.[33] It had not been popular with low income users, who preferred face-to-face help. It was used by only 6 per cent of the divorcing population, mainly the more affluent and educated, who found it helpful for the early stages of seeking information, but they often did not proceed to the end of the process to reach settlement. The constant nudging towards 'harmony' seems to have been at the expense of seeking fairness. Maurits Barendrecht, Research Director at HiiL, recognised a 'submission problem', namely, that 'getting "the other party" to the table and parties voluntarily agreeing to use the same procedure often just does not happen'.[34] It has been suggested[35] that the company had over-extended in trying to develop its business internationally and had run into difficulty. The Dutch legal aid authority might have been prepared to continue funding, but HiiL could not sustain the economic position. A new private fully commercial service, 'Justice42' has commenced, recommended but not funded by government.[36] This service has had 100 users in its first nine months.[37] There may be lessons to be learned for the Out of Court Pathway project. In the Netherlands, use of ADR remains low, and private legal insurance on the German model[38] is increasing. In 2017 legal expenses insurance cover was recorded as reaching 42 per cent of the population.[39]

In England and Wales, previous government interactive website expertise has been mainly in the field of benefit claims, where the individual user is in dialogue with the state provider about eligibility rules. A Civil Legal Advice (CLA) telephone helpline is available for advice regarding matters for which legal aid is available. This involves initial eligibility assessment and, if this is successful, reference to

---

and fall (and potential resurgence) of the Rechtwijzer': http://www.legalvoice.org.uk/decline-fall-potential-resurgence-rechtwijzer/ (last accessed 31 May 2018).

[33] See N Hilborne 'Relate puts pioneering online divorce project on hold': https://www.legalfutures.co.uk/latest-news/relate-puts-pioneering-online-divorce-project-hold (last accessed 301 May 2018).

[34] M Barendrecht, 'Rechtwijzer: Why Online Supported Dispute Resolution Is Hard to Implement': http://www.hiil.org/insight/rechtwijzer-why-online-supporte-dispute-resolution-is-hard-to-implement (last accessed 19 June 2018).

[35] See Smith (n 32).

[36] www.uitelkaar.nl: See also *Scheiden zonder Schade*, 2018, published by the Rijksoverheid (a report from members of parliament, officials, and the Ministry of Health with the Ministry of Justice on divorce reform recommending moving away from the online approach, and supporting the use of a single lawyer rather than one for each party with the aim of reducing conflict): see https://translate.google.co.uk/translate?hl=en&sl=nl&u=https://www.rijksoverheid.nl/documenten/kamerstukken/2018/05/09/uitvoeringsprogramma-scheiden-zonder-schade&prev=search (last accessed 19 June 2018).

[37] S Peters and L Combrink (of the Dutch Legal Aid Board), 'Customer Journey Research within the Legal Aid Reform', Paper given at the Access to Justice and Legal Services Conference (University College, London, June 2018).

[38] Because fixed costs are common in Germany, it is easier to acquire insurance cover, so private legal insurance is the norm, with public legal aid available only if private insurance would not be affordable, or is not provided as an employee benefit: see M Trebilcock, A Duggan and L Sossin (eds), *Middle Income Access to Justice* (Toronto, University of Toronto Press, 2012) 263.

[39] www.rvr.org/binaroes/content/assets/.../12835_legalaid-brochure_2017.pdf (last accessed 19 June 2018).

a 'specialist' (who makes a second eligibility assessment). Since LASPO it has operated as a mandatory gateway in applications for legal aid in relation to debt, discrimination and special educational needs. Face-to-face advice is possible, but an evaluation of the mandatory gateway showed that only 3.1 per cent of users were referred to this (mostly in debt cases) in the first 12 months after LASPO came into effect, although evidence showed more users would have wanted this. 'Users with complex cases were particularly disappointed at not being able to speak to someone in person and expressed a preference for at least one face-to-face meeting.'[40] How far this service would be successful in family matters is unclear. For the Pathway to succeed in keeping parties out of court, the second party must agree to join the process, and this will depend on the emotional state of the parties. Here the purchaser is the MoJ, the providers are the Digital team, and the users are the parties. In the commercial field, the user has some power, but this is not the case in family issues. Furthermore, the legal framework within which they must operate is shaped by the best interest of a third party: the child. To devise commercially viable web-based assistance for dispute resolution where third party interests are paramount, where emotions run high, and where the focus is on the future needs of the parties, not the culpability of past actions, may still be an aspiration rather than a reality.

Using web-based technology for giving information, and for processing forms, may well help to reduce costs and delay in the family justice system but dispute resolution is a different matter. The costs of the various existing approaches to the various parties also need further examination. A First Hearing and Dispute Resolution Appointment (FHDRA) on a child matter before a judge may cost the MoJ £600–£900 to run, and a final welfare hearing £1,500.[41] This would be avoided if the parties resolved the matter out of court, thus transferring the cost to them alone. The applicant would still pay £550 for the divorce decree. If, in the case of a children dispute, the parties take the mediation pathway, then, on the basis of three one-hour mediation sessions (on average £160 per hour for each party but costed at 90 minutes to include administrative expenses), and £70 each for the MIAM, and a fee of up to £500 for documents, including a Memorandum of Understanding if agreement is reached, or in a finance cases a statement of income, assets and outgoings, the total cost to them could be £2,080. Add to this the legal help needed for a finance case requiring a Consent Order for enforceability, perhaps £500 each, VAT, and court fees (£215 court application fee for child arrangements even where a Consent Order has been prepared), and the total is likely to be well over £2,000 each.[42] If the parties used a free website, the cost

---

[40] A Patel and C Mottram, *Civil Legal Advice mandatory gateway: Overarching research summary* (Ministry of Justice, 2014) 3: https://assets.publishing.service.gov.uk/government/uploads/system/uploads/attachment_data/file/384307/cla-gateway-research-summary.pdf (last accessed 31 May 2018).

[41] These estimates are based on preparatory work for the Ministry of Justice, *Mediation Task Force* (2014).

[42] These figures are drawn from the work of the Mediation Task Force (n 41) and data from the fieldwork for M Maclean and J Eekelaar, *Lawyers and Mediators* (Oxford, Hart Publishing, 2016).

to the government, assuming triage, assessment, updating, checking, support and possible face-to-face contact has yet to be fully costed but might not be very much cheaper than the court process. For the parties, if the impact of making access to court difficult were to result in additional collateral legal problems or social disadvantage, there might be additional costs. The British Columbia Civil Resolution Tribunal (CRT), which deals with small claims and certain condominium disputes submitted and processed online, could provide a model, but it does not deal with family issues.[43]

C. Government Support for the Litigant in Person Support Strategy

As stated earlier,[44] family cases where both parties are litigants in person (LiPs) rose from 16 per cent in 2013 to 34 per cent in 2016, and cases where both were represented fell from 38 per cent to 21 per cent over the same period.[45] This has placed a heavy burden on court staff and the judiciary. The study by Liz Trinder and colleagues for the Ministry of Justice[46] gives a clear account of the problems of establishing what is at issue where neither side is represented. Particularly difficult situations have arisen when a person (usually a woman) has made allegations of violence against her partner, who is unrepresented and therefore seeks to question her in court. This is discussed further in chapter six.[47]

Some additional training has been provided for judges in how to help where there are two LiPs and one may be more vulnerable. In addition, government has supported the Litigant in Person Support Strategy (LiPSS), established in 2014, the Minister for Courts and Justice stating in 2017 that it had provided £3.5 million for strategy since 2015.[48] LiPSS does not give individual assistance but is a collaboration of services which do. It is overseen by a committee of the chief executives of six organisations, the Personal Support Unit (PSU), which is a charity (described in detail in chapter seven) in which volunteers, according to its website, 'help people to represent themselves more effectively in civil and family cases and tribunals', and has a presence at 20 courts,[49] the Royal Courts of Justice Advice (RCJ Advice), LawWorks, Law for Life (incorporating AdviceNow), the Bar Pro

---

[43] see info@crt.bc.

[44] See p 19.

[45] Ministry of Justice, *Family Court Statistics Quarterly, England and Wales, Annual 2016* (2016), Figures 1 and 8; Ministry of Justice, *Legal Aid, Sentencing and Punishment of Offenders Act 2012: Post-Legislative Memorandum submitted to the Justice Select Committee*, October 2017 (Cm 9486), paras 166–67.

[46] L Trinder, R Hunter, J Miles, R Moorhead, L Smith, M Sefton, V Hinchley and K Bader, *Litigants in person in private family law cases*, Ministry of Justice Analytical Series (2014).

[47] See pp 96–7.

[48] Sir Oliver Heald, Westminster Hall Debates (11 January 2017), col 137.

[49] The Personal Support Unit, *Report and Financial Statement for year ended March 2017*: https://www.thepsu.org/media/1318/psu-annual-report-201617.pdf (last accessed 4 September 2018).

Bono Unit and the Access to Justice Foundation. These organisations work closely with the Ministry of Justice, and their individual roles will be discussed later. The strategy is able to take an overview on and coordinate the wide range of support available to LiPs on a national and local level, identifying where there are gaps in provision and avoiding duplication of effort.' LiPSS is sharing premises in Chancery Lane with the Bar Pro Bono Unit, LawWorks, the Legal Action Group and the Access to Justice Foundation. The Legal Education Foundation (LEF) supports Law for Life (AdviceNow) which is now offering a central portal which advertises their one-stop shop, but does not offer help directly.[50]

The latest LiPSS activity is the launch in April 2017 of a Litigant in Person Network, an online platform where professionals can share, discuss and collaborate across sectors 'connecting the community working to improve access to justice' including the legal professions, judiciary, academics, and court staff.[51] An update on 18 May 2017 included information about a new collaborative family advice clinic in Exeter, the extended PSU service in Southampton, the Time Together Contact Centre at the Central London Family Court, a new PSU in Chester, and the new self booking appointment online service at RCJ Advice. The Ministry of Justice works closely with the group, which also offers LiP engagement groups with HMCTS.

III. Government Information Provision

In 2011 government accepted the recommendation of the Family Justice Review[52] chaired by Sir David Norgrove that information should be provided through an accessible knowledge hub, while the family court system should be made clearer and more transparent. The knowledge hub has not developed under that title or in the universal format proposed, but various initiatives have been taken. One is a Family Justice Bulletin produced by the Ministry of Justice which lists and summarises ongoing and recently published research both from this jurisdiction and international sources, and is widely read in electronic form by those working in the justice system, academics, and policy makers in a number of jurisdictions.[53] Another was the widely criticised website 'Sorting out Separation', developed by the Ministry of Justice, with the Department of Work and Pensions (DWP), referred to later.[54] In addition, the Civil Legal Advice (CLA) Line,[55] open from

---

[50] See https://www.advicenow.org.uk/ (last accessed 27 September 2018).

[51] http://lipnetwork.org.uk (last accessed 4 September 2018).

[52] Ministry of Justice with Department of Education and Welsh Government, *Family Justice Review Final Report*, November 2011.

[53] See eg Ministry of Justice, *Family Justice Research Bulletin*, January 2018: available at https://assets.publishing.service.gov.uk/government/uploads/system/uploads/attachment_data/file/706672/family-justice-bulletin.pdf (last accessed 19 June 2018).

[54] See p 40.

[55] See https://www.gov.uk/civil-legal-advice: (CLA Direct 0845 345 4345).

9 am to 8 pm and on Saturday mornings, offers guidance on legal aid eligibility. The government website, www.direct.gov.uk, explains (among other things) the basic legal framework relating to family issues and the essential steps that need to be taken regarding obtaining a divorce and arrangements for finance and children, including detailed information on how to apply to court, what orders are available and the court fee. But users are told: 'You can get advice and information about legal paperwork and making arrangements from Sorting Out Separation, Citizens Advice and Advice Now'.

There are also government websites listing local courts, where to find a mediator, and how to apply for civil legal aid. The DWP Options website[56] gives clear information on child support arrangements and offers a free telephone helpline. The extent to which child maintenance agreements can be reached and, to an extent, implemented using online services was explained in the previous chapter.[57] The Cafcass (Children and Family Court Advisory and Support Service) website[58] provides detailed information on arrangements for children, including a parenting plan template (plus a pilot scheme for phone and face to face advice in six areas). For native English speakers used to handling quite complex instructions these services provide an accurate and accessible guide around to the system. Their success can be contrasted with 'Sorting out Separation' (SoS), referred to above,[59] which, however, had sought to deal with a wide range of matters, not only children issues. This was not satisfactory when launched, whether in the quality of information provided (an early version famously began with a reference to UK divorce law, whereas the law in Scotland has long been significantly different from that in England and Wales) or in coverage, where there is little material on pensions in financial arrangements on divorce. When accessed in May 2017 SoS listed the names of two mediators and four law firms who offer work on pensions. The site overall does not provide information but supports links to other sources ('seperation' spelt thus in places).[60] It suffers by comparison with other resources such as AdviceNow, the independent not for profit website run by the charity Law for Life, discussed later.[61]

IV. Conclusions

There are inevitably limitations to what can be achieved by these various means, especially in disputed cases. The issues have perhaps been most thoroughly considered in Canada, where in 2010 the then Chief Justice Warren Winkler

---

[56] See https://www2.dwp.gov.uk/contact-cmoptions/en/contact.asp.
[57] See pp 20–3.
[58] See https://www.cafcass.gov.uk/.
[59] See https://www.sortingoutseparation.org.uk (last accessed May 2017).
[60] J Albeson, 'The Sorting out Separation Web App: Fit for Purpose?' (2014) 44 *Family Law* 878.
[61] See pp 154–5.

described the family justice system as 'a system in crisis'.[62] A period of intense reform effort followed. In Ontario a programme of policy oriented research known as the Ontario Project was initiated, with a Family Justice Working Group which had an Action Committee on Access to Justice in Civil and Family Matters and an inquiry into National Self Represented Litigants, both of which reported in 2013, followed by the main report.[63] The report focuses on the 'entry points' to the system, and its policy aim was not to keep people out of court, but to increase access to justice 'through the provision of sufficient information and assistance to enable family members involved in family disputes to make a decision about *whether* they want to enter the family legal system and if so *how* to take the subsequent steps.'[64] Furthermore, the Commission emphasises that, although it focuses on 'entry points', 'it is crucial that the access points meld smoothly into the court system in cases where judicial adjudication or assistance is required and that the courts are available to family members to resolve their disputes when other methods are unsuccessful or the situation is, for one reason or another, legally complex or of high conflict'.[65]

The report stresses the limitations of information whether in print or on the internet. 'It quickly becomes complicated and difficult to navigate. There are many different sources, each emphasising its own mandate, While the internet may make it easier for many people to access information, for others, it is difficult because they do not have ready access to computers or possess computer literacy and in some cases because they live in remote areas lacking high speed internet. People with low levels of literacy or whose first language is neither English nor French are likely to find written information particularly inaccessible and, even if they can read it, may find it almost impossible to apply to their own circumstances.'[66] The Commission emphasises the need to take a holistic view of family problems, and asks, for example, whether the resolution of financial or mental health problems might mean a couple finds they do not need to break up. The development of inter-professional services in health care was taken as helpful analogy.[67]

The Ontario Report is particularly useful in setting out a series of 'benchmarks' which it recommends must inform a developing strategy in regard to access to justice. These can be summarised as being to provide initial information that is accessible to people in their everyday lives; insofar as it is provided online, to do so through a single 'hub'; to make written information available to those without the internet; to provide assistance (through a 'trusted intermediary') for those who might have difficulty in accessing, reading, understanding or applying the information to their circumstances; to help people to understand whether a dispute is

---

[62] Law Commission of Ontario, *Increasing Access to Family Justice through Comprehensive Entry Points and Inclusivity* (Toronto, February 2013), p 5, available online at www.lco-cdo.org.
[63] ibid.
[64] ibid, p 1, emphasis added, and p 9.
[65] ibid, p 28.
[66] ibid, p 1.
[67] ibid, p 3.

'really' a legal dispute; to minimise duplication of persons with whom the individual must deal; to respond to diversity and domestic violence; to take into account financial capacity; to recognise the multiple problems that can accompany family problems, and to offer a 'seamless' process to final resolution.[68]

Of course the Ontario report is a statement of intent, and there are many obstacles to be overcome. But it stands out as a well expressed, carefully thought out set of goals against which it is useful to measure the situation as it is in England and Wales. There is also currently debate in Ontario about the provision of family legal services by persons other than lawyers in family matters, such as paralegals, who are licensed and regulated by the Law Society of Ontario, law students, law clerks, and family court support workers.[69] In a report to the Attorney-General of Ontario, Justice Annemarie Bonkalo recommended (among other things) greater use of unbundled services by lawyers (with safeguards), creating a special licence for paralegals to do family law work in areas 'that are typically (but by no means always) less complex than others' (such as custody, access and simple child support), and clarification of when law students required supervision. These too are matters which will be covered in what follows.

---

[68] ibid, p 11.

[69] *Family Legal Services Review, Report submitted to the Attorney General of Ontario by Justice Annemarie Bonkalo*, December 2016. https://www.attorneygeneral.jus.gov.on.ca/english/about/pubs/family_legal_services_review/ (last accessed 12 September 2017). This report includes a useful definition of the distinction between information, which is given in response to a question which has a right answer, and advice which will provide and evaluate a number of options. However, Justice Bonkalo acknowledges that it is often 'challenging' to distinguish between them.

3

The Response of the Legal Professions to LASPO: I Solicitors' Innovative and Pro Bono Activity

I. Innovative Practices

We have seen that it was the government's view that the legal profession was primarily to blame for the overloading and eventual collapse of family legal aid, although we noted that this overlooks various other factors. But whatever view is taken on the causes, this collapse posed challenges for lawyers. How might they be expected to respond to the government's cuts and the increase in unmet need for family legal help? This chapter focuses on the actions taken by solicitors.

One option has been for lawyers to become more engaged in mediation, and in fact many have done this, to the extent that of the 1,535 mediators registered with the Family Mediation Council in 2015, approximately three-quarters were lawyers, many of them members of Resolution, an organisation mainly of solicitors committed to non-confrontational practice of family law.[1] However, as we have seen,[2] mediation has not succeeded in replacing legal advice as formerly provided under the previous legal aid dispensation. Lawyers have needed to develop other ways of trying to meet this need. How might they do this? Perhaps by making themselves more attractive and affordable in the market place? Or perhaps by providing free or substantially subsidised legal assistance, usually called work pro bono publico?

Taking the first option,[3] there have been a number of developments since LASPO arising from a range of different motivations. Lawyers began to offer free introductory advice more frequently, as well as fixed-price deals, and 'unbundling', whereby the lawyer contracts to carry out specific items of work rather than taking

---

[1] M Maclean and J Eekelaar, *Lawyers and Mediators: The Brave New World of Services for Separating Families* (Oxford, Hart Publishing, 2016) 72.

[2] See p 16.

[3] See also M Maclean and J Eekelaar (n 1), chs 2–3; M Maclean, 'Delivering family justice: new ways of working with lawyers in divorce and separation' in H Sommerlad, S Harris Short, S Vaughan and R Young (eds), *The Futures of Legal Education and the Legal Profession* (Oxford, Hart Publishing, 2015).

on a client in order to deal with the entire matter at issue. Offers for free initial advice and certainty over costs are helpful, but are at least in part a marketing exercise intended to attract business. Unbundling offers the client an apparently clearly defined contract, but this has not been without problems, in particular concerning the need for very clear client care letters at the beginning of a piece of work to make sure that the client is aware of where the boundaries lie. In *Sequence Properties Ltd v Kunal Balwantbhal Patel*[4] a costs order was made for the late filing of an appeal bundle that was not served on the opposing party. Even though the party's solicitor was on a 'limited retainer', the party was treated as having the assistance of a solicitor. However, in *Minkin v Landsberg*[5] the Court of Appeal upheld a decision that a solicitor on a retainer limited to re-drafting a financial remedies Consent Order had no wider duty to advise on the merits of the underlying agreement. This is seen as encouraging 'unbundled' work and in February 2017 it was reported that the Solicitors' Regulation Authority (SRA) was keen to publish guidance that would promote the practice.[6] In addition, solicitors are increasingly using more sophisticated IT to develop ways of routinising day-to-day activities such as appointments and billing, and in more innovative ways, such as asking new clients to use an interactive website to present their story before a first meeting, so saving lawyer time.[7] Some lawyers are working from home, using skype and email, and only renting office space for occasional meetings. Also interesting is the development in Australia where lawyers are anxious about their future, and in December 2017 were being offered the services of Automio, the law robot advertised as 'your very own lawyer in the cloud' … 'automating your client onboarding process' … 'doing all the stuff you don't like' which 'interviews your clients and frees you from tedious legal work. So you can save time and earn more'.[8]

Despite these innovatory moves, the Law Society's Baseline Survey of solicitors firms[9] published in 2012 found that even before the LASPO changes, in the period 2007–08 to 2010–11, turnover had decreased in over 30 per cent of the smaller firms who were the most likely to be offering family law services. This was attributed to the economic crisis and the increased bureaucracy associated with legal aid income. Costs were being cut, more legal executives were hired, and solicitors were training as mediators to increase their range of services. During interviews carried

---

[4] Unreported: discussed in Gazette newsdesk, 'New Judgment kills unbundled legal services', *Law Society Gazette* 24 May 2016. See also M Sefton, R Moorhead, J Sidaway and L Fox, 'Unbundled and Pro Bono advice for litigants in person: a study for the Cabinet Office' (Office for Civil Society Transition Fund, 2011).

[5] [2015] EWCA Civ 1152.

[6] See J Hyde, 'SRA keen to lift barriers to solicitors offering unbundling' *Law Society Gazette* 1 February 2017: https://www.lawgazette.co.uk/news/sra-keen-to-lift-barriers-to-solicitors-offering-unbundling/5059645.article (last accessed 4 June 2018).

[7] See Siaro project, A Larkin, Family Law Partners Bristol: https://www.legaltechnology.com/latest-news/startup-corner-siaro-has-tremendous-possibilities-for-family-law/ (last accessed 4 June 2018).

[8] Automio: https://autom.io (last accessed 4 September 2018).

[9] P Pleasence, N Balmer and R Moorhead, *A Time of Change: Solicitors Firms in England and Wales* (Law Society, Legal Aid Board and Ministry of Justice, 2012).

out in our study of lawyers and mediators,[10] we found one family law legal aid firm had been taken over by a larger more commercially minded firm, and even a long established specialist family law firm with high wealth clients had begun to offer fixed-price initial interviews at which a plan would be developed and costs estimated. Even with the formation of small networks known as pods to share overheads and employ expert consultants, maximum use of technology to simplify administrative procedures, more targeted use of paralegals, and improved market-ing, it was clear that the provision of family legal help to the group within the population who had formerly relied on publicly funded help was dwindling, and that this is the group least able to benefit from free online information and advice.

Some more radical suggestions which would involve structural changes to the role of the profession and its relationship to the courts have been made. There is renewed debate about the possibility of one lawyer helping two clients at the early stages of a divorce, to provide an outline of the possible range of outcomes. As Marilyn Stowe, an experienced lawyer and mediator asks: 'If it is possible for a single lawyer to mediate a couple and to arbitrate a couple, why is it impermis-sible for one lawyer to advise a couple – with legal aid?'[11] The Handbook of the Solicitors' Regulation Authority 2011 states[12] that this is possible 'where there is a client conflict and the clients have a substantially common interest in relation to a matter … if you have explained the relevant issues and risks to the client …; all the clients have given informed consent in writing to you acting, and you are satisfied it is reasonable for you to act for all the clients and it is in their best interests …'.[13] We have been told by solicitors that clients ask for this, and that some are respond-ing by providing a joint early stage options meeting at which both parties can be given information specific to their situation though if either needed to instruct a solicitor they would have to go elsewhere.[14]

This kind of help is available in other jurisdictions, for example in the Netherlands one lawyer serving two clients in this way has been established for over 40 years, but lawyers generally have been reluctant to do this unless there is a mediation agreement on the table as they do not wish to be thought to favour the stronger party.[15] This practice is very similar to our own suggestion[16] of 'lawyer-assisted mediation', which would be a form of mediation conducted by a legally-trained mediator permitted to proffer legal advice to both parties and designed to achieve an agreed outcome. One group of barristers has commenced such a practice as an Alternative Business Structure approved by the Bar Standards Board (see www.thedivorcesurgery.co.uk). Another suggestion is for the creation of a commissioner solicitor who would work with both parties to try to settle the

---

[10] Note 1.

[11] M Stowe, 'One couple: one lawyer?' (2017) 47 *Family Law* 737.

[12] Para 3.6.

[13] ibid.

[14] See M Maclean, 'Can one lawyer help two clients?' (2016) 46 *Family Law* 212.

[15] Personal communication from Bregde Dijksterhuis, Free University for Amsterdam, August 2017.

[16] Maclean and Eekelaar (n 1) 129–31.

case and, if this failed, would make a recommendation to the court on the outcome which would be considered by a judge rather in the way that Consent Order is scrutinised.[17] Yet another that has emerged is that a solicitor might be appointed by the court to act as an intermediary who could help unrepresented parties to understand the process and thereby facilitate and support negotiation and settlement during a hearing.

If even the kind of innovative help designed by family lawyers to be affordable becomes unaffordable, or is inadequate to meet the needs of particular individuals, what remains? Apart from the kinds of help that may be provided by non-lawyers, which we will discuss later, there is another route open to the legal profession: to work pro bono. Not surprisingly this latter option developed earlier and to a greater extent in the United States where state support was never substantial, and we begin by looking to developments there to illuminate our understanding of the limited nature of pro bono family work in this jurisdiction.

II. Pro Bono Activity

A. The American Experience

As was the case in England and Wales before World War II, assistance with access to legal assistance for people without sufficient financial means has always been meagre in the United States. However there was no equivalent to the post-war Rushcliffe reforms. To the contrary, fears of federal funding for legal aid in the 1950s led the American Bar Association (ABA) to play up what it perceived as the moral responsibility of lawyers to allocate some of their time to provide free services to low-income groups. But this was no more than aspirational. The Legal Services Corporation (LSC) was set up in 1974 to assist the poor (defined as people with an annual income of below 125 per cent of the poverty line). With an annual budget of $321 million by 1980, this could provide two lawyers for every 10,000 poor people. But during the 1980s the Reagan administration, incensed by use of LSC funds in public interest litigation, which it perceived as being politically motivated, sought its dissolution. This was unsuccessful, but it achieved severe cutbacks in LSC funding which terminated many of the already inadequate services, which David Luban in 1988 described as a 'disaster'.[18] While subsequent administrations, especially that of President Obama, were more supportive, funding in 2015 was barely above what it had been in 1980.[19] The first budget of the Trump administration proposed to eliminate the LSC in order to 'encourage non-profit organizations, businesses, law firms, and religious institutions to develop

---

[17] Personal communication from Peter Harris, Exeter College, Oxford.

[18] D Luban, *Lawyers and Justice: An Ethical Study* (Princeton University Press, 1988) 242.

[19] See http://www.lsc.gov/lsc-funding (last accessed 4 June 2018).

new models for providing legal aid, such as pro bono work, law school clinics, and innovative technologies'.[20]

These inadequacies in legal assistance for the poor have led to suggestions that pro bono provision should be mandatory, but these calls were rejected by the ABA in 1983 in favour of a more concrete exhortation that lawyers should allocate at least 50 hours per year for pro bono work.[21] But this was applied differently among the state bar associations. The New York State Bar, for example, called for only 20 hours.[22] Like those made in England and Wales before the post-war reforms, discussed earlier, such appeals to altruism seem to have had relatively little success. Writing in 2000, Deborah Rhode, who has made a distinguished contribution to pro bono promotion, observed that 'few' lawyers met the ABA's goal. The average time allocated was less than half an hour a week, with about half of lawyers doing none at all. 'Nowhere' she wrote, 'is the gap between professional ideals and professional practice more apparent than on issues of public service'.[23] In 2009 it was estimated that, while three-quarters of attorneys did 'some' pro bono work, only 27 per cent met the 50 hour standard.[24] Even where pro bono work is done, it faces many problems. It often does not reach those who need help the most. Much of what lawyers did do has been for family, friends and clients who had failed to pay,[25] for government agencies and political candidates, or has taken the form of giving legal talks or sitting on boards of non-for-profit organisations.[26] The provision is likely to be driven by the needs of the firm, in what has been called 'strategic philanthropy',[27] whether it be corporate policy for branding, corporate image, and marketing, or 'as a stop gap measure to keep their new hirees employed but at a reduced salary and an uncertain job future'.[28]

The match between the little that is provided and people's needs is weak. Firms, especially large ones, might be anxious to take on high-profile cases that would enhance their image and provide publicity, whereas there is little attraction in dealing with high conflict family cases, as was found in pre-war London.[29] James Gocker's account[30] of the Buffalo Housing Court, where volunteer attorneys provide one three-hour session on four Saturday mornings a year, raises analogies

---

[20] See *Major Savings and Reforms, Budget of the US Government, Fiscal Year 2018* (May 2017) at 98.

[21] See R Granfield and L Mather in R Granfield and L Mather (eds), *Private Lawyers and the Public Interest: The Evolving Role of Pro Bono in the Legal Profession* (New York, Oxford University Press, 2009) 3–4.

[22] C Feathers, 'Bar Politics and Pro Bono Definitions: the New York Experience', in Granfield and Mather (n 21), 268.

[23] DL Rhode, *In the Interests of Justice: Reforming the Legal Profession* (New York, Oxford University Press, 2000) 37.

[24] Granfield and Mather (n 21) 5–6.

[25] Rhode (n 23) 37.

[26] Granfield and Mather (n 21) 12.

[27] Rhode (n 23) ch 12.

[28] Granfield and Mather (n 21) 6.

[29] See p 7.

[30] JC Gocker, 'The Role of Volunteer Lawyers in Challenging Conditions of a Local Housing Crisis in Buffalo, NY' in Granfield and Mather (n 21) ch 11.

with a hospital Accident and Emergency unit (one attorney described it as a 'MASH' unit), dealing with particular segments of problems without the ability to 'cultivate an effective rapport with clients' and also without the facility to pass clients on to more intensive legally assisted help where this was necessary.

Despite these limitations, pro bono activity is an important component of what assistance in legal matters is available to the poor in the US. In 2009 Rebecca Sandefur calculated that it amounted to one third of the supply of civil legal assistance.[31] This has led to serious attempts by law schools to inculcate in law students the virtues of doing pro bono work, so as to be able to counter arguments questioning why lawyers should work for free. In 1996 the ABA had called for law schools to encourage students to participate in pro bono programmes. However Deborah Rhode noted that in 2000 only ten per cent of law schools 'required' such participation, usually for less than eight hours a year. But this was better than nothing, for, as she wrote: 'Particularly among low-income communities, some access to legal assistance is preferable to no access at all, which is their current situation.'[32] It also had the benefit of exposing students to the needs of the poor and (perhaps hopefully) inspiring long-term commitments.[33]

In 2005 the ABA *required* law schools to offer 'substantial opportunities for student participation in pro bono activities',[34] and by 2009 152 law schools did this.[35] Subsequent research however has shown that mere participation in pro bono activity, whether mandatory or voluntary, had not significantly enhanced the provision of pro bono services. Cynthia Adcock therefore concluded that such participation alone is insufficient: it should be accompanied by *instruction in* 'the value' of pro bono service ... as they teach other skills and values'.[36] Another strategy has been for law schools to be involved in providing legal help to *pro se* litigants (litigants in person). This has taken many forms, described in detail for many states by Margaret Barry in 1999,[37] frequently as group 'workshops' where law professors, lawyers, law interns and students 'provide general information about the law, procedure and practice to a group of litigants or prospective litigants who share a common category of legal issues'[38] sometimes giving participants forms to

[31] RL Sandefur, 'Lawyers' Pro Bono Service and Market-Reliant Legal Aid' in Granfield and Mather (n 21) ch 5.

[32] Rhode (n 23) 205.

[33] ibid, 206.

[34] In Canada also strong emphasis has been placed on developing the contribution of law students with the establishment in 1996 of the Pro Bono Students of Canada to ensure 'that each generation of lawyers enters the profession already schooled in and committed to pro bono philosophy and practice': see *Family Legal Services Review, Report submitted to the Attorney General of Ontario by Justice Annemarie Bonkalo*, December 2016: https://www.attorneygeneral.jus.gov.on.ca/english/about/pubs/family_legal_services_review/ (last accessed 6 June 2018).

[35] C Adcock, 'Shaped by Educational, Professional and Social Crises: The History of Law School Pro Bono Services' in Granfield and Mather (n 21) ch 2.

[36] ibid, 48.

[37] MM Barry, 'Accessing Justice: Are Pro Se Clinics a Reasonable Response to the Lack of Pro Bono Legal Services and Should Law School Clinics Conduct Them?' (1999) 67 *Fordham Law Review* 1879.

[38] ibid, 1883. However it is stated that in 1993/4 law students interns and pro bono lawyers assisted around 28,000 individual petitioners with document preparation in domestic violence cases: ibid, 1906.

complete as 'homework'.[39] While there are concerns about the accuracy of some of this, projects have been developing innovative methods of distributing court-approved forms and step-by-step instructions, for example, through touch screen multimedia kiosks. These programmes are of course primarily what in this jurisdiction we would call public legal education, and the beneficiaries are not necessarily principally seen as being the litigants, for Barry concludes that the groups 'respond to legal needs of communities and, more importantly, by inculcating their students with a sense of responsibility for affirming the legal rights of the poor and the disenfranchised'.[40]

At the other end of the lawyer's career in the US there is the tradition of offering pro bono work through and during retirement, for example, 'Senior Attorneys Initiative for Legal Services' of the DC Bar Pro Bono Center.[41] Sadly a similar exercise in England and Wales, 'The International Senior Lawyers Project' in the City of London failed to attract widespread support in 2016. Perhaps this is because of a culture where pro bono is seen as being what senior lawyers ask junior lawyers to do as part of their professional development. It seems clear, however, that even if all these measures are as successful as they can be, they fall far short of supplying the amount of legal assistance needed for the poor in the US.

B. The Development of Pro Bono Activity in Family Justice in England and Wales after LASPO

In his description of the strengths and weaknesses of what he holds to be the four possible 'delivery mechanisms' for legal assistance, Richard Abel distinguishes between the state, the market, philanthropy and self-help. While all have their benefits, he is clear that 'the state must take primary responsibility'. The other methods can only be 'supplementary'.[42] He suggests that self help is egalitarian but that this route, like philanthropy, offers no guarantee of quality of service. Market provision elevates the status of the consumer, but only where there are the necessary resources, while the other routes may be stigmatising. Only state help can guarantee affordable quality service. But despite that advice, and even if

---

[39] ibid, 1896.

[40] ibid, 1920. In 2006, the Family Law Education Reform Project, sponsored by Hostra University and the Association of Family and Conciliation Courts stressed the importance of inter-disciplinary knowledge for family lawyers, and a programme at the University of Denver has placed law students with students in other disciplines in inter-disciplinary teams to provide, under supervision, advice and support to potential users of the family court: MK Pruett, A Schepard, L Cornett, C Gerety and RL Kourlu, 'Evaluating the University of Denver's Center for Separating and Divorcing Families: The First Out-of-Court Divorce Option' (2017) 55 *Family Court Review* 375; 'Law Students on Interdisciplinary Problem-Solving Teams: An Empirical Evaluation of Educational Outcomes at the University of Denver's Resource Center for Separating and Divorcing Families' (2018) 56 *Family Court Review* 100.

[41] For another example, see the Volunteer Lawyers Project, 99 Chauncey St, Boston MA 0211.

[42] RL Abel, 'State, Market, Philanthropy and Self-Help as Legal Delivery Mechanisms' in Granfield and Mather (n 21) 304.

the story of pro bono publico legal help in the US is not encouraging, with what Gocker calls its struggle to marry profit and principle,[43] after LASPO it has become necessary to look closely at the current state of pro bono provision in England and Wales. Hopes have even been expressed for the long-term potential of legal education to be a means for recruiting future lawyers to pro bono activity which would then hopefully develop and increase,[44] though we have not gone as far as the US as to require law schools to offer 'substantial opportunities for student participation in pro bono activities'.[45]

Part of the difficulty in describing pro bono activity in the US arose from the differences between legal cultures across the country. In this jurisdiction we have less geographical variation but there are substantial differences in motivation and practice between the Bar and solicitors, between large and small law firms, between firms with high asset clients and those with low income clients, and also by degree of specialisation. In what follows in this and the following chapters we are most grateful for the help of the Law Society, LawWorks, the Bar Pro Bono Unit, CILEx the National Pro Bono Centre, and individual practitioners including members of the judiciary, court staff, the Bar, solicitors and paralegals, academic supervisors and students. This has enabled us not only to draw on published material but also on interviews, meetings and observations of work in practice in our attempt to describe the complex and courageous current state of family legal help. Our duty of confidentiality as always prevents the individual acknowledgments which are so richly deserved, but all those whose views are quoted have been given full opportunity to comment on or correct this report.

i. Overall Objectives of Pro Bono Work

What is considered pro bono work could cover a wide range of provision. Does it include specific items for which no charge is made? Does it include additional work on an existing case where funds have run out or where the legal aid provision is limited? Can it cover part of the work needed on a matter, a single session of advice or a letter, or should it include handling a case in full (end-to-end casework) with representation? We may also bear in mind the need for appropriate expertise: it may not be helpful for a client with an urgent child arrangements case to be seen by a lawyer whatever the stage of their career whose expertise is not relevant. In addition there are concerns about professional indemnity insurance, and about student and paralegal involvement, discussed more fully later.[46]

As in other jurisdictions, there are mixed messages about the various purposes of pro bono work. They could include establishing a socially responsible image for

---

[43] Gocker (n 30).

[44] D Nicolson, 'Legal education, ethics and access to justice: forging warriors for justice in a neo-liberal world' (2015) 22 *International Journal of the Legal Profession* 51.

[45] See p 48 above.

[46] See pp 52–3, 56, 59–60.

the legal profession (especially following the government's expression of negative views about lawyers generally); providing professional development experience through training in an additional specialism and meaningful client contact for young lawyers doing commercial work where this is rare, and in this way assisting in recruitment; providing therapy for stressed commercial practitioners; or perhaps just allowing opportunities for straightforward altruism. National Pro Bono (NPB) Week, held in London in November 2016, opened with a keynote paper describing Australian research into the mental health benefits for the practitioner of pro bono work by preventing problems such as anxiety and depression.[47] The Law Society's Pro Bono Manual (discussed further below) sets out a 'business case' for pro bono work which includes all those matters. It would be surprising if pro bono activity did not comprise a mixture of some of these motives, and also a determination not to be pushed into letting government 'off the hook' when cuts to legal aid are made. When Michael Gove, then Secretary of State for Justice, expressed the desire that the professions should be doing more rather than using funding from taxation,[48] the opposition was immediate and vociferous,[49] as indeed had been the experience in the United States, described earlier.

ii. Sources of Support

Despite these uncertainties, pro bono activity at individual, firm, professional organisation and family court level is responding to the new and increasing level of unmet need for family legal help after LASPO. Sources of support and funding for this activity include the government, through the Litigants in Person Support Strategy (LiPSS),[50] major foundations (such as the Legal Education Foundation (LEF)), the Bar Council (through the Bar Pro Bono Unit (BPBU)), the Law Society (through the LawWorks network of clinics) and the Access to Justice Foundation (which is a collaboration between the Bar Council, the Chartered Institute of Legal Executives, the Law Society and the voluntary sector, represented by the Advice Services Alliance). In addition there are individual firms, ranging from former legal aid firms offering help to former clients, to multi-national corporate enterprises such as DLA Piper which aims to provide legal assistance to 'under-served regions' around the world including the deprived communities near their London office,[51] or providing effective help by paying the salary of a lawyer working in a law clinic with the aim of both training the lawyer in a secondary specialisation, and finding new clients. For example, Simmons and Simmons, which has

[47] Amy Roach, Paper given at National Pro Bono Week, November 2017.
[48] Speech 23 June 2015 at the Legatum Institute by Michael Gove, Secretary of State for Justice. See https://www.gov.uk/government/speeches/what-does-a-one-nation-justice-policy-look-like (last accessed 4 June 2018).
[49] See eg https://www.theguardian.com/law/2015/jun/23/michael-gove-rich-law-firms-help-secure-justice-for-all (last accessed 4 June 2018).
[50] See pp 38–9 above.
[51] https://www.dlapiper.com/en/us/focus/probono/pro-bono (last accessed 4 June 2018).

215 partners, paid the salary of a lawyer working part time for the South West London Law Centres and claimed 7,711 pro bono hours to the value of £2,259,261 in 2011. Others have funded niche work, such as the Allen & Overy funding of a legal adviser specialising in immigration law at the Coram Children's Legal Centre (the Centre specialises in education), or the funding of the development of specialised websites such as CourtNav, described in more detail later.[52] Universities are providing opportunities for clinical education and these are coming together in the Clinical Legal Education Organisation (CLEO), also described later.[53] And, as we will describe, individual lawyers are quietly offering time in a law clinic or advice centre.

iii.   *The Law Society and the Pro Bono Protocol, Charter and Manual*

The Law Society has worked with the Bar and CILEx under the auspices of the Attorney General's Pro Bono Coordinating Committee in setting the National Pro Bono Centre (NPBC) in Chancery Lane in 2010 and produced the Pro Bono Protocol,[54] quickly followed by the Pro Bono Charter[55] and the Pro Bono Manual and Practice Notes,[56] launched at the NPB Week in November 2016. The Protocol sees pro bono work as 'legal advice or representation provided by lawyers in the public interest including to individuals, charities and community groups who cannot afford to pay for that advice or representation and where public and alternative means of funding are not available'. The work must be 'free to the client, without payment to the lawyer or law firm (regardless of the outcome) and provided voluntarily either by the lawyer or his or her firm'. The Protocol adds, pointedly, that it should always be seen as an adjunct to, and not a substitute for, a proper system of publicly funded legal services. The Protocol sets out the standards lawyers must achieve and observe. These include that it should always be done to a high standard; the terms must be clear, and the work only undertaken by a lawyer who is adequately trained, has the appropriate knowledge, skills and experience no less than would be required for paid work, should be given the same priority and attention as would be given to paid work, and covered by adequate insurance. The Protocol also states that a commitment to the delivery of Pro Bono Legal Work is encouraged throughout a lawyer's professional life, from being a student, through practice, to and including retirement, though this last point has not yet been taken up to any extent in this jurisdiction.[57]

---

[52] See pp 79–80.

[53] See pp 122–3.

[54] https://www.lawsociety.org.uk/Support-services/Practice-management/Pro-bono/The-pro-bono-protocol/ (last accessed 14 June 2018).

[55] http://www.lawsociety.org.uk/support-services/practice-management/pro-bono/pro-bono-charter/ (last accessed 14 June 2018).

[56] ibid.

[57] See above p 49.

The Pro Bono Charter invites firms, Alternative Business Structures (ABS) and in-house legal teams to sign up to a commitment to achieving access to justice via pro bono work which, re-iterating the words of the Protocol, it affirms will be an adjunct to and *not* a substitute for state funded services. This involves developing a pro bono policy, with an identified person or committee responsible for pro bono work, and endorsement of the Protocol. The Charter provides opportunities for developing future protocols, contributing data for monitoring purposes and publication in a biennial report.

The Law Society's Pro Bono Manual, a comprehensive and detailed document available from the Law Society website,[58] is designed as a practical guide and resource kit for solicitors planning pro bono work. It acknowledges the support of the Australian Pro Bono Resources Centre for allowing use of content and information from the Australian Pro Bono Manual. The Manual, which incorporates the Protocol discussed above, deals with planning, developing and maintaining a pro bono policy and culture within law firms, then with procedural and practice issues, including insurance, and then with precedents, pro formas and other information.

The first eight chapters describe incorporating the Pro Bono Protocol into the firm's practice, and recommend specific criteria for the firm's work, planning a checklist for the firm's activities, and making the business case for pro bono and building a pro bono culture. For example, a firm might set out the areas of work where they will not act, based on areas where they do not have expertise. A requirement that the firm accepts only matters where it has appropriate expertise is often included as a separate criterion. The firm might decide to accept all meritorious pro bono work where they do have expertise, or might restrict its casework to public interest matters where the legal work is intended to advance the interests of a broader group rather than an individual client, such as where it affects a significant number of people, raises matters of public concern or impacts on disadvantaged or marginalised groups. Firms are advised of the difficulty of applying precise means tests to clients and to use instead a broader 'capacity to pay' assessment. Firms should also think about potential conflicts of interest, about their profile in the community, about offering staff who are working pro bono opportunities for training or education, about the level of commitment, about supervision and management, and about the possibility of working in partnership with commercial clients in a pro bono matter.

The business case for pro bono mentions pride and loyalty within the firm, the impact on graduate recruitment, attracting paying clients, and attracting and keeping high quality staff. There is a need to set a budget and ensure efficient allocation of resources, to give staff time and recognition, if possible to treat pro bono work as billable hours, to ensure recognition in staff reviews and evaluations and circulate annual pro bono reports. Part 2 of the Manual sets out current models of

---

[58] www.lawsociety.org.uk/support-services/practice-management/pro-bono (last accessed 4 June 2018).

pro bono service delivery, including end-to-end case work with individual clients, or the clinic model which involves working with other organisations, including pop-up or outreach clinics, clinics run with other local legal advice organisations or student clinics (which will be discussed in more detail below[59]), secondment to legal advice organisations, assistance for not-for-profit organisations, IT-based services, law reform and policy work, Public Legal Education and international pro bono work. As in the United States, the lawyer can also provide information and education, for example by sitting on a board of trustees.

Firms are advised that receiving requests for help directly from the public is not an effective way to obtain pro bono work, and brings difficulties in controlling the flow of work and assessing an individual's request. Larger firms are said to prefer not to have individuals approaching them directly but to see individual clients at pro bono clinics which are run with a community organisation such as Citizens Advice or a Law Centre. For many firms, a 30 minute slot will be the only time in which they see such clients, while others run end-to-end programmes which will take the individual through the case. Many firms work through a charity or NGO, while others join a referral organisation. Some solicitors work in partnership with an experienced welfare lawyer and offer advocacy or organisational skills. Non-lawyer staff within a set of chambers or firm should be able to make the same contribution they would make to a paid piece of work.

Firms need a clear policy on costs and disbursements, to be communicated to the client up front. As to costs, clients need to be aware of the potential for claiming costs from the other side in contentious matters. According to the accepted indemnity principle, the losing party pays the successful party no more than the successful party has to pay their lawyers. But this cannot apply when the successful party is assisted pro bono, so in that case section 194 of the Legal Services Act 2007 allows some courts to order the losing party to pay an equivalent sum to a charity, which has been designated to be the Access to Justice Foundation. But it is also important for the client to be aware they may be at risk, if an action is unsuccessful, that they may be liable for the opposing party's costs under an 'adverse costs order', or under a settlement agreement. Chapter 15 of the Manual gives guidance on working with barristers, especially in a situation where counsel has agreed to attend a hearing and is then required for a hearing on the same day in a paying case. The solicitor must ensure that standard procedures are observed in dealing with counsel's clerk and making clear when the pro bono relationship is deemed to have ended and counsel's professional obligations discharged.

Chapter 18 of the Manual deals with risk management, the key points being that pro bono matters must be dealt with in the same way as any other matter in the firm and subject to conflict searches and covered by the professional indemnity insurance of the firm. For solicitors in England and Wales, professional indemnity insurance generally extends to pro bono work so long as it is undertaken

---

[59] See chs 8 and 9.

in connection with the practice of the firm, and subject to the same supervisory arrangements as paid work.[60] Appendix B of the Manual contains a list of Training Courses and Providers. From our point of view, it is interesting that there is no reference to training in family law apart from one course on children's rights, provided by the Coram Children's Legal Centre. However LawWorks (which is supported by the Law Society, and discussed later[61]) does offer training in family law for solicitors who attend clinics they support. We attended a LawWorks training session in public family law for practitioners working in in other fields. After three hours in a group of 15 with an expert and well prepared handouts, the attendees, including young trainees from city firms, and older non-specialists, felt confident to advise advice centre clients. A current issue arising is, however, whether the activities of LawWorks are limited by continuing with firm-based memberships, rather than opening up to individual membership.

iv. Solicitors' Pro Bono Work

In 2016, drawing on the Practising Certificate Holder Survey for the Law Society 2015, the Law Society published a report, *The Pro Bono Work of Solicitors*, which showed that of 1,502 solicitors interviewed between May and August 2015,[62] 37 per cent had done at least one hour of pro bono work over the previous 12 months, down from 42 per cent for the previous year. Mostly these were solicitors in private practice, where 55 per cent of sole practitioners have done so compared to 43 per cent in larger firms. Pro bono work in firms of 2–4 and 5–10 partners showed particularly sharp falls, although pro bono work in firms of 11–25 partners in fact increased from the previous year. For those who did pro bono work, the average number of hours across the year was 52, although this amounts to only 19 hours of work if averaged across all solicitors.

For large international firms, pro bono activity is simply part of branding, and does not conflict with their paid work. Extra work to comply with an estimated bill is not regarded as pro bono. These large firms have a code to record their pro bono work, but there is still no common definition of what is included in the term. In small legal aid firms there had always been extra work carried out beyond what was covered by the legal aid contract, but this would not be defined as pro bono according to the Pro Bono Protocol. Although large firms are ready to offer the time of their junior staff, it appears that the former legal aid practitioners find that this is not always useful, and would prefer them to make a contribution to a fund from which relevant help could be subsidised.[63]

---

[60] On the BPBU, see ch 15, p 66 of the Manual, and on Student clinics, see para 5.2.3, p 27 of the Manual.

[61] See p 56.

[62] www.google.co.uk/search?q=Practising+Certificate+Holder+Survey+2015&oq=Practising+Certificate+Holder+Survey+2015&gs_l=psy-ab.3...327592.329587.0.329698.5.5.0.0.0.0.160.463.3j2.5.0....0...1.1.64.psy-ab.0.3.237...33i160k1.neZ3MPPgZdA (last accessed 18 September 2017).

[63] Information based on personal communications and discussions at several LawWorks roundtables in 2017.

The Law Society has developed guidance on family work so that non-specialists might help with, for example, an emergency application in a public law child protection case. But we understand that the Law Society membership as a whole is not supportive of further targets for pro bono work or mandatory engagement, but is concerned with risk avoidance and professional indemnity insurance protection not only to protect the profession but to ensure client confidence in the universal availability of redress in case of negligence.

v. *The LawWorks Clinics Network, Including Law School Clinics*

The main contribution of the Law Society and its members to meeting unmet need for legal help comes through their support (£200,000 per year) to LawWorks, which is the operating name for the Solicitors Pro Bono Group which aims to connect volunteer lawyers with people in need of legal advice. Their Networks Programme brings together over 200 law clinics, who make a financial contribution to LawWorks as members. There are over 100 members, including international and city firms, and regional medium and small charities needing legal advice who pay a fee to become members. Clinics can access free legal resources, with both face-to-face and online training, regular Round Table supportive and informative meetings, and online materials via www.lawworks.org.uk/solicitors-and-volunteers. Apart from the Law Society, LawWorks receives funding from a variety of sources, including the Ministry of Justice and a number of charitable trusts and foundations. Membership of LawWorks remains firm-based, not individual, as a result of accreditation and insurance requirements.

The LawWorks Clinic Network has complied with the Law Society's Pro Bono Manual and collected the necessary information to compile annual reports. The student clinics have also been the subject of a study by the University of Ulster.[64] The LawWorks Strategy for 2015–17 states that 'the most effective way to impact on the needs of large numbers of people is through legal advice clinics … through these clinics individuals receive vital advice and support'. But it accepts that some clinics need more comprehensive support than others and states that LawWorks 'will work with partner stakeholders to strengthen and deepen the legal expertise on offer in response to particular areas of identified need for instance through secondary specialisation'.

According to the Report published in November 2016,[65] over the period April 2015 to March 2016 there were 223 clinics (including one which consolidated 36 previously recorded separately), 36 per cent being law school clinics. The report uses data from surveys of volunteers, student volunteers and interviews

---

[64] See O Drummond and G McKeevor, *Access to Justice through University Law Clinics* (Ulster University, 2015) ch 8 for further detail.

[65] LawWorks Clinics Network Report, April 2015–March 2016 (LawWorks, November 2016). https://www.lawworks.org.uk/solicitors-and-volunteers/resources/lawworks-clinics-network-report-april-2015-march-2016 (last accessed 18 September 2017).

with clinic representatives. 88 per cent of clinics were offering initial advice, 41 per cent written advice, 25 per cent form-filling, 19 per cent casework and 14 per cent representation. There had been 53,000 individual inquiries, an increase by 24 per cent over the previous year. 35,000 inquirers were given legal advice, and 11,000 were given information or referred to other sources. Family overtook employment issues as being the most common category of problems at 21 per cent (a 37 per cent increase), followed by employment (17.4 per cent), housing (17.1 per cent), asylum and immigration (14 per cent), consumer and contract law (8 per cent), welfare benefits (2.4 per cent) and debt (2.2 per cent). 4,824 individuals had volunteered to work in the clinics, over a half being students and over a third being lawyers or trainee lawyers. Based on client surveys in Wales, after attendance at a clinic, 81 per cent felt less stressed, 67 per cent felt their physical or mental health had improved and 44 per cent felt that (where applicable in their case) they had avoided going to court. Family advice was available in 42 per cent of clinics. 20 per cent of clients are returners. 70 per cent of clinics reported increased complexity of cases, and while 38 per cent were finding it difficult to source and retain pro bono lawyers to provide the necessary expertise and supervision often with reduced funding, 33 per cent reported an increased willingness to volunteer among students and lawyers.[66]

Although the Law Society's Pro Bono Manual[67] refers to the traditional 'full service' legal assistance (which it calls 'end-to-end' casework) as being the 'archetypal form of legal assistance', this is not often available at a clinic, as can be seen from the low proportion of clinics offering casework or representation. There has been a marked increase in the availability of advice following extensive training and support activity by LawWorks.[68] The 2016 report states that 46 per cent of inquiries at law school clinics received legal advice, compared to 71 per cent across the networks as a whole.[69] Although 89 per cent of LawWorks clinics offer legal advice, only 39 per cent of clinics are reported[70] as being able to offer family advice. On reading through the individual website information provided by 219 clinics listed in 2016, only 58 (26 per cent) clearly indicated that the help offered (which did not necessarily include legal advice) covered family matters. Of these 58 clinics, 27 indicated that they used student volunteers,[71] seven were primarily

---

[66] For a comprehensive ongoing evaluation of LawWorks' monitoring and existing practice, see J Sandbach and M Gregor, 'Hearing the Client's Voice in Pro Bono – What helps and What gets in the Way?', Paper given at the Access to Justice and Legal Services Conference (University College, London, June 2018).

[67] Law Society, *Pro Bono Manual*, 25.

[68] Mavis Maclean attended an excellent face to face training session on private family law for non-specialists in May 2017.

[69] LawWorks Report (n 65) 17.

[70] LawWorks Report (n 65) 18.

[71] Two BPPP clinics, City University, Sussex, Liverpool John Moores, two Manchester clinics, Brunel, Hull, two Birmingham clinics, Central Lancashire, York, Greenwich, Huddersfield, Kent, University of Law clinics in Chester, Guildford, Bloomsbury, and the Universities of Leeds, Liverpool, Manchester, Sheffield, South Wales, Westminster, Southampton and Plymouth.

based in law firms,[72] a further seven clinics were attached to Citizens Advice offices (including at the Royal Courts of Justice), eight to charitable foundations such as Access to Justice Worcester, seven were Family Support Advice clinics which specialise in contact issues, and three were attached to courts in the Cardiff Family Advice Clinic, Leicester Family Court Pro Bono Service and the Oxford Combined Court Clinic (children matters).

As stated earlier,[73] students are a key element in the LawWorks pro bono workforce, with a steadily increasing level of activity within Law Schools, and constitute over half the volunteers in LawWorks clinics. The work of law school clinics will be examined in detail in chapter eight. Here we note that, just as the pro bono work of the legal professions combines altruism with other motivating factors in what Rebecca Sandefur[74] calls a state of market reliance, paid for by firms to enhance members' attachment and performance, student involvement too is underpinned by a complex set of motivations. 80 per cent of student clinics are without external funding and largely supported by their institution, so from the universities' perspective the spirit of altruism is supported, perhaps dominated, by educational arguments. Participation in pro bono legal work is termed 'clinical legal education' (CLE), with its own journal (the *International Journal of Clinical Legal Education* based at the University of Northumbria in Newcastle) and an academic association, CLEO, (the Clinical Legal Education Organisation) which held its annual conference in 2017 in Northumbria on Clinical Legal Educators in the 21st Century University.[75] And even within this academic heading, there are differences in the emphasis placed on education, which is a good in itself, and training, which is of value to the individual, particularly students from ethnic minorities or mature students in helping them to access a legal career by securing training contracts and pupillage.[76]

There are complex debates about what form of organisation to use, the level of supervision and assessment and what students can or should do within the range of activities which constitute legal help, from simple clerking and support, to giving initial information and advice, perhaps followed by written advice under the supervision of a practitioner who may be employed by their institution, or even undertaking full casework and representation. There are questions about professional indemnity insurance for students and supervisors.[77] In order to demonstrate the strengths and vulnerabilities of student involvement, we later[78] give an example

---

[72] Allington Hughes Free drop in Wrexham, Caveat Solicitors London, Centre 70 Pro Bono Clinic London, Nucleus Pro Bono Service London, Spicketts Patrick Family Law Clinic Cardiff, Temple Legal Centre London, The Chichester Evening Law Clinic made up of nine firms plus CAB support.
[73] See p 56.
[74] R Sandefur, 'Lawyers pro bono service and American-Style Civil Legal Assistance' (2007) 41 *Law and Society Review* 79.
[75] CLEO will be discussed in more detail in ch 8, p 119.
[76] See Nicolson (n 44).
[77] See p 124.
[78] See pp 70–4.

of practice in a university-based legal advice clinic which offers family help as a member of the LawWorks Network, and which works in conjunction with the university's Family Court Help Desk set up on a 'McKenzie model' (discussed in chapter seven[79]) and based in the local family court. Students nationally may also participate as volunteers outside university-based centres in other advice settings, including local independent advice centres. But in these settings their role is often more limited, and the activity sits further away from the driving force for joining many university clinics of developing a springboard for their future career. The activity also enables the university to collect data for research into meeting legal need.[80]

Despite this information, given the range in methods of organisation and sources of support and staffing, it is difficult to form a coherent picture of what exactly is available as family legal help. To be affiliated to the LawWorks Clinic Network, each clinic must be independent and self managed, and signed up to the Pro Bono Charter described earlier. They generally (to quote the Network Report introduction) 'involve a partnership bringing together a mix of law firms, in-house legal teams, barristers and law schools working with advice agencies and other charities to support individuals in the local community.' The clinics team at LawWorks offers consultancy, free training, trouble shooting on issues such as regulatory requirement, resources (including legal research tools), secure document storage solutions as well as fact sheets and tool kits, networking and awards for excellence. Student clinics require less support as they are supervised by their institution, and, using the framework Initial Advice, Next Steps and then Guidance, the students usually act as a sounding board for clients by carrying out administrative tasks such as taking the history, helping with form filling and drafting letters of advice after consultation, using a template and under supervision. They would only see clients after screening and by appointment, usually for 30 to 45 minutes. Their most common tasks are note-taking and intake or triage. Other volunteers included administrative volunteers, trainees, paralegals and legal executives.

vi. Paralegals and Legal Executives

The contribution of the paralegal and legal executives to pro bono work can take the form of support for the solicitors or barristers they work with. But we also met with a paralegal pro bono group, whose members included a group of students who had completed their course and were either looking for or beginning to work pro bono while on a training contract. A group known as Horizon had identified the process of application and appeals concerning Personal Independence Payments (PIPs) and the Department of Work and Pensions (DWP) as an area

---

[79] See pp 113–7.
[80] See pp 103–4.

of law that was not too complex, and where they could handle cases from end-to-end before a tribunal, not a court, and reach the maximum number of clients. They were able to hold two sessions a week in an office provided at a low rent by another charity and were supported with supervision by five firms and a salaried part-time specialist lawyer solicitor to check every document which left their office.

They had a success rate of 85 per cent in terms of awards made and appeals succeeding and had quantified the level of expenditure that this advice would have cost in the open market. But they too felt the need to pay over £1,000 a year for Professional Indemnity Insurance (PII) partly because they dealt with some mentally unstable clients and large sums of money were in issue and, although confident of the quality of their work, they did not want any queries to be attached to their record which might affect their future career. They did not rely on their firm's cover because their documents did not refer to their employing firms, but were checked by their own employed expert, and they wanted to avoid any risk of complaint from a mentally ill client as it might damage their future career prospects.

III. Regulation and Liability

A. Regulation

The Legal Services Act 2007 removed the regulation of solicitors from the sole responsibility of the profession to the independent Legal Services Board which oversees a number of regulators including the Solicitors Regulation Authority, an independent Board of the Law Society. While the giving of legal advice is not in itself regulated, there is a general requirement that, in order to practice as an accredited solicitor, the solicitor must, first, be admitted to the Roll which recognises possession of the necessary qualifications and professional training, and apply annually for a practising certificate which enables solicitors to work as sole practitioners or in law firms and other entities where solicitors are employed with non-lawyers and licensed as Alternative Business Structures, all of which must have professional indemnity insurance (PII).[81]

In addition, according to the Legal Services Act 2007, exercise of the right of audience and conduct of litigation are reserved legal activities[82] and only *authorised or exempt* persons may carry them out (other reserved activities relate to matters of conveyancing or probate, and are not usually relevant to family issues). Under the SRA Rules 8.1 and 9.1 solicitors are so authorised if they are 'involved

---

[81] SRA Practice Framework Rules, October 2017, rr 1, 9 and SRA Handbook Indemnity Insurance Rules 2013, r 4.1.

[82] Legal Services Act 2007, ss 12, 13.

in legal practice' and practising as a solicitor (ie, and hold a practising certificate, or are exempted from doing so). Usually the pro bono work of employed (in-house) solicitors will be covered by this. But such solicitors may also take on pro bono work outside that of their employer, for example, by participating in a pro bono programme, which could be LawWorks, though others can be accessed through other law firms like DLA Piper. They are permitted to do this if '(a) the work is covered by an indemnity reasonably equivalent to that required under the SRA Indemnity Insurance Rules; (b) either: (i) no fees are charged; or (ii) a conditional fee agreement is used and the only fees charged are those which you receive by way of costs from your client's opponent or other third party and all of which you pay to a charity under a fee sharing agreement'.[83]

Furthermore, Rule 4.16 of the SRA Rules allows solicitors *employed* by a 'Law Centre or Advice Service' to 'give advice to and otherwise act for members of the public' if operated by a charitable or 'similar non-commercial organisation', under certain conditions. These are that: '(a) no funding agent has majority representation on the body responsible for the management of the service, and that body remains independent of central and local government; (b) all fees you earn and costs you recover are paid to the organisation for furthering the provision of the organisation's services; (c) the organisation is not described as a law centre unless it is a member of the Law Centres Federation; and (d) the organisation has indemnity cover in relation to the legal activities carried out by you, reasonably equivalent to that required under the SRA Indemnity Insurance Rules'.

These provisions therefore allow solicitors employed by qualifying law centres (such as LawWorks Network clinics) to give general legal advice. However, employed lawyers may not undertake any *reserved* legal activities unless the provision of relevant services to the public or a section of the public (with or without a view to profit) is not 'part of their employer's business'.[84] The result seems to be that, while in-house solicitors can participate in programmes that provide pro bono advice on most family issues, such solicitors can only conduct litigation or appear in court on a pro bono basis if they are acting on behalf of their employers or if that is not part of their employer's business, which the Law Society's Pro Bono SRA Manual interprets to mean that if they do this, they will be acting in a 'personal' capacity.[85] This may be the case if the employer is, for example, a university (and the university is a charity). If, on the other hand, this was considered to be part of the business of the centre, on a strict reading of the rules,[86] this could not be done unless the centre was managed by authorised persons (solicitors), or either exempt or licensed. As regards exemption, the 2007 Act[87] allows persons

[83] SRA Practice Framework Rules, 2011, r 4.10 (a) and (b).
[84] ibid, r 4.10 (c).
[85] Law Society, Pro Bono Manual, 83. However, pro bono work that an employer requires, or where the employer pays the insurance, or supervises the work, will be considered part of the employer's business: ibid.
[86] SRA Practice Framework, rr 1 and 13.
[87] Legal Services Act 2007, s 19 and Sch 3.

to carry out certain reserved activities without authorisation: but these are very specific activities, such as exercising rights of audience with the court's permission, or 'conduct litigation' with such permission. Perhaps a court could authorise a clinic to perform such activities. If not, the clinic would need to be licensed, either as an Alternative Business Structure[88] or as a 'special body'.[89] 'Special' bodies include not for profit bodies and indeed any other body that may be prescribed by the Lord Chancellor on the recommendation of the Legal Services Board.

B. Liability

Solicitors can be professionally liable either in contract or in tort. A solicitor must always act with reasonable competence, which, depending on the facts, could involve ensuring that the client fully understands their position and, if the client is about to take a disadvantageous step, that the client fully explores their reasons for doing that. This is so whether or not the client is charged for the advice.[90] Normally the extent of the liability can be controlled by the contract, subject to specific regulation. For example, solicitors cannot exclude liability when they would otherwise be liable when conducting 'contentious' business (ie business done in or for the purposes of proceedings before a court or arbitrator[91]) and nor can they exclude it for non-contentious business because section 57(1) of the Consumer Rights Act 2015 states 'a term of a contract to supply services is not binding on the consumer to the extent that it would exclude the trader's liability arising under section 49 (service to be performed with reasonable care and skill)'. However, they may limit this liability but this is heavily qualified, in particular by section 62 under which 'an unfair term of a consumer contract is not binding on the consumer', a term being 'unfair' if, 'contrary to the requirement of good faith, it causes a significant imbalance in the parties' rights and obligations under the contract to the detriment of the consumer'. Effectively, this means that any such limitation will be subject to a 'fairness' test.

It is common in standard matters for solicitors to limit any liability to the extent of the insurance cover they are required to have under the SRA Indemnity Insurance Rules. In the case of pro bono work, it is recommended that solicitors use a 'Letter of Engagement' that sets out what is agreed between the solicitor and the client. This is described terms of 'managing expectations' and it also sets out what the client is expected to do (which may include paying some costs for 'disbursements'). This therefore seems to be a contract, and the Law Society Pro

---

[88] ibid, Pt 5.

[89] ibid, s 106.

[90] *Padden v Bevan Ashford Solicitors* [2011] EWCA Civ 1616. In this case, involving advice during a free half-hour interview, the Master of the Rolls thought there was an implied contract [para 51], but it does not seem that this was crucial to the finding that the solicitors were liable for falling short of their duty.

[91] Solicitors Act 1974, s 87, as amended by the Consumer Rights Act 2015.

Bono Manual, which provides templates for such letters, comments that 'many firms choose to limit their liability for pro bono matters to the minimum required by the SRA Indemnity Insurance Rules'.[92]

The SRA, however, is aware of the impact of insurance on the costs of legal services, and is currently considering a programme of reform to bring about a more innovative competitive market by removing restrictions on where and how solicitors can practice and also looking again at the minimum amount of professional indemnity cover a firm should be required to hold. George Hawkins, of the SRA, has observed[93] that the current minimum cover is set to £2 million per claim for sole practitioners and partnerships, and £3 million for incorporated businesses. Insurance claims can be as high as 8 per cent of a firm's annual turnover. But analysis of claims over a 10 year period shows that 95 per cent of payments were settled for less than £250,000 and 98 per cent less than £600,000. The average payment was around £70,000 and conveyancing problems were responsible for 50 per cent of the total value of payments. The SRA will therefor suggest that the minimum level of cover can be reduced whilst still maintaining public protection.

The Terms and Conditions of the online Family Law Panel[94] providing access to a small group of solicitors, barristers and mediators which offers 'free initial conversations' appear to seek to avoid liability by including the following:

(a) The information gained from this website is for general guidance on the issues raised and should not be relied or acted upon without taking detailed advice from an appropriately qualified person.
(b) If you need more details on your rights or legal advice about what action to take, please contact a professional advisor or a solicitor.
(c) The Family Law Panel will not accept liability for any loss, damage or inconvenience arising as a consequence of any use of, the inability to use, or the reliance upon of any information gained via this website.
(d) Whilst the Family Law Panel makes every effort to provide a service of the highest quality, we cannot guarantee that our service will be totally error-free.
(e) We are not responsible for claims brought by third parties arising from your use of this website or the information displayed on it.

It also describes itself as a 'free service for members of the public to access initial professional and independent family law information'. Notice the word 'information'. There is something slightly odd in a service which is run by qualified professionals that states that the information it provides 'should not be relied upon without taking detailed advice from an appropriately qualified person'. However, it is probably explained by the clear intention not to be seen to be 'assuming responsibility'.

[92] Law Society, Pro Bono Manual, 79.
[93] G Hawkins, 'Using Insurance Claims Data to Determine Appropriate levels of Public Protection in a Regulated Market', Paper given at Access to Justice and Legal Needs Conference (University College, London, 2018).
[94] https://thefamilylawpanel.org/.

Similarly, Law for Life's AdviceNow website[95] displays a Disclaimer, saying that: 'This Guide is not Legal Advice'. It goes on to say that it 'will only give you an overview of what you need to do if you have a civil (non-crime) law legal problem'. But if it suggests what you 'need' to do, that is surely some form of advice? This seems to be a common form of exclusion: eg, the Guide on How to get repairs done at your privately rented home[96] states:

> Disclaimer: The information in this guide applies to England only. The law is complicated. We recommend you try to get advice from the sources we have suggested.

Despite this possibility, it seems that solicitors undertaking pro bono work do not seek to exclude their liability. The requirements in Rules 4.10 and 4.16 of the SRA Practice Framework that the work be covered by an indemnity reasonably equivalent to those required under SRA Indemnity Insurance Rules, and frequent reminders that adequate insurance cover should be taken out for pro bono work indicate that there could be liability for pro bono work. The argument made in support of this position is that non-paying clients deserve the same level of protection as private clients.

The focus on PII in this jurisdiction was of interest to Australian delegates at the National Pro Bono (NPB) Week in November 2016 who described how the Australian government had intervened to help to institutionalise pro bono work not only by requiring any firm awarded a government contract being required to do pro bono work but also by paying for insurance for in-house lawyers to take part. No claims have been made in the ten years of the operation of the scheme so far. Of course the risk is low, and small sums are involved. But in this jurisdiction government has not intervened so far in this way, though the SRA appears to be considering change. Meanwhile the concerns of the lawyers in England and Wales remain focused on the greater likelihood of mistakes being made by young lawyers working outside their areas of expertise, and the injustice of not offering to vulnerable clients the protection afforded to the private client.

[95] http://thejusticegap.com/adviceguide/finding-affordable-help-advice-now/.
[96] http://www.advicenow.org.uk/guides/how-get-repairs-done-your-privately-rented-home.

4

Legal Advice Clinics:
Observational Data

Chapter three described the organisational basis of pro bono activity by solicitors, which was largely (but not exclusively) carried out through LawWorks Legal Advice Clinics. In this chapter we will describe visits to and observations made at three very different LawWorks clinics offering family legal help. All were members of the LawWorks Network as at June 2017 but represent three different models: a law firm model where the clinic is staffed by lawyers from local law firms, a university-based model where students work with local practitioners in the clinic under faculty supervision, and an advice centre-linked model where a clinic is associated with another advice-giving agency, such as a CAB or Law Centre. These models can be further subdivided, for example, by whether or not they are court-based, and whether they offer only initial advice or casework and representation. In addition, there are other models, including a specialist model with services offered, for example, by experts in domestic violence (Rights of Women) or child education issues (Coram Children's Legal Centre).

I. Clinic A: A Court-based Family Legal Advice Clinic (Staffed by Solicitors Assisted by PSU)

Clinic A opened in 2015 following an approach by the Law Society pro bono unit, LawWorks, to the local family judges, with a view to exploring the feasibility of setting up some way of helping Litigants in Person (LiPs) appearing in court in family matters. There was a local Families need Fathers advice group offering specialist help with contact, but no court-based service offering help with family matters. The court already had a voluntary support court service in the form of a Personal Support Unit (PSU), whose work will be described later,[1] and also a housing advice clinic run with student help for debt and repossession cases. They had tried to set up a family mediation pilot scheme whereby mediators would be present in court on two mornings a week to provide initial Mediation Information and Assessment Meetings (MIAMs) where needed prior to a First Hearing Dispute Resolution Hearing (FHDRA) in children cases, but the mediators were no longer

[1] See pp 106ff.

attending as they had attracted so little work. With this experience, and an enthusiastic response from the local Designated Family Judge (DFJ), a draft plan was developed to work further with local practitioners and the Bar, local universities, and charities involved in assisting with the provision of non-legal lay support from 'McKenzie Friends.'[2]

It was accepted from the beginning that any scheme would not be able to fill the huge gap in advice and representation which followed LASPO, and that there would need to be a balance between, on the one hand, the needs of the LiPs, their expectations and financial constraints, and on the other, the level of altruism on the part of the professionals. The original objective was therefore agreed as being to provide steps leading to advice and possibly representation at the FHDRA stage. Local counsel were asked to explore how far the Bar Pro Bono Unit[3] might be able to take on full representation in selected cases. The PSU, which had reported that 60 per cent of their enquiries were about family matters, would act as a resource for signposting to other possible agencies for help. The PSU has played a major part in enabling this LawWorks clinic to function, by dealing with client referral and other aspects of basic administration as they are visibly present in court every day and well signposted. They have also made their WiFi system available for clinic staff to carry out checks for conflicts of interest in case a party is already advised by a firm involved in the scheme. The court service (HMCTS) has made a room next to the PSU available, newly decorated with judicial encouragement (and paint).

The clinic is staffed by one or two practising local solicitors from legal aid firms on two mornings each week, and can offer six sessions by appointment at each, which are regularly fully booked. Five firms are now involved. Local barristers came to the planning meetings but have not been able to follow up with clinic time, though some offer Direct Access[4] help in money cases. The mediators were originally supported by court staff, but no longer attend. The solicitors to whom we spoke reported that there had initially been some difficulty with clients coming in about financial issues who could afford to pay for legal help, and for whom the clinic staff did not have the required expertise. There was also concern about the number of repeat attenders. But people are now limited to one visit, unless the solicitor agrees more. This clinic does not use students in the family advice clinic. The DFJ takes the view that students can be trained for work on benefits or housing, but that family law is more difficult for them. McKenzie Friends are not encouraged in this court. Overall the DFJ is delighted with the work of the family advice clinic, saying 'these solicitors are worth it'. The judge commented that they may be able to persuade clients to try mediation because they are seen as 'on their side' in a way that court staff, although supportive of mediation, are not. The only frustration was that the clinic does not offer representation.

---

[2] For more on McKenzie Friends, see below pp 113ff.
[3] See pp 86–90.
[4] See pp 83–5.

On visiting the clinic, the outer room is used by the PSU, a tiny office but with tables along the wall in a wide pleasant corridor with racks holding copies of forms, redacted judgments and orders, a mobile phone and computer with printer (their property). They are able to photocopy up to five pages for a client on their machine. There is also a court counter service upstairs. They are open all day every court day. There are core volunteers, including retired judges, and students over 21 who can take down details and make appointments. Most clients come to the PSU via Citizens Advice, Cafcass or Social Services, and have been referred at an early stage for information or advice. The PSU had 2,000 contacts last year, over 1,000 being family cases. About 80 per cent are fathers seeking contact. The PSU cannot advise but can inform their decision making. Volunteers explain about MIAMs and C100[5] forms, and hand out a flow chart describing a child arrangements case. The manager said: 'if you know what you want to do we can act … if a father comes in wanting to make his wife comply, we can act … if in doubt we send him to the counter, and we refer along to the clinic two days a week. We fill in a two page advice form for the judges to see how PSU is going. The solicitors arrange their rota, and we do the appointments. It's not a burden. We give the forms for the day to the solicitor in the clinic'.

The judge had explained that the judiciary would like the clinic to expand so as to include offering representation by solicitors as well as advice, but the PSU and the solicitors at the clinic are unwilling, partly because it would limit the number of cases the clinic could handle. At present the clinic sees 360 cases a year. If they offered representation this would fall to about 60 a year. The PSU can prepare clients for seeing the solicitors by giving out the correct forms and helping with witness statements, not telling people *what* to write but advising on what is relevant and making it comprehensible. To give two examples: not just writing 'I want to see my children', but being specific about what they are asking the judge to do; or when the C100 asks on page 1 'are you asking for permission to make this application if this is required', it does not say, but the PSU can, that this applies if you are a grandparent or a father not on the birth certificate. At the counter no forms are given out. People have to download their own, 'so we do it here and can use the HMCTS photocopier for a C100 as it is so long': as the manager said: 'PSU must say "I can't tell you what to do, but I have a redacted court order and I can show it to you, and template orders."'

Two solicitors were working at the family advice clinic on the morning we attended, a local legal aid family practitioner and her trainee. The solicitor started by explaining that she can give advice on procedure and how to get a court hearing if the court office has not told the applicant about a MIAM. She commented that 'no one comes for a MIAM as it costs £70 for nothing, they don't want mediation, and the voluntary mediators have given up coming'. Two-thirds of clients come to the clinic via the PSU, but there is also a large poster in court saying that there is free family advice here. Most clients come before making

---

[5] This form must be completed when making an application for a 'child arrangements' order.

an application to the court, or sometimes in public law if there is a care order in place and they want it discharged. The solicitors only deal with children cases, not with money. Each comes in for one morning every six weeks, and they usually have two appointments in the morning, two drop-in clients and two phone calls.

The first client on the day of our observation was a husband referred as a drop-in by the PSU, but he may need to come back another day as they need to run conflict of interest checks in case either party is a client of their firm. The second appointment, ten minutes later, is a care case where the mother and her partner were seeking more unsupervised contact with their children. They had previously lost care of the children due to their substance abuse, and had separated, but were now together again. The children had gone to the mother's aunt under a Special Guardianship Order (SGO), which the parents wanted lifted. At present they only had supervised contact separately with each child weekly. The solicitor explained that she could not go into the hearing with them because she did not have the insurance needed.[6] She later referred to an earlier case where there had been a Cafcass report saying the child should stay with the father, which the mother wanted to challenge. The solicitor had tried to get legal aid for the mother and helped her as much as she could.

The second client by appointment was a young father, K, with his support worker who spoke for him. There had been a hearing five weeks earlier where a Special Guardianship Order (SGO) had been made in favour of the grandparents with whom his daughter, T, is living. He also has two other children living with their mother, and the mother of his daughter, T, has another daughter with a different father.

> The solicitor (S) reads the order and notes which K hands him, and sees that he had opposed the SGO. The solicitor asks: 'are you happy for T to live there, under a Special Guardianship Order?'. K replies: 'I don't want the SGO'. S explains what an SGO means, that as father 'you don't lose parental responsibility, they just have it as well so they can make day to day decisions, they already do ... you are not less important'. K says 'OK'. The solicitor continues: 'so you need to make it quite clear whether or not you oppose the SGO. If you want to make application to the court you can, you have parental responsibility, but they (the grandparents) have to apply for permission to apply to the court ...'.

> It is becoming clear that it is primarily K's opposition to the SGO which has brought him to court. He says T has been living with the grandparents for a year. S asks: 'have you made the application? Do you have some concerns?' The support worker replies that the father has not seen T since she has been living at the grandparents, and that he thinks they turn the child against him. He asks if that is grounds to oppose the SGO, and if the solicitor would advise him to oppose? S says: 'yes, he should make the court aware of this concern before the court starts thinking about whether to continue the SGO'. S is reading the notes, and sees the father of the mother's other child is in prison. To clarify, she asks: 'so were you just asking for access at that last hearing, not opposing the SGO'? K loudly agrees. S asks: 'you made an application for contact last year, when'? K says it was in the summer. S asks which judge heard the case. K does not

---

[6] See pp 60–2 for discussion of liability and insurance issues.

remember. S asks why the application did not succeed, and gently asks 'was it drug addiction'? K replies: 'Heroin. I'm on methadone now, for 4 years'. S says: 'so you are stable'? K agrees. S asks if he was offered contact in a contact centre. K replies: 'I was able to see her at first, not through court, 3 times it was agreed with mum but then she didn't show so I went to the house but the order …'. S asks: 'was it a restraining order'? K simply says: 'I got angry'.

The support worker asks: 'can they do that? Stop him seeing the children'? S answers: 'it can be used, if you are not complying with orders, if there is a meltdown. The court might want a contact centre, supported not supervised, and then you go into the community. Have you got the papers from the previous proceedings? Then we can see what it's best to touch on. You need to show substantial changes from the previous proceedings to show what has changed between last year and this year'. K says: 'yes, I've got 7 days to do this statement: it says send copies to the court'. S says the order will be sent to you, but asks: 'is this your correct address'? K says: 'No it isn't, but they know my address, I told the court before the last hearing'. S suggests just popping up to the first floor court office and asking them to note the correct address, not to wait for the hostel where he lived to forward it, it causes delays,

Looking at the papers, S says: 'you didn't give them your address … make sure you do. It says the baby is with mum and the local authority is assessing them. Christmas card granted last year. You need to go through the paperwork and make reference to the original assessment when the order was only for a Christmas card, to show you are ready for direct access. Give us a call and come in. I'll make a note so you know what papers to look for. You need to set out for the judge: 1. what has changed since your last appointment; 2. your position re the SGO application, pro, oppose or neutral, that is not agreeing or opposing and you would like the court to decide. Say, about the application I remain neutral, because I have concerns that they have not permitted contact between me and her and I don't think they would going forward. You need to look at the reasons given on the Christmas card order and for the last refusal. You can say you are ok with the contact centre being supervised. Give us a call, we can have a quick word. Any domestic violence'? K says: 'no'. S asks: 'Any (social services) investigations into the case'? The support worker says not that he knows of. S says: 'I am seeing if we can put you in for legal aid. We can't do the statement for you but we can tell you what needs to go in. Anything else? I'll pop these into an envelope'. K thanks and leaves.

The solicitor then commented to the researcher that other clinics have more representation. The solicitors wait outside court, but 'you can't help so many that way. What if another hearing was not on a Tuesday or Thursday when we are here? We couldn't help more than one case a day and not fully after the first hearing'.

The last case that morning was a father with his own mother, the grandmother, about contact. An order had been made in 2014, and an enforcement hearing held in 2015.

The grandmother (GM) says that she sent information to the solicitor and is just waiting and waiting. The solicitor asks which solicitor that was, and recognises the name of a colleague. GM says the order is for the contact centre. 'Two and a half hours a week was ordered, but she, the mum, is never there, she is lying, she hasn't contacted the solicitor. I think she has moved. I have contacted E, the solicitor, but she won't give me information. I said, can I say happy birthday to him. His dad has parental responsibility, but doesn't know anything, not where they are'.

S says: 'let me look at the papers'. She says it is the exact order redone after the first one, and that Cafcass didn't say anything in the hearing the next year. GM says: 'the baby was going to come to my house and I was going to supper with my son with contact, the court has got everything, she (mum) says she hasn' t got anything'. The father says that he emailed E (the solicitor) and she did not respond. S says the file would have been closed and archived as a legally aided case (on Mum's side), and that is why she is not responding. GM says the mother was rehoused, she had an order, we had it, even the contact centre had it, but she's (mum) not replying …'.

The father says 'the judge said to her, "if I see you in court again it will be a fine or prison". She's had another baby now, she is trying to stop me'. GM interjects: 'prison? I don't want that for her, she can come back with P (child) so he's not worried. I asked her and she said yes and never did anything. It's affecting my court order too, I want to see him.' The father says: 'my dad was sick, we wanted him to see his grandson before he died but she never …'. S says to GM: 'you can enforce your order separate from your son's, if you can show you've tried to deal with it outside court'. GM: 'It's going on and on'. S: 'she has a court order and she needs to comply. We will help with the enforcement application' The clients leave.

In our view, the service was effective: accessible, informed, clear, not offering the traditional full legal service of end-to-end casework, but covering all the essential points of the case and offering precise specific advice on the next steps to take. The positive relationship with the PSU was important in easing the administrative burden, and offering a pleasant environment and some office and storage facilities. The strong support of the local judge was helpful in many ways, but did not override the reluctance of the clinic, in line with LawWorks policy, to take on representation, and they did not wish to use student help. Solicitors staffed the clinic, and saw their participation as arising from the policy of their firm, not as an individual decision. In addition, they had picked up two legal aid cases in the last month, which provided some financial compensation for the time of one family legal aid solicitor and her trainee for three hours every six weeks. The barristers had not managed to find a way of contributing, and the mediators had given up trying.

II. Clinic B: A University-based Clinic Comprising a Legal Advice Centre with Local Practitioners and Students and a Separate Student Family Help Desk at Court, Run by a 'Pracademic' (A Faculty Member with a Practising Certificate as a Family Solicitor)

A. The Legal Advice Centre

At Clinic B, the Legal Advice Centre is run by a 'pracademic' (a faculty member with a practising certificate) with an administrator, and staffed by pro bono solicitors with supervised students. A family session is offered one evening a fortnight in term time depending on availability of the solicitor. Family matters are limited to private children cases (contact and residence) and exclude finance or public law. The Court Help Desk for family LiPs is run by the same faculty member who has a practising certificate as a solicitor, and supervises students who offer support and information but not advice. The desk is open on Mondays in term time for children FHDRA hearings.

The Legal Advice Centre is open two mornings a week in term time, offering a drop-in service open for clients to give details of their case and receive information and referrals to other sources of help, including appointments with the specialist advice session which takes place one evening a week during term, with a solicitor working pro bono. The Centre offers initial advice, form-filling help, and written advice. The students can take a history, and observe the solicitor giving advice. They then prepare an advice letter to be checked by the external solicitor, sent out two to three weeks later. The students do not give legal advice. The organiser, a member of the law faculty, is experienced in practice as a family solicitor doing legal aid work and has maintained a practising certificate as a solicitor on the Roll, but has also worked with trainee solicitors offering courses in family law for non-specialists for many years. The Centre is situated in a university building campus close to public transport in a ground floor, highly visible, office suite, with a clear logo in the window. The outer office has a counter, a table for initial introduction and recording information, two banks of work stations with computers and filing area, and a small interview room.

On the evening session observed, two appointments had been booked in at hourly intervals. The first client was received by the administrator and looked after by two students (second and third year) who talked to her in the outer office, taking her story while waiting for the solicitor to arrive. She was a lady who had divorced some years ago but now planned to relocate to the north west with the children to be nearer family members as she had health problems, and she needed to make arrangements for the children's schooling within a few weeks. There was no immediate crisis, and she said that her former husband had consented verbally to the plan. The solicitor, a young woman from a local practice, arrived and took her and the students into the interview room where the first task was to make it clear that written consent for the relocation would be needed. The solicitor (S2) suggested a check for legal aid eligibility. S2 did not think she was likely to be eligible, but that she might qualify for partial remission of the court fee if an application was made to the court. The client left, and the students confirmed that they would send her a legal aid application form and draft an advice email for S2 to check at the next session. It was not clear whether the client would need to come back, as apparently there had been issues of domestic abuse in the past. S2 suggested that she might come to see her at her firm, where her charges are £180 an hour or she could see her for a lower rate.

The second client (C), a slight young black man, visibly distressed, arrived at 7pm. S2 introduces the students and the observer, and says that the students will do the interview (though in effect she does the interview herself). C tells his story. His wife had left with the children four days ago, and he does not know where they are. He had told the police and given them her phone number. He had tried to call himself but there was no answer. He had called the family court the following day. S2 asks which court, and comments how difficult it is to get through there, but C says that the court told him how to contact the Legal Aid Agency, and the CAB and told him to get legal advice and a C100 form. He goes on to describe how the couple had housing benefit arrears, that he gave her money for the rent and that she gave some back as she had been working. 'I give her everything. I just see if she can pay anything but I support the family. She stopped talking to me; I stopped talking to her a month ago now'. S2 asks if there had been any domestic abuse. C says that in January (six months ago) 'she tried to fight me out, I called the police, she slapped me out, they called an ambulance and while it was coming she told them I was attacking her, the police took me that night, they released me in the morning'. S2 asks if there was no further action. C says: 'yes, no further action: I'm just trying to hold on for the children (son, 5, daughter, 9)'.

S2 asks: 'have you contacted the school to see if the children have been there'? C says 'no', but he has asked the police and they won't tell him. S2 tells him that the school must tell him if the children have attended, but that they do not have to give him any new address. But he will know they have been to school. She says: 'I think she is likely to be in a refuge, and the police are doing a welfare check. All these refuges keep their addresses secret. They will find a place outside this area. This will be a considered as a 'danger area' for her by the police. You will have to seek an order for the children's whereabouts, not just a C100 but a C8, to keep addresses secret. Put in as much detail as possible to enable the court to locate her. Is she claiming any benefit'? C says 'no'; child benefit and tax credits come to his account. S2 tells him that the court can ask the school or bank, anyone, to disclose her address to the court, and they will not disclose it to him but will keep it in a sealed envelope. 'The court will tell her that you are seeking a hearing, a child arrangements order, and they will send you to x court, or to the Central Family Court in Holborn but it is not very quick'.

S2 asks if he is working. He says 'yes' and she says: 'then it will cost £215 to issue proceedings, cash or card. The court here will try to deal with it, will contact DWP, and when they have the whereabouts they might send the case back to the other court. Sometimes files get lost in the system. But when they have her address they will send a date for the FHDRA. Cafcass will contact you and have a phone interview with you and mum and give advice to the court which the judge will follow. It might be a district judge or a magistrate. Sometimes you get into a safeguarding check, social services or police, making sure everything is OK. It's a good thing. In the past they used to do this in the middle of a case. A dad could be on bail. It took longer. Last week's incident (where C had made a disturbance outside the house and police had been called but no action was taken) will come up and the 2016 incident. If you can't agree, the judge might ask Cafcass for a report. It can take 6 to 10 weeks'.

C asks: 'When will I see my children'? S2 replies that if Cafcass is saying no contact until the case is heard unless you both agree, based on what you have said, the court might say at a contact centre, supervised, but you have to pay. 'There is one near you. And you will need a MIAM … but if you don't know where your wife is you are exempt'. She goes on to say that the students will help him fill in the C100, and that he will need four copies: for mum, the court, Cafcass and himself. C asks when he will need the £200. S2 tells him that he will need to pay when he goes to court tomorrow. But she adds: 'You have got parental responsibility, there is no reason why you shouldn't have contact, but it doesn't always work as it should, But you can contact the school for information, they are used to dealing with separated parents'. C reflects: '2016 was a turning point for me. I had been living with someone who … she turned on me, I saw what happened, what should I apologise for'.

S2 says: 'You want to go to court tomorrow? You don't want any more allegations against you'. C says he will contact the school in the morning. S2 asks if he has any questions. He says: 'Yes, but I will take them one at a time, we are on the same side'. S2 advises him not to think too much about divorce now, but to sort the children out first. C asks what will happen next. S2 replies that the girls (the students) will write to him. C says: 'I will do it tomorrow'. S2 agrees that he need not wait for the letter. A student says: 'It usually takes 10 days, all our service is free'. C says he can't believe it. S2 says the girls work very hard, and she has the C100 online, adding: 'Tick don't know on p 12 and then you will be exempt from the MIAM'. She says: "Fill it all in, do one and sign it and then photocopy each one and sign. Check with the court, you might need an appointment to go to the counter there. If you do, go through security and pick up the phone and say you have an appointment and they will buzz you in'. C remembers that he went there last year, that he tried to go to court but his wife had apologised and cried, so he had contacted his lawyer and said he was not doing it.

S2 asks who the lawyer was, but C cannot remember. S2 says: 'Don't worry … but there are very few legally aided divorces now'. C says that the solicitor was with him at the court when his wife cried and cried and said 'bring me back' so he dropped it and six months later she started again, maybe she has mental health issues, she can be so loving and then this. 'You can't be there if your partner is not stable. I worked, I love my children, everything. But I've had enough. Need to sort it out'. S2 says: 'We are making progress'. C asks her to pass his gratitude to M, the receptionist: 'She reassured me at my lowest point, please thank her … I went to CAB and they gave me this number and I rang'. He leaves, in tears.

The students then ask questions of S2 about whether the court will talk to the children. She says 'no, not unless they are over 9, and the police will not talk to them'. She thinks there might be an injunction coming, and he will need to get representation. 'It looks like he petitioned for divorce and relented, you get some people so abused they think it's the norm, keep going back. At the Family Justice Centre (a specialist domestic violence organisation where she volunteers) every Tuesday morning we have these meetings for victims, case studies, and they say "it's me!"' The second student asks if she sees men who are being abused. She says 'yes', that no one wants to listen but that is changing. It is more about the police getting used to it, and there are no refuges for men. She thinks these two will get together again, but the children will watch … 'we'll see …'.

Another student says that C is Nigerian, like her, and 'I know the community encourages them to stay together. It's not right, I think he is right about the mood changes …'. S2 says that Cafcass might want her to go to Freedom (a centre for victims of domestic abuse) and him to go on a perpetrators course, but 'if he can't pay then he won't see the children till he saves up and pays. If Cafcass seek a contact direction, then they pay'. She says: 'you have to be direct and clear with a client. You have to sort of say "now I've heard enough"'. She says that she is used to being in the CAB 'where we have a queue, so I've learned that' and the student agrees. This young solicitor also works at the One Stop Shop which offers help with housing, and for domestic violence victims at Centre Point, a police refuge, and the Family Justice Centre in Croydon with IDVA (Independent Domestic Violence Adviser) and support workers, one for young women and one for older women, with outreach, picking up vulnerable women who might end up in sex work.

B. The Family Court Help Desk

The Legal Advice Centre was an impressive service, with expert input from the volunteer solicitor who had expertise in domestic violence. The students were learning a great deal. But the resources expended per case are considerable. To complement this service the faculty organiser has developed a separate Family Court Help Desk situated in the local family court to provide practical and procedural advice for LiPs on the day of a hearing, but not 'legal advice' which would include the kind of strategic suggestions being made by the solicitor in the Legal Advice Centre. The Help Desk was not a LawWorks Clinic, but supported entirely by the university.

The Help Desk began by opening weekly on the day when First Hearing Disputes Resolution Appointments (FHDRAs) are held, but only in term time. It is sometimes possible to stay open during vacation if enough local students are around, and the organiser continues to attend throughout the year. The organiser is in court one day a week, and has a practising certificate and would be able to offer advocacy. There will be eight students in the building, and their participation in the scheme forms part of the their assessed course in Dispute Resolution. There are two courtrooms, which usually have six cases listed in each. There are two Cafcass officers in court but they only speak to parties where a Cafcass letter has not been filed and served. Cases often run late.

The students at the Help Desk follow the model of activity of McKenzie Friends (to be described later[7]) in providing all the help which falls short of legal advice and representation. The two Lead Students will be shown the list of cases for the day by the court usher, and are able to make a note of who is not represented. They start by giving each LiP a leaflet and letting them think about whether they would like help. If after consideration the LiP requests help they will be asked to read and sign the agreement for service, and a student will take the litigant to a side room

---

[7] See pp 113ff.

or corridor space to go through the ways they can help. They will sit with LiPs before the hearing, check that all paperwork has been filed, especially the C1A and C8 forms, help manage expectations (eg, that it could be a long day and that the case might not be resolved at this first hearing), accompany them into court and make a note of the order, go over this with the LiP after the hearing and make sure the LiP has a note of key dates, and keep the parties apart, and alert security if a LiP is afraid of leaving the building. The students have pro forma forms to fill in to make sure they have all the key information, and they give parties a leaflet after the hearing with a note of the order written in it. They are given careful instruction about keeping the parties separate, and not discussing any aspect of the case.

The court has requested only second and third year students, and this is accommodated by means of 24 students each term, half of whom are experienced, with eight on the rota each week. The two students who sit at the usher's desk will bring clip boards, name badges, forms, leaflets etc for the Help Desk and take the lead in identifying LiPs. The Desk helps both parties at the request of the judges. This was not what was expected when planning the service. The organiser had expected students to be in court with LiPs, making a note of the hearing, but in practice they have been asked to spend more time with the parties both before and after the hearing, offering emotional support.

But there are issues of confidentiality and impartiality. The service is very careful to make sure that parties know that the students are supporting both parties when this happens, and that both parties know that notes are not kept other than the record of the hearing which is not confidential. The university requires each Help Desk client to sign a client agreement, which refers to confidentiality and collection of data for research purposes. The wording is as follows: 'I have read the above explanation of the service. I understand that the student supporter is not qualified to give me legal advice but can support me in court and before the hearing'. Details of proceedings are recorded when first speaking to the client (who issues, what type of order is sought, whether a position statement has been filed with the court and served on the other side, whether they have received a position statement from the other side, whether safeguarding checks have been completed, and whether they have had legal advice). There is a further section to deal with safety in cases of domestic violence. The student also writes a summary of the court order and directions, with date and time of the next hearing. After the hearing the student records whether there was legal advice before the hearing, whether safeguarding checks were completed before the hearing, whether there are allegations of domestic violence, or drug or alcohol abuse. They note position statements, reports and other evidence directed by the court to be acquired, such as SPIP (Separated Parents Information Programme) Orders, whether the case is listed for fact finding, and whether there has been a final order or an adjournment. If the clients want to make an appointment with the Legal Advice Centre after the hearing, this is done on a first-come-first-served basis.

The nature of proceedings is categorised as being about starting contact, reducing or increasing contact, or regulating or stopping contact. This is followed by a section on changes about with whom the child lives, a specific holiday or school issue, change of name, removal from jurisdiction or disputes over paternity or any other issue. The students will have attended a training session with discussion of examples, and been given a detailed handbook describing process, court etiquette (including suitable dress), directions to the court, and how to explain the service. There is a list of don'ts (for example, 'do not share information with anyone other than the organiser', 'do not chew gum ... this could lead to you being removed from the court room' ... 'remember the court is not open to the public', 'do not give the litigant their summary leaflet without having it checked by your supervisor'). Key terms are defined and the student must sign a Family Court Project agreement.

The students are not holding themselves out to be lawyers, and not conducting advocacy, which is a 'reserved legal activity'.[8] The project is therefore not professionally regulated except insofar as this is provided by the university, but the organiser, as a practising solicitor, is subject to professional regulation, but can give advice as an employee of the university by reason of paragraph 4.16 of the SRA Practice Framework Rules 2011 and therefore should be covered by the university's insurance.[9] It seems that the solicitor could also undertake representation in her 'personal capacity' under that paragraph as representation is not part of the university's business, but in practice she avoids speaking to LiPs as she might inadvertently speak to both parties in the same case, giving rise to conflict of interest issues. But views on this issue vary from clinic to clinic.

The majority of cases are about regulating contact, but over a third involved domestic violence issues. Between September 2016 and March 2017 the Desk helped in 98 cases, evenly divided between applicants and respondents. 35 involved domestic violence issues but without legal aid at this stage, 33 a Section 7 report (where the court directed Cafcass to report on the child's welfare). Safeguarding before hearing, involving protective intervention by the local authority,[10] had taken place in 15 cases; there were drug or alcohol issues in 21 cases and a finding of fact in only four cases. In 46 cases a final order was made, and in 34 the case was adjourned, The most common issues were restarting, increasing or regulating contact (64 cases), enforcement (seven cases) and eight SPiPs. There were Christian, Sikh and Muslim parents, the majority aged 25–45. 26 were above the Rowntree minimum income (a poverty measure) and 22 below. 20 clients (now LiPs) had received legal advice before the proceedings.

The first case observed concerned a father, who had representation, asking for contact with his 10 year old daughter on weekend afternoons and one midweek contact, but no staying contact. The lead student, a recent graduate, dressed in

---

[8] See pp 60–1.
[9] See pp 60–2.
[10] That is, there had been a need for intervention by the local authority to protect the child.

a suit and looking very much the part of a solicitor, invited the unrepresented mother through her interpreter to sit in a quiet corner with him where he checked whether she had filed a position statement and, if one had been needed, he would have helped with the drafting. He then went to find the applicant father's solicitor to ask if a statement had been filed and it had not. He returned to his client just as the Cafcass officer arrived to speak to her, and it appeared that there was no disagreement about contact being resumed but that the mother wanted it to be regular. She was tired of the father just turning up and not saying when he would return the child.

We were called into court where the magistrate asked who everyone was, asked the parties to speak to the court, not to each other, and heard first from the Cafcass officer that agreement had been reached. The magistrate congratulated the parties on this, but then asked why an order should be drafted, given the no order presumption. The mother, with whispered support from the student, managed to say that she needed the certainty of an order, and the applicant's representative said the same. The magistrate accepted this, and the father's solicitor offered to draft the order by the end of the day. The magistrate ended by firmly telling the parents that if they had further disagreements they should attend mediation and not come back to court. The court rose, the student accompanied the mother to a quiet corner and made sure she understood what had happened, what to expect, and that she was free to go home. It was not difficult to imagine how different this woman's experience would have been without the calm 'professional' support of the student, even though she had an interpreter. The court building was crowded and confusing, and at one point an angry father in another case tried to snatch his ex-wife's phone from her, causing quite a disturbance. The student commented that without lawyers to manage people who are very upset, respect for the court and for the law itself is being damaged.

The students appeared fully integrated into the busy court setting, well known to court and security staff, and to be making a valued contribution. They were learning, but also giving real and much needed assistance to the litigants in person. They were able to assist with all the FHDRA cases that morning, and were invited by the judge to help with two Dispute Resolution Appointment (DRA) cases which had moved on to the next stage of dispute resolution. The FHDRA is a particularly appropriate setting for their contribution as it involves applicants and respondents who are not familiar with the court process but may not yet be deeply entrenched in their dispute. The principal actor is the Cafcass officer, who has already spoken to both parties and has a good idea of whether the dispute can be resolved. Cafcass values the part played by the Help Desk students in keeping the parties calm, answering questions, and generally supporting both parties. Over half of these cases reach agreement at this stage.

We were also able to observe a university-based clinic which combined both legal advice (as in Clinic A) and court support (as in Clinic B), which we will describe in chapter seven.

III. Clinic C: A Family Legal Advice Clinic Linked with an Advice Agency

A. Family Advice

This family law clinic is embedded within the Royal Courts of Justice Advice Bureau (RCJAB), incorporating Islington CA, with family advice provided by salaried solicitors, supported by volunteers (no students). Family Advice was set up by the judges in 1978 at the Royal Courts of Justice (RCJ), now known as the Central London Family Court. There are two to three full-time salaried solicitors and between 20 and 40 pro bono legal assistant volunteers who, if they have completed the Legal Practising Certificate, can do initial interviews, some witness statements, run papers to court and provide triage. The service also has a debt team, a civil law team and immigration lawyers, and can signpost to other family providers such as CORAM, Rights of Women (ROW), and the BPBU,[11] for whom this CAB is a major referrer. Volunteer lawyers must be at least two years post-qualification, and their rotas are supervised. The service is open Monday to Friday from 9 am to 5 pm, but there is a high level of demand and the service has moved from drop-in to telephone appointments and now only sets appointments for a week ahead. These are all taken by 11 am on a Monday morning.

Since LASPO, the client groups in many agencies appear more vulnerable, with more complex problems, more domestic violence, and 85 per cent do not have English as their first language. This represents a significant change in the kind of work required of this service which did not see legal aid clients before LASPO. Because of the pressure of demand, each client is limited to three half-hour sessions. Family Advice (FA) at the RCJ carries out a form of triage with a separate form for family matters on the new website.[12] If someone cannot fill it in, they can drop in early on a Monday morning for help. Conflicts of interest and legal aid eligibility are checked, but the service decided not to seek a legal aid contract. The form asks if the person is coming to court, what stage any proceedings have reached, dates of hearings, any vulnerabilities, and whether any other advice has been sought. Three out of four applicants have some form of disadvantage, such as having a family member in prison. There is a PSU at the court which offers emotional support and will help with forms.

The FA at the RCJ advises on content but does not fill in forms. It hosts a separate public law rota inherited from a nearby court which has closed, and picks up some legal aid work. There are also plans for a trainee programme in advocacy, which the law schools are asking for. But, as explained earlier,[13] there is no current

---

[11] See pp 86–90.
[12] http://www.rcjadvice.org.uk/family-law/ (last accessed 5 June 2018).
[13] See pp 66, 70.

scheme that uses volunteer barristers. A number of attempts were made but none has succeeded. The key gap in post-LASPO provision is thought to be provision of early legal help: people are just not getting initial legal advice. The 30 minute client interviews with the experienced in-house solicitor offer the kind of advice formerly available under the legal aid scheme, and the lawyer is experienced in making effective use of the time available. For example, in a case where a single mother seeks a lump sum from the father, the lawyer is able to identify the relevant facts, explain the applicable legal provisions, including the Child Maintenance Service and the possibility of regularising contact while warning that everything might depend on the father's resources, so that it would be worth checking on benefit and housing entitlement, and possibly considering mediation.

B. CourtNav

Given the pressure on the services of the solicitors, the RCJCA has turned to trying to find ways of making best use of resources to reach more clients, and free up their lawyers to deal with the more demanding work. It would like to send more people on to a solicitor for unbundled work, but this has not been possible as the clients simply do not have even the smaller amount of money required for legal help. But with funding for development from a large city firm, the service has developed an interactive website known as CourtNav to be used initially by clients seeking to fill in a divorce application. The triage process carried out by the service consists in discovering whether the client has a computer and can use it, and has a sufficient command of the English language. It provides a pathway. Developed with the experience of the Citizens Advice family solicitors and the technical expertise provided by external finding, CourtNav helps the user along the divorce journey from petition to decrees nisi and absolute. There is a shutdown and save button for the safety of users in threatening domestic circumstances. Citizens Advice simply sends the link, which is now nationally available, and sets up a separate email and password. There is a progress key which identifies a response to a question as incomplete, requiring attention, or locked in. The information provided in response to the carefully structured set of answerable questions will be checked by a CourtNav lawyer. If all is complete, and the petitioner confirms that they wish to go ahead, the information will be used by the website to populate the divorce petition which will be sent to the court. Nothing will be printed without the client's agreement.

From the first 500 cases using the system so far, none have been returned by the courts for correction. For all other forms of application, the return rate nationally was over a third[14] and this is unlikely to change while there is a very limited

---

[14] L Trinder, 'Losing the particulars? Digital divorce and the potential for harm reduction' (2017) 47 *Family Law* 17. See p 33.

counter service in the family courts, and the new divorce centres are finding it difficult to answer calls. The process works smoothly as it was designed by people with experience of the application process. For example, as the majority of the 40 per cent of petitions returned to applicants not using CourtNav had errors in the response to the request to state the place of marriage, CourtNav asks the petitioner to photograph, upload and send a picture of the marriage certificate via the website. Another trouble spot in the petition is the lengthy and complex section on jurisdiction, determining whether the applicant may divorce in this country. CourtNav knows that 85 per cent of petitioners are UK residents and therefore simply asks 'are you generally resident in the UK? ... is your spouse generally resident in the UK?'. This deals with the great majority of cases without the applicant ever needing to see the jurisdiction section in the petition. Similarly the divorce petition no longer contains a long section on child arrangements, but there is still a rather clumsy section on children. CourtNav instead has a simple heading 'Your Children' and asks for names and ages.

CourtNav has an extra section not in the petition called Personal Information in order to check whether the applicant's address should be revealed. This section opens the dialogue on legal aid and the possibility of an injunction, highlighting the process. The courts need the case reference number, not the case details, so this is what CourtNav asks for, and finally, concerning the Prayer (that is, what the applicant seeks), there is an opt-in structure on page 8 of CourtNav, where clients are advised to tick all boxes so that they are not prevented from following various actions in future. If they choose not to do so, they are asked to say why they made that choice. The applicant is encouraged to use the behaviour condition for divorce, and is advised that this is because this depends only on what the applicant states so there will be no bargaining and minimal difficulty. If adultery or separation and consent are given as the basis for the divorce, there may be disagreement over dates, or consent may be withdrawn. A soft acceptable sentence is given as an example for how to choose behaviour with minimum distress: for example, 'my spouse is not responsible with money and after many conversations and attempts cannot improve'. The process includes access to the GOV.UK website 'Check if you can get legal aid', and to the fee forms and information on remission of fees. Every section is checked and requires a green tick before going on to print out and submission. CourtNav is a rare example of a website which benefits both the client through the legal advice embedded in the structure (such as the advice regarding choosing the basis for the divorce), as well as the service which can reduce the need for more appointments for advice further down the road to divorce.

IV. Concluding Observations

These examples illustrate only a small part of the range of ways in which the LawWorks clinics are organised, and the services they offer in family matters.

The advice provided by lawyers who give time as members of their law firm to work in clinic, despite the reservations of the profession about working without payment letting the government 'off the hook', is clearly of great importance. This can make a significant contribution which is particularly visible in the court setting where those without representation, whether present as applicants with some degree of choice or respondents without, face the need for immediate help. The extent to which clinics provided 'representation' however was limited, and litigants might have to rely on support from the lay volunteers of a PSU or, as described in the context of Clinic A, a student serviced Help Desk.

What is less clear is how the parties find their way to the clinic, and the impact of the help and support received given that visits are usually limited to one half hour without follow-up other than a single letter of advice. When we observed a trainee from a major city firm offering advice at a weekly community advice centre, not however on a family matter as these were excluded from most such schemes, we could see how such a session could be of limited value. A middle aged man with poor English had been dismissed from his junior management job with a cleaning contractor for behaviour which he denied, and received notice that if he wished to appeal he must do so within a few days. The trainee solicitor from a major city firm was kind and supportive, but found it difficult to elicit relevant information. After the allotted half hour had extended to 45 minutes, the trainee discovered that the man had not been given the required seven day notice of appeal, and that he could write in immediately to ask for more time. The man asked for and was given help to write this as his English was poor. But little was achieved beyond hopefully some extension of the time limit. The trainee explained that he was not a lawyer and could not give legal advice, but nevertheless the client was grateful, as he said everything had happened so quickly and no one else had listened to him.

For the lawyers, this pro bono work carries little risk, in that the activity is defined and insured through their firms. The main issues for practitioners in this sector are concerned with recognition of the work as billable, in meeting targets, being appreciated by the firm and even acquiring a secondary specialism. LawWorks provides the organisational structure for solicitors to provide simi-lar services pro bono on an outreach basis. We have seen the way in which such services can be useful, but availability remains limited, and the transition from a single advice session to representation and full case care remains very problematic.

5

The Response of the Legal Professions to LASPO: II Barristers in Action Pro Bono

I. Structural Issues

Chapters three and four showed the pro bono activity of solicitors as being varied and visible, usually taking the form of initial advice rather than full case work, and organised mainly through the activities of LawWorks, which does not provide assistance directly but supports the work of member clinics acting as the pro bono arm of the Law Society, often with student involvement. Individual solicitors give additional help in the form of free initial meetings or by going beyond what is required by a legal aid contract, or through in-house lawyers participating in coordinated pro bono programmes, but the main body of work takes place through LawWorks.

The pro bono activity of the Bar is also coordinated through its key professional organisation for promoting pro bono work, the Bar Pro Bono Unit (BPBU). The Unit is a charity, established in 1996, and describes its role as to 'match members of the public who need help with barristers who are willing to donate their time and expertise in deserving cases for those who are unable to obtain legal aid and cannot afford to pay'.[1] The BPBU has published its own Protocol,[2] developed with LawWorks, which sets out a concept of pro bono work in the same way as the Law Society Pro Bono Protocol, described earlier.[3] The differences between the professions are described in detail below.[4]

Like the Law Society, the Bar also supports a range of diverse pro bono activities by its members and has various strengths and weaknesses. The key differences between the branches of the profession arise from the working practices of the Bar, where there is a different organisational structure and perhaps a greater degree of specialism. For example, a barrister, who is normally an independent

---

[1] https://www.barprobono.org.uk/overview.html (last accessed 5 June 2018).
[2] Bar Pro Bono Unit, Joint Protocol for Pro Bono Legal Work: https://www.barprobono.org.uk/pro_bono_protocol.html (last accessed 5 June 2018).
[3] See p 52.
[4] See pp 82–4.

practitioner, has less flexibility than a solicitor, who is part of a law firm, to attend clinics or be 'on call' as a duty lawyer in court-based services. Barristers also appear less able to organise ongoing supervision of law students, and so seem less likely to be drawn into student pro bono activity. There is as yet little clinical legal education including advocacy for potential members of the Bar, as the dominant model for student activity is closer to that of the lay support offered by McKenzie Friends who support their clients in court but do not usually speak in court.

But it is also possible for barristers to operate as a group, for example as a limited company managed by lawyers (who need not be barristers), or managed by lawyers and non-lawyers. Such 'BSB entities' may be authorised or licensed by the Bar Standards Board (in the latter case, as an Alternative Business Structure), focusing on entities that specialise in advocacy, litigation, and specialist legal advice. In those cases the entity must ensure that the work of barristers employed within the structure is covered by adequate insurance.[5] It was reported in 2015 that one of 32 such entities 'is to put on free advice and litigation clinics, including one at Yarl's Wood Immigration Removal Centre',[6] which is a charity funded by donations and assistance from solicitors from DLA Piper's pro bono unit.

As representing a client in litigation is a 'reserved activity', those carrying it out (whether barristers or solicitors) must have the appropriate qualification. Attempts to introduce advocacy experience into clinical legal education give rise to issues about the practicality of supervising advocacy experience as well as arranging appropriate insurance. The University of Law advocacy training scheme has been able to function more freely as a result of having achieved Alternative Business Structure status as this allows its legally qualified employees to practice as such and carry out 'reserved' legal activities.[7]

In the past, clients could only engage the services of a barrister through the intermediary of a solicitor, but since 2003 criticism by the Office of Fair Trading forced the Bar Council to allow barristers to take instruction directly from a client (known as Direct, or Public, Access) if they have undergone the specified course and received appropriate certification.[8] A barrister need not, however, have such certification in order to take instructions from the BPBU, since the unit is licensed to give such instruction. However, the most common working practice still is to take instruction from a solicitor. This structure may make it more difficult to organise pro bono work, which is often needed at short notice. In this regard a solicitor, who works in a law firm and has greater individual flexibility as a result of team work with input from paralegals, legal executives and

---

[5] *Bar Standards Board Handbook* (February 2018), gC113: https://www.barstandardsboard.org.uk/media/1918141/bsb_handbook_1_february_2018.pdf (last accessed 14 June 2018).

[6] See D Bindman, 'BSB-regulated entities reach 32, with pro bono and solicitor-run start-ups' at http://www.legalfutures.co.uk/latest-news/bsb-regulated-entities-reach-32-with-pro-bono-and-solicitor-run-start-ups (last accessed 5 June 2018).

[7] See pp 60–1.

[8] *Bar Standards Board Handbook* (n 6), rC119, rC120.

administrative staff, is at an advantage over a barrister who works as an individual within a set of chambers making it difficult to commit to setting time aside for a pro bono client.

Barristers in pro bono clinics may however be less likely than solicitors to be limited to giving initial advice or be led into attempting to give advice outside their area of expertise. They may be less likely than solicitors to be encouraged to develop a useful secondary specialism as offered through the LawWorks training. They are however sometimes involved in what the Canadians call 'secondary consultation', whereby they give advice to advice workers, not on a specific case, but on a particular issue which occurs repeatedly.[9] Examples are advice given to Gingerbread and the Coram Foundation, referred to elsewhere.[10]

II. Liability and Insurance

Pro bono work done by a barrister will normally be provided as Direct (Public) Access. If the matter were not pro bono, there would be a contract between the barrister and the client, and the standard letter of engagement contains no limitation of liability clause, though reference is made to the possibility of the client making a complaint to the Legal Ombudsman, who could award compensation.[11] In the case of pro bono work, however, the client receives a letter from the BPBU informing them of the barrister allocated to them, and told that the barrister has agreed to 'help you with the piece of work on the standard terms of work that apply to all cases accepted through the Unit' and saying they may receive these terms 'on request'. The terms include the clause: 'Duty of care: A barrister will exercise reasonable care and skill in carrying out instructions. This is however subject to any immunity from suit which the barrister may enjoy under the general law in respect of any work done in the course of carrying out instructions'.[12] Since the decision of the House of Lords in *Hall v Simons*[13] ended the immunity from suit in tort for negligence for advocates, the position of barristers is essentially the same as for other professionals.

The clause is striking in that, unlike most Terms of Engagement for pro bono work, far from seeking to exclude or restrict liability, it in fact asserts responsibility.

---

[9] 'Secondary Legal Consultation in Ontario, an approach to outreach in which the clinic lawyer provides advice to service providers in agencies within the community to help them assist their clients ... depends on the legal clinic establishing deep ties with the community ... early indications are that it is going well':. Ab Currie, Senior Research Fellow, Osgoode Hall Law School, York University, Toronto: Personal communication, 4 June 2017.

[10] See pp 52, 147.

[11] *Bar Standards Board Handbook: The Public Access Scheme Guidance for Lay Clients*, para 42:. https://www.barstandardsboard.org.uk/media/1580314/public_access_guidance_for_lay_clients_-_jan_2014.pdf (last accessed 14 June 2018).

[12] Bar Pro Bono Unit, Terms of work for work accepted through the Unit, cl. 6.

[13] [2000] 3 WLR 543.

This may be because this engagement is not perceived as a contract, so the barrister's liability could only arise in tort, and this depends on an assumption of responsibility, although in some circumstances it may be imposed simply on the basis of 'proximity', 'foreseeability' and 'fairness'.[14] In any event, under the Bar Code of Conduct,[15] barristers are told that they must 'ensure that you have adequate insurance (taking into account the nature of your practice) which covers all the legal services which you supply to the public'; and, if self-employed (which is the standard case) they must be a member of the Bar Mutual Indemnity Fund (BMIF). Barristers taking cases through the BPBU are however covered for insurance purposes by the BPBU's block access licence.

Having set out the organisational context in which most barristers operate, we now seek to provide evidence of how pro bono work is handled in practice. To do this we have carried out interviews with members of chambers engaged in pro bono activity either directly through chambers or through the BPBU, and in court-based duty services in family courts. We deal with their role in giving advice in the advice sector agencies later.[16]

III. Interview Data

As examples of this range of activity, we will present here the views of the head clerk in a chambers well known for its pro bono work on the implications for chambers of such work, the views of those working with the Pro Bono Unit on the process of reviewing applications for help and the question of matching need to availability on providing services, and finally the views of barristers attempting to offer help via duty schemes in family courts.

A. The View from Chambers

A senior clerk first described how there are new ways of working which, while not pro bono, nevertheless attempt to cut the cost of legal help to the client. Where a client is paying fees but has a liquidity problem, chambers can help with payment methods, including access to loans. Some barristers offer Direct Access as a low cost, sometimes fixed fee, option through the Direct Access Portal (DAP)[17] which is the official and exclusive Bar Council website. Direct Access avoids the cost of paying a solicitor, but from the clerk's perspective, Direct Access usually carries a

---

[14] *Hedley Byrne v Heller* [1964] AC 465; *Henderson v Merrett Syndicates* [1995] 2 AC 145; and *Williams v Natural Life Health Foods* [1998] UKHL 17; *Lejonvarn v Burgess* [2017] EWCA Civ 254.
[15] See *Bar Standards Board Handbook* (note 6) rC76 and rC77. Pro Bono Protocol, 2.9.
[16] See pp 123, 147.
[17] www.directaccessportal.co.uk (last accessed 5 September 2018).

premium to cover the additional administrative costs which have to be carried by chambers, particularly the extra work for the clerks in assembling bundles, and making sure the client is aware of times and dates of hearings or meetings. But if a barrister works pro bono, without a solicitor, there is no provision to meet these costs.

There are also limits to the work which can be done. Although Direct Access barristers can advise on the law, evidence and procedure, draft letters and help with applications to court, and represent the client in negotiation meetings and at court, they cannot always conduct the litigation if this would be outside their area of expertise. When a barrister takes a case pro bono, there is usually additional pressure on the clerk and therefore the functioning of chambers as a whole is affected. There is also a need for pro bono training. The clerk told how the chambers used to encourage their members to sign up for pro bono training with the BPBU, but that they no longer do so as the training has changed and now impinges on pupillage in chambers by requiring the release of a pupil for two months out of a six month pupillage. The clerk described the changing context for pro bono family work where demand is increasing but the lack of resources to pay for it is causing problems, especially on the fringes of public law cases where, although there is still legal aid for the parents, it is not available for the wider family, such as grandparents and, in adoption cases, if the proposed adopters cannot afford legal representation and the local authority will not fund them.

Despite these difficulties regarding pro bono work, the clerk said that 'all the non-selfish ones do it'. The senior barristers may be too busy to take on very much, but for more junior members of the Bar there are non-monetary rewards in taking particularly interesting cases, and appearing before particular judges who 'may see them differently if they come asking for money for a rich wife if they have seen them arguing for a woman without money in difficulty'. Solicitors refer cases individually when a client has run out of money, but also when there are particular issues such as cases where the respondent needs representation for the other side in a domestic violence case 'to stop the perpetrator from cross-examining the victim'.[18] However, the structural issues are such that the time barristers can devote to pro bono work is very limited, and finding a pro bono barrister raises many problems, as explained below.

B. Organised Pro Bono Work

i. *The Bar Pro Bono Unit (BPBU)*

Pro bono work does not often result from an individual barrister's choice of a client, but is usually part of organised pro bono activity. There are two main forms

---

[18] For more on this, see p 96.

for this, either on a national basis through the BPBU or through a local court-based voluntary legal help scheme such as that run by the Central Family Court in London.

As explained earlier, the BPBU does not help directly but helps to find free assistance from their list of barristers (now approaching 4,000) for those who need it. Individuals cannot apply directly but must be referred, usually by a solicitor or advice agency such as Citizens Advice or a Law Centre, and increasingly often by their MP. The decision whether to refer is taken by the solicitor, or by the referring agency. The Unit needs at least three weeks' notice of a referral before any hearing date or deadline in the case, and the application form must be fully completed with all relevant information and copy documents. The Unit will then correspond with the solicitor or referrer up to the point where the decision is taken whether or not to take on the case, and it then becomes their responsibility to inform the applicant of the outcome. Help is given on a step-by-step basis and is reviewed at each stage.[19]

The Unit is licensed to accept a case where there is no instructing solicitor but the decision whether to accept a case is determined not only by financial factors but also by how much work it is estimated will be required from the volunteer. It also advises potential applicants of the risk that 'an assisted party may be ordered to pay the costs of the other side'. This can happen when the case is lost or even if only part of the case is lost, and the successful party obtains an order that their own legal costs are paid by the losing party. The fact that the applicant is being assisted by the BPBU is no protection and will not prevent any such order being made. But on the other hand it is also possible for a costs order to be made in favour of the assisted applicant under section 193 of the Legal Services Act 2007 which requires a losing party to make a payment to the Access to Justice Foundation charity (the Bar pro bono charity).

The BPBU provides access to high quality, full professional legal assistance for cases of merit for which there is no alternative source of funding. But it is well defended against the problem of overwhelming demand even before the stage of screening applicants for financial suitability and the merits of their case. The pathway to receiving help is complex, and the applicant has many obstacles to overcome after identifying a legal need, as the case must not only be suitable but the applicant must be matched with a volunteer barrister with the appropriate skills and availability. The workload has increased significantly since LASPO. By 2015–16 it was reported that the unit had seen a 30 per cent increase in applications year on year since 2012, and the number of family cases helped almost doubled from 244 in 2013 to 471 by September 2015.[20] In 2012 family matters had constituted 12 per cent of the Unit's work,[21] but by 2015 family was the largest

[19] See https://www.inbrief.co.uk/legal-system/bar-pro-bono-unit/ (last accessed 15 September 2017).
[20] C Baksi, 'The Politics of Pro Bono' *Legal Action* March 2016, 8–9: https://www.lag.org.uk/article/202002/the-politics-of-pro-bono.
[21] Bar Pro Bono Annual Report (2012).

area of law covered (32 per cent: followed by property at 12 per cent).[22] The number of barristers registered as able to volunteer in 2012 had been over 2,500, of whom 100 act as reviewers of applications. It is currently thought to be close to 4,000. The CEO of BPBU has a staff of 20 caseworkers who have legal training of at least two years, and interns with one year's training, as well as a smaller core of salaried staff.

We visited the Unit and are grateful for the information provided by the Chief Executive, the Chief caseworker and a senior reviewer. Core funding comes from the Inns of Court (not the government) plus charitable help. An optional sum of £30 is added to the cost of a Practising Certificate and over 50 per cent of barristers pay this contribution. The reviewer told us that, by their criteria, 95 per cent of family cases should be accepted, but that because of the level of demand, more than 60 per cent were being turned away. When a case is accepted, it is helped with review at each step, as the applicant may be found able to manage on their own after initial help, but there is also a vulnerable group who will always need help. The reviewer said:

> I had a woman so frightened she could hardly walk into the FHDRA.[23] We expect our volunteers to offer 3 days a year, and so part of the review process is to estimate how much time is needed. But cases often 'balloon', and also members of the Family Bar often have their own cases ending up as part heard and have to stand down from their agreement to volunteer. The arrangement is that each barrister should find their own substitute in cases where they cannot appear, but this does not happen. On the other hand if a PB case overruns the barrister must stay with it, just as in any other case.

The review process itself is currently under review. There have been requests for fuller information about reasons to be given when a case is not accepted, and this work is being developed. It had not been the usual practice previously, as any reasons given that involve a legal argument could have been seen as legal advice and not all the caseworkers were practitioners with the necessary qualifications or insurance cover to give this. There is also interest in developing a digital interactive website for triage and review on the lines of CourtNav but in mid-2017 this was still at the planning stage.

The BPBU has also been criticised for its lengthy triaging system. The chambers clerk cited above drew a parallel with emergency medical services in World War II, with which a friend of his had been involved, and who had found that the original system that used five categories of seriousness was slow because, although it was relatively easy to identify very serious (level 5) or minor (level 1) cases, it took time to determine the distinctions between levels 2, 3 and 4. A simpler three point scale was subsequently adopted with great success. The clerk also described how

---

[22] Bar Pro Bono Unit, *Justifying Justice, Annual Review 2015*: Exhibit One: https://barprobono.org.uk/public/downloads/guf-3/Bar%20Pro%20Bono%20Unit%20annual%20review%202015.pdf (last accessed 14 June 2018).

[23] First Hearing Dispute Resolution Appointment in a children case.

members of chambers used to offer a day monthly, then quarterly, and then half a day a quarter, but now the hours were irregular. A barrister of five to seven years call would take a case all the way, and when a case comes to the BPBU its length is usually determined, though it may run over, in which case the 'decent' barrister will stay with it. The review process does not, however, depend on a tight means test. For example, the reviewer recently took on a medical practitioner who had an income but also debts and mental health issues which made financial management difficult. The reviewer agreed that the BPBU can sometimes help to avoid the need for court hearings by offering early advice.

What kinds of cases would be rejected? According to the reviewer, these might include vexatious litigants, clients who appear to have resources, but also a first appointment in a children case as these meetings are meant to be accessible for a LiP. The new 2016 Review Guidelines look at the mechanics of reviewing. The reviewer takes about one case a week, which takes about an hour, including preparation of the necessary papers, turnaround time, and completing the review form. The new Guidelines also discuss the factors contributing to making the decision. These include the general nature of the case, the degree of urgency, the scope of barrister involvement needed, a merits test and whether there are alternative sources of funding. Then an overall assessment is made as to whether a barrister is needed, or whether a solicitor or legal executive would suffice, and, finally, if needed, whether a barrister is available. It is always helpful if the referring solicitor can stay with the case.

The Guidelines now include special criteria for family cases.[24] These note that family cases are particularly difficult to place since the lack of public funding means many applications to the Unit are made with insufficient counsel ready or able to step forward, and therefore a family case is required to be especially deserving to be accepted on review! There is no categorisation into children or ancillary relief work, but generally the case is given priority if points of law or stark injustice have or may occur, such as where grandparents are not eligible for public funding, and cases where public funding has been refused on a negative Cafcass report which is of doubtful quality, and also Child Support Agency appeals and variations of periodical payments. It is acknowledged that some cases are just too big to be assisted pro bono, but reviewers are asked to bear in mind the possibility of limited assistance. The merits test is described[25] as assessing whether there are 'sufficient prospects of success, and special circumstances, eg loss of children, loss of home, legitimate sense of grievance, let down by previous lawyers, ill, or having English as a second language.' The reviewer said:

> we record the advice being given (at each stage) of the proceedings, but cannot give advice unless the case is accepted. It may be possible to give telephone advice if there is no representation. We do not give reasons why a case is rejected (as this would be legal advice) and we could be sued … but we are looking at this, we think people are entitled to some information about the reasons for rejection.

[24] Guidelines, 16–7.
[25] Guidelines, 8.

In its early days the BPBU used to work informally in a single office as a tight-knit group. The group is now expanding, and appreciates the need for more formal management. But the caseworkers are very experienced. There is some discussion of finding a larger role for students, perhaps in writing rejection letters, or helping barristers who are working without solicitors. There is also discussion with CILEx about extending the role of its members (legal executives), who are offered block Personal Indemnity Insurance, and extending the current joint scheme known as Joint Ilex and Bar (JIB), established in 2010 whereby CILEx members prepare papers for the barristers. Interestingly, the application form to take part in JIB states that CILEx members do not need to inform their employers about their activity if they are doing this work as they are acting individually as providers and not on behalf of their firms.

ii. Court-Based Duty Schemes Involving the Bar

One example of such a scheme, in central London, was described by a founder member and barrister (XY), and a clerk who for several years convened the group. There had been a great deal of interest and goodwill from members of the Family Bar, with the support of the local family court judges, in setting up essentially a duty lawyer pro bono scheme to help people coming to court without legal representation. A rota was set up, which was circulated for members of the Bar to sign up. But it had failed to work. There was never sufficient channelling of clients towards the barristers when they were available and who had the relevant skill set. XY told of being offered a room in court where the advice service would send clients who were in need of help. XY duly sat there for three full days, and for two days saw no one. On the third day he was asked to help with a FHDRA,[26] went straight into court, and was not available to help anyone else for the rest of the day.

The duty rotas were sent to the clerks, some of whom were active in getting support, others less so. (It should be noted that when barristers work pro bono, this can affect the pay of the clerk). This unit struggled to find clients with various referral systems, and in the end accepted cases directly. XY had suggested telephone access using the number of a local chambers set, whereby barristers would be on call for short telephone advice consultation, or be able to attend court at short notice. This was tried, using mobile phones, but without success, as it did not have the same impact as the actual presence of the lawyers. There was simply not sufficient flexibility in the individual barrister's work schedule to make the scheme feasible. (Unlike solicitors who have a range of colleagues to call on and were often able to justify the loss of billable time and any impact on colleagues by being able to pick up legal aid cases for their firms in sufficient numbers to cover their costs.)

---

[26] See n 23.

The local senior clerk had taken responsibility for convening the rota, but it had lapsed due to lack of support.

At the same court a duty solicitor scheme to cover public law children cases had worked steadily for a number of years. Children's Panel specialists are available every day, and each offers one or two days a year and drop-in help on the spot, but not end-to-end casework. A solicitor interviewed described it as 'just doing your best, dealing with whatever comes in and if the matter is beyond your competence just say so, there are no referral routes elsewhere'. There are minimal management data, just name, date, and advice given. The names are not kept. Only raw data is analysed. There was a similar account from a judge in the south west, who had set up a duty scheme for LiPs in family cases, only to find it faltering from lack of demand despite the level of unmet need following LASPO in the area as seen by the increase in LiPs. The solicitors who had been instrumental in setting up and administering the scheme had left the area, and the local members of the Bar were simply not able to organise the scheme. The judge and colleagues considered the possibility of funding the post of organiser.

IV. Conclusions

The discussion above has shown how the rigid diary constraints of the Family Bar and the added burden of working without the support of a solicitor create difficulties for pro bono family work by barristers. This is not to say that some barristers do not make valuable contributions. We found that a young barrister could, diary permitting, take on pro bono work with approval from chambers when approached by a solicitor, especially in a high profile case of legal interest or in a case before a particular judge. A recent extreme child treatment case involving an unusual medical procedure was taken pro bono by a young barrister at the direct request of the solicitor who was already acting pro bono and succeeded in attracting legal funding for the child as the case progressed.

However, a second young barrister described the difficulty of working with the BPBU. She said that too little information was provided about the case when a request for help was made for the barrister to decide whether there were diary constraints, and that the notice given for court hearings or other deadlines at various stages in the course of the case was too short. This young barrister had been asked to do a four day final hearing in a care case at two days' notice, which she felt was impossible, especially as she would be working without a solicitor. She thought that many cases are not taken for this reason. She compared this with the way work is organised by COAS, the Court of Appeal scheme which offers pro bono advocacy help to litigants in person seeking leave to appeal in civil matters, including family. She had taken part in four such cases. Requests for help come to the Royal Courts of Justice advice desk. There is a mailing list sent out monthly giving a two-line summary of cases seeking leave to appeal. If a lawyer replies, they receive the papers and the court date. Insurance is provided by the BPBU through COAS. The barrister will meet the client if there is time, rewrite the ground, represent and feed back to COAS. Young barristers are keen to get involved as 'it's good for your career'.

This barrister described a 'tidal wave' of family work since LASPO. Even paid work is difficult, as diaries are always changing. In private law hearings a judge will estimate three days, but often cases 'balloon' and are part heard or unfinished within the listed time. In care cases local authorities are so short of money that they give no proper instructions. Legal aid stops when an order is made, and if further advice is needed, it is poorly recompensed. The example given was of having to read over 500 pages in 24 hours for a fee of just over £100. Preparation is usually unpaid. She described standing in a hot corridor at court, trying to interview a man about his alleged attack on his wife, holding a laptop, pen and pad, as there were no interview rooms, and looking at the water machine but unable to drink a glass of water as the court had run out of plastic cups and couldn't afford to buy more.

6

Judicial Initiatives

I. Introduction

LASPO has deeply affected the ability of both branches of the legal profession to help those with family legal issues but limited means, and we have described in preceding chapters some of the initiatives developing in the profession in response to the unmet needs of this group of the population. But the primary target of the dual policy of saving money and promoting individual responsibility in private family matters was of course restricting use of the courts. LASPO was clearly designed to encourage alternative dispute resolution, various forms of private ordering, and to reduce the need for adjudication from the bench.

As we noted in chapter one, although the number of private law children applications in 2016 was only slightly lower than in 2012, the year before LASPO was implemented, private family law cases where neither party was legally represented rose from 16 per cent in 2013 to 34 per cent in 2016. But cases where both were represented fell from 38 per cent to 21 per cent over the same period[1] and hearings took longer. In the sample of LiPs in courts studied by Liz Trinder et al, the majority were unrepresented because they were unable to pay or obtain legal aid.[2] The great majority of those felt they would have done better with a lawyer.[3] The researchers concluded that there appeared to be no relationship between being highly educated, professional and articulate and being able to handle family court proceedings.[4] Almost all fell between being 'procedurally challenged' and 'vanquished' (totally out of their depth).[5] A group of LiPs had obtained legal aid for part of the proceedings, but would be unlikely to obtain it at all after LASPO. Yet they had high levels of drug, alcohol and mental health problems.[6] The researchers noted that cases with LiPs had a higher rate of listing for a further hearing,

---

[1] See p 19. Ministry of Justice, *Family Court Statistics Quarterly, England and Wales, Annual 2016* (2016), Figures 1 and 8. These figures were sustained over the first quarter of 2017: *Family Court Statistics Quarterly, England and Wales, January to March 2017*, Figure 4.

[2] L Trinder, R Hunter, E Hitchings, J Miles, R Moorhead, L Smith, M Sefton, V Hinchly, K Bader and J Pearce, *Litigants in Person in Private Family Law Cases* (Ministry of Justice, 2014) 13.

[3] ibid, 19.

[4] ibid, 24.

[5] ibid, 25.

[6] ibid, 105.

and a lower rate of settlement. They concluded that LiPS need more than 'passive' web-based information, but also face-to-face 'emotional' support and information about the court process.[7]

So, instead of fewer litigants, we have seen fewer legal advisers in court, but this has simply increased pressure on the judiciary who now need to help applicants who are not sure what forms they need to complete, what they want to ask the court to do, what arguments they need to present in order to do so, and what evidence they need to support their case. They may not understand the limit of the court's powers. They may not have English as their first language. They may have health or mental health issues which have made them unable to resolve their family problem with no more than the help of friends and family. Some may have had some initial help from a lawyer but run out of funding, others would have been eligible for legal aid prior to LASPO, but are now unable to afford even an unbundled fixed price package of legal help. The lack of help with preparing for a case means either that cases collapse early in proceedings, or take longer to resolve.

II. Specific Problems and Initiatives

The judiciary, however, anticipated this. In July 2013, three months after LASPO was implemented, a Judicial Working Group published a report on how to respond to the expected increase of LiPs in civil and family cases.[8] The Group set out the potential difficulties that LiPs could face, and also potential problems for judges, who would need to hold a fine balance between helping the LiP without eroding confidence by other parties in their impartiality. Its recommendations included asking the Ministry of Justice to produce audiovisual material to inform LiPs what is required and what to expect when going to court; to ensure through a review of web-based information that LiPs had access to the information they need; to ensure that the training of judges should take into account the expected increase in LiPs, including through a 'LiP Toolkit' and to develop an online resource for staff and the judiciary to identify nationally what sources of advice and assistance are available for LiPs. The group also recommended that the Judicial Office should consider various modifications to procedural rules which would allow courts to address better the needs of LiPs, including the rules governing rights to reasonable assistance and regarding the right to conduct litigation and exercise rights of audience; and that judges should deal robustly with vexatious litigants.

Developments in a number of these areas are considered elsewhere in this book. As far as procedure in court is concerned, significant problems have remained. In 2016, in *Agarwala v Agarwala*[9] (not a family case, but one in which neither

---

[7] ibid, pp 100–01.
[8] Judiciary of England and Wales, *The Judicial Working Group on Litigants in Person: Report* (July 2013).
[9] [2016] EWCA Civ 1252.

party was represented, it seems, by choice) Lady Justice King concluded her judgment by saying that the case had taken up 'countless court and judge hours as both parties, incapable of compromise, have bombarded the court with endless applications', and that 'the court staff and judge have been inundated with emails, which they have had to deal with as best they could, with limited time and even more limited resources'. She concluded: 'Whilst every judge is sympathetic to the challenges faced by litigants in person, justice simply cannot be done through a torrent of informal, unfocused emails, often sent directly to the judge and not to the other parties. Neither the judge nor the court staff can, or should, be expected to field communications of this type. In my view judges must be entitled, as part of their general case management powers, to put in place, where they feel it to be appropriate, strict directions regulating communications with the court and litigants should understand that failure to comply with such directions will mean that communications that they choose to send, notwithstanding those directions, will be neither responded to nor acted upon'.[10]

While that case focused on the difficulties caused to judges and court staff by unrepresented litigants, it has been said that similar difficulties are faced by represented parties when facing LiPs: 'It is frequently and unfairly that the party who can afford solicitors often subsidises the LiP with the cost in preparing bundles, drafting additional court documents and indeed often replying to a similar torrent of informal, unfocussed emails ... It is sadly becoming all too common for LiPs to email directly the courts and judges where solicitors and barristers would never dare ... Litigants in person should not by accident or design obtain an unfair advantage at the expense of others by a lack of legal knowledge or understanding'.[11]

Yet if coping with some LiPs can cause such difficulties to judges and legal representatives, what of the LiPs themselves? Sir James Munby, President of the Family Division, has been very active, judicially and extra-judicially, in seeking to mitigate the disadvantages that could be experienced by litigants as a result of the absence of representation. In 2014[12] he sought to resolve the issue in cases involving unrepresented fathers against whom serious sexual misconduct was alleged by assuming that the Family Procedure Regulations allowed judges to order representation to be provided for a litigant in such cases at public expense in order to 'cause' questions to be put to a witness. But the Court of Appeal disallowed this.[13] In *D and K and B (a child)*,[14] in which the possibility arose that a mother (who was legally aided) would be cross-examined by the unrepresented father, against whom she had made an allegation of rape, and who had failed to secure

---

[10] ibid, paras 71 and 72.

[11] J Haden, 'Do Litigants in Person have an Unfair Advantage?' *Family Law Online* 3 February 2017 http://www.familylaw.co.uk/news_and_comment/do-litigants-in-person-have-an-unfair-advantage#. WcKQAf6Wxyt (last accessed 5 September 2018).

[12] *Q v Q; re B (A Child); re C (A Child)* [2014] EWFC 31.

[13] *K & H (Children)* [2015] EWCA Civ 543.

[14] [2014] EWHC 700 (Fam).

legal aid for representation, HHJ Wildblood expressed grave concern that the father was not represented, adding that he felt profound unease at questioning the complainant himself. He therefore pleaded with the legal aid authorities to reconsider their decision, but thought this was 'highly unlikely to be granted'. Such cross-examination would be prohibited in a criminal court, but was common in family cases, but could be prevented only by statutory reform, which Sir James Munby had been urging for some time.[15] A survey of judicial views on the matter showed a range of opinions. One suggested solution was for potential questions to be submitted to the judge in advance for clearance.[16]

Research published in 2018 suggested that probably around a quarter of women who made allegations about abuse were questioned by the alleged perpetrator.[17] The Prisons and Courts Reform Bill 2016–17 contained measures to prevent the practice by prohibiting such cross-examination by persons who have been prosecuted for or convicted of certain offences, or when so directed by the judge if (among other things) cross-examination (or continued cross-examination) by the individual would be likely to cause the witness significant distress greater than if cross-examined by someone else. In such circumstances a publicly-funded independent advocate could be appointed to carry out the cross-examination. But the Bill fell with the dissolution of Parliament for the general election in May 2017, and has not been re-introduced. In May 2017 Hayden J again protested against the practice, describing it as 'a stain on the reputation of our Family Justice system that a Judge can still not prevent a victim being cross examined by an alleged perpetrator'.[18]

On 27 November 2017, after extensive consultation, including with the Children and Vulnerable Witnesses Working Group (CVWWG), set up by Sir James Munby in June 2014 to examine the related issues of how the family justice system accommodates the needs of children attending court to give evidence or to visit the judge, and the needs of vulnerable witnesses and parties, and with the Family Justice Council and Family Procedure Rules Committee, Part 3A of the Family Procedure Rules and Practice Direction 3AA took effect. These require courts to take into account the vulnerability of court participants and adopt various measures, such as not seeing another participant, and using intermediaries or live links, provided that no public funding is used. Sir James commented that 'this undoubtedly marked a big step forward, though it had taken over three years to get this far, but the new arrangements could, and, in my view, should, have gone further' and called for further changes and resources so that 'the family justice system can meet

[15] Sir James Munby, *View from the President's Chambers (16) Children and vulnerable witnesses – where are we?* (19 January 2017) https://www.judiciary.gov.uk/wp-content/uploads/2014/08/view-from-the-president-of-family-division-16-jan-17.pdf (last accessed 5 June 2018).

[16] NE Corbett and A Summerfield, *Alleged perpetrators of abuse as Litigants in Person in private family law* (Ministry of Justice, 2017) 15–18.

[17] J Birchall and S Choudhry, *Domestic Abuse, Human Rights and the Family Courts* (Women's Aid Federation of England and Wales, 2018) 25.

[18] *Re A (a minor) (fact finding; unrepresented party)* [2017] EWHC 1195 (Fam) para 62.

the aspirations and accommodate the needs of children who want to come to court themselves, whether to see the court, give evidence or meet the judge'.[19]

Individual judges have been taking various initiatives to ameliorate the position of unrepresented parties, although they are of course constrained by the law, as in the case of cross-examination by an alleged perpetrator discussed above. In an example of imaginative case management in a case where a 14 year-old child wished to give evidence, but his mother and stepfather and the experienced Cafcass officer disagreed, Peter Jackson J decided that the child should give evidence briefly at the beginning of the hearing, but, instead of being questioned directly by either of his parents, each of them should prepare five questions which the judge put to the child himself. Additionally, the judge gave his judgment in the form of a letter to the child.[20]

If a case is semi-represented (where one party only is represented) the judge may be able to call on a representative for one party to help provide some guidance for both, or may give additional judicial support to the unrepresented party. Or there may be neutral third party in court in children cases, such as Cafcass, who will help with working towards a settlement. But it takes time and skill to handle this kind of imbalance. Some judges become more actively interventionist and even inquisitorial in trying to make up for absence of legal help. But as observed earlier, Trinder et al concluded that LiPS need face-to-face support and information about the court process. Court staff are unable to give advice, and the PSU support services which, as described in chapters four and seven, are providing excellent help in some courts, are available in only a minority.[21] McKenzie Friends, described also in chapter seven,[22] may be present but are unregulated and vary in their approach and contribution. That study clearly identifies the LiPs' need for 'practical support and tailored legal advice' (help with paperwork, with advocacy in court, with gathering evidence and framing their cases in legal terms), all work that would have been done by lawyers and the court process assumes still will be done by lawyers.

We have discussed the way the legal profession has tried to help in these matters pro bono, with limited success, due largely to the constraints on their time and availability. But by 2016 there was a considerable amount of discussion of judicial initiatives in supporting the setting up of duty lawyer schemes in the family courts. The scheme set up by Judge Stephen Wildblood in Bristol was attracting attention.[23] In this scheme the local judge was enthusiastic, local solicitors' firms

---

[19] Sir James Munby, 'Because it is the right thing to do', speech at the 6th Annual 'Voice of the child' FJYPB Conference in Manchester 24 July 2018, 3. See https://www.judiciary.uk/wp-content/uploads/2018/07/pfd-speech-fjypb.pdf (last accessed 25 July 2018).

[20] *Re A (Letter to Young Person)* [2017] EWFC 48.

[21] See pp 106ff.

[22] See pp 113ff.

[23] HHJ Stephen Wildblood QC, Claire Wills Goldingham QC and Judi Evans, 'The way we are: accessing the court after LASPO' (2014) 44 *Family Law* 1597.

provided pro bono time, the local PSU helped with the administration and the service was working well. But although the judiciary are interested, for practitioners there are a number of hurdles. In November 2016 the Law Society published a detailed Practice Note about setting up of such a service,[24] referring to 'certain risks in terms of ensuring compliance with professional duties'. The success of housing and criminal court duty schemes is acknowledged, but these help clients who are within scope for legal aid.

The particular difficulty for family legal help is that it will have to be provided pro bono, but it must be noted that solicitors with a practising certificate remain subject to the SRA Code of Conduct in full, and those without, such as retired solicitors, always need to comply with the Principles set out to uphold the rule of law, maintain integrity, and public trust. The November 2016 Practice Note gives detailed guidance about how solicitors should deal with pro bono cases under duty schemes, including setting out what matters it can deal with (such as children only, or finance also), following the welfare paramountcy principle, being aware of domestic abuse, and referring where possible to mediation. The Practice Note draws attention to specific risks a duty solicitor may face, such as that 'Advice based on inadequate information is a significant risk with duty scheme advice and care should be (taken) not to make any assumptions about the facts' and concludes with a check list of actions to take before becoming involved in such schemes. The solicitor should 'ensure your documentation is consistent with the specimen wording and client letter in the Practice Note; ensure your PII insurer is notified; ensure the scheme is covered by rules or a protocol which covers the points addressed in the Practice Note; ensure your internal procedures (eg conflicts searches, anti-money laundering) are amended to reflect the priority of requests where advice is being provided at court under the duty scheme; ensure any solicitors from your practice are aware of this best practice guidance and the steps required to minimise your exposure to regulatory risk; risk register – this should reflect the practice's potential risk arising the duty scheme (compliance, legal and operational risk)'.

So it can be seen that any judge experiencing the additional pressures after LASPO and hoping to assist LiPs by encouraging a duty solicitor scheme in family cases needs to overcome practitioner nervousness about the level of risk set out by the Law Society for its members. There is also no funding available from government to support such schemes, though in California there are funded schemes to help LiPs at least manage the court process, with sessions on form filling and using the available IT and judicial support.[25] Richard Zorza[26] describes how the good

---

[24] Law Society, 'Court duty scheme for private family clients', Law Society London 2017, available on the Law Society website: https://www.lawsociety.org.uk/support-services/advice/practice-notes/court-duty-scheme-for-private-law-family-clients/ (last accessed 5 June 2018).

[25] BR Hough, 'Innovations in Self Help in California's courts', Paper given at Access to Justice Conference, University College, London, June 2018.

[26] R Zorza, 'Towards the best practice in complex self represented cases' (2012) 51 (1) *Judges Journal* 36.

judge is expected to set the stage, explain process, elicit the necessary information, and allow the LiP to speak, dividing the matter into topics and probing for detail. Finally the judge is expected to involve the LiP in the decision-making process before explaining any order and what will happen next, not forgetting the importance of body language.

III. Observational Data

With the help of the President of the Family Division, Sir James Munby, at the beginning of September 2016 we carried out a survey of Designated Family Judges[27] asking: 'do you currently have any form of duty solicitor scheme in your court?'. We received 26 responses from the 42 judges, of whom seven said that they did have such a scheme, and five said they had tried or were in the process of trying to set up such a scheme. Of these five cases where the outcome was not yet clear, in one court local solicitors had raised insurance issues; in another, a scheme to have a solicitor/mediator present for FHDRA days had been tried but was no longer viable; one DFJ would have liked to have such a scheme but had not yet succeeded in setting one up; another was awaiting an agreement with the local PSU for administrative help, and the fifth had set up a scheme with the local university to use trained and supervised student helpers. 14 replied that they had no such scheme. For the remaining 16 DFJs we have no information. We spent one or more days in five of the courts where schemes are running in a variety of forms, and with various levels of cooperation with other forms of service, such as Citizens Advice or PSU, or a student initiative. We have chosen three of these courts to illustrate the range of services provided. These were:

1. An ambitious scheme aiming not only to offer support and advice but to change the relationship between the family court and the community.
2. An effective scheme, involving a court working successfully with the local PSU and adding a small clinic.
3. A university-based outreach clinic, invited into court and offering help but not advice.

1. An ambitious scheme

The ambitious scheme was established through the initiative and energy of the local Designated Family Judge (DFJ) who had worked hard to make the family court more accessible to families, and more effective in involving the local legal profession and advice and support workers through a newsletter, and open

---

[27] DFJs are the circuit judges responsible for leading all levels of the family judiciary in their area, with a responsibility to build and maintain relationships with others involved in the family justice system, working with court staff, and acting as the liaison point with the Family Division Liaison Judges and through them with the President under the Designated Family Centre Operating Model.

meetings and discussions on issues such as adoption. Before the duty scheme began work, a clear detailed statement was issued about the status of their volunteers. These would be solicitors or barristers with one year post-qualification experience, covered by the BPBU insurance for members of the Bar or by the firms' insurance in the case of solicitors. These lawyers would be offering two days a year, providing advice but not representation. Public law cases were excluded. The local PSU would help by making 30 minute appointments for two lawyers one day a week, and the court service would provide a room at court. Clients would receive a written report of the advice given and a copy would be kept securely by the service. A local member of the Family Bar had worked with the DFJ, playing a key role in getting the scheme up and running.

The service began in an area where there was already a strong PSU and Citizens Advice, a voluntary solicitor scheme operating one evening a week, a postgraduate student scheme offering legal assistance and representation on the day, but not fully conducting litigation, and other charities. After LASPO the family court began to set up an extensive website bringing all these activities together and added the duty lawyer scheme in early 2015. But there were difficulties. The key barrister moved away from the area. There seemed to be a lack of 'advertising' for the new service. Although the court has an open, friendly, entrance with a number of notices clearly visible in one corner giving details of mediation and support services, as well as how to apply for legal aid with PSU, when we visited there was no information on display about the duty scheme. The lawyers responsible for getting the service off the ground remained full of enthusiasm, but acknowledged their local difficulties. They had received hostile communications from the pro bono lawyers and described how insurance issues had been used to delay their start by up to a year. Their aim was to provide a holistic service, following the recommendations of the Low Commission,[28] which stressed the way people experienced social problems in clusters. They had hoped to 'tap into' the Citizens Advice work in this way but so far without great success. Even the PSU had been raising difficulties about record storage. The rota members were failing to find a substitute when they are unable to attend, as had been agreed.

There was surprisingly little consumer interest. At first there were one or two clients a week. By 2016 there were perhaps four or five, but still less than half the capacity of 12. The founders of the scheme were afraid that local lawyers were unwilling or unable to get involved with the administrative aspect of running the clinic. It was suggested that students could be more willing to do these tasks as it would strengthen their CV and job prospects. The local judges expressed a wish for better outreach and above all for an administrator/facilitator to coordinate activity in court. They were afraid that there was a certain amount of distrust of the legal system in the local community and wanted above all to develop the family

---

[28] Low Commission, *Tackling the Advice Deficit: A strategy for access to advice and legal support on social welfare law in England and Wales*, Legal Action Group, 2014 paras 1.4, 2.7.

court as a resource for the community, a welcoming place where help is available. We were reminded of the German family courts[29] which act as a hub for access to social services help where all families with issues over parenting arrangements are seen as families with problems rather than disputes. But in the meantime this scheme was struggling to become an established part of the local scene despite the number of enthusiastic individuals willing to share their time and expertise.

Sadly difficulties with the court building led to suspension of the scheme but a separate new scheme, working with three local universities, has been launched in which students offer sessions for potential LiPs, explaining court process and what the court is able to do. In addition, the DFJ provides an accessible and informative newsletter, organises debates on topics, including how the court can offer a better service to the community, and has developed a form of teaching through interactive examples of how a family problem coming to court is perceived by the various actors, including parents, social workers, and the judge.

2. An effective scheme

The DFJ in this area had been in post for three years, and had been working hard to improve the running of the court given the 20 per cent increase in public and private family applications experienced during that period. The problems with LiPs had become so prevalent that the DFJ had personally prepared a pack to be handed by court staff to anyone alone in the waiting area. This included a leaflet on accessing AdviceNow on 'Going to court about a family issue', and a 25 page typed A4 booklet entitled *'I'm representing myself': Guidance for people representing themselves in the X Family Court*. This begins by saying:

> Lots of people represent themselves in the family court, These notes are intended as a brief introduction to the way the court works and how you get the best from your involvement with it. They are mainly about Child Arrangement cases but may be useful to you if you are involved in a different type of case. **They are not a substitute for legal advice**.

This is followed by a list of the kind of family cases which the court hears, contact details for Cafcass and Sorting out Separation, and a reminder that 'an appointment with family mediation **must** be made before any court application can be started'. Mediation and the MIAM is explained, stating that this will be free to anyone eligible for legal aid, and the contact number of Community Legal Advice Direct is given. The Child Arrangements Programme is explained, and the various orders described. The reader is told to begin with the form C100, and access to a video on making the application is given. Urgent applications,

---

[29] See Thomas Meysen, Director of the German Institute for Youth Human Services and Family Law, Heidelberg, 'The German approach in family court proceedings and the interplay with support services from the child and youth welfare system', Paper to the High Conflict Divorce Conference, The Hague May 2015 (Ministry of Security and Justice and Ministry of Health Welfare and Sport). Since 2008 the court controls proceedings, managing the interaction between parents, but does not make decisions, instead referring parents to support services.

injunctions and involvement in care cases are also set out, although the last are begun by the local authority.

The booklet also explains about communicating with the court, the possibility of bringing someone along for support, what happens at a first appointment and a FHDRA, the need to attend but not discuss any aspect on social media, the issue of confidentiality, how to address the judge, court orders, the need for a statement which is not just telling the judge what happened as everyone involved needs to read it, attaching an example. It ends with a glossary of terms used, and links to further sources of information including AdviceNow and Parent Connection, a website offering advice to divorcing or separating parents. The final annex attempts to cover access to legal advice but can offer no more than suggesting going to Citizens Advice, Resolution, the Law Society, the Bar Council, and government websites for checking legal aid and legal services. It is a clear, comprehensive and helpful document. But it cannot provide legal advice, and states clearly that the court staff cannot do so as they are not trained to do it.

The main source of support in this court is the very effective PSU which has 30 volunteers (including retired judges) supported by a small number of local students. Training for everyone consists of one day plus three in-service days on court procedure, but *not* on giving legal advice. PSU volunteers do not speak in court but can signpost to the new Legal Advice Clinic which is open one morning a week, staffed by a rota of pro bono solicitors supported by students supervised by practitioners, not academics (for whom the experience will not be part of their course).

The PSU in this court has volunteers with such clearly relevant practice experience that it is particularly hard for them to avoid giving advice, but their manager is strict, and they can now refer a small number of cases to a new Family Advice Clinic. They told us that 70 per cent of their clients were seen by appointment and 30 per cent on a drop in basis. There are about 20 family applications to the court each week, 70 per cent of which are children cases, 10 per cent divorce and the rest include probate and other matters. While protesting that advice is *not* given, the PSU staff described how they are trained to 'get the story' and then, if they can see that the client has a clear aim, if they are able, help them achieve this. 'We can take them to the counter and ask for the right form, as we know which it is, and if the matter is 100 per cent clear, eg eviction, we go ahead and act.' The question of whether the counter staff give advice was carefully avoided. The PSU approach was described as: 'We encourage people to think about possibilities.' There has not been a strong pro bono tradition in this area except for public law children cases (where legally aided cases may be identified). But the underlying issue in this court revolved around the reduction in HMCTS (the court service) resources leading to the impending closure of their counter system, together with the move to electronic filing of applications which they feared would be problematic if under-resourced. This was not unlikely, given the continuing loss of experienced staff. The IT systems in this court were described as being notoriously unreliable (one judge spoke of being unable to print out his orders for some months as his printer was not working, another of taking 20 minutes for her laptop to function on arrival) and that they have been advised that with the introduction of the new technology, their court staff will be reduced by 50 per cent.

So again, as in our first example where the DFJ's efforts had been limited by lack of administrative support and the loss of a key barrister, here too judicial initiatives had been frustrated. The DFJ's excellent booklet for LiPs with all the necessary information (but stopping short of advice) was limited by having no sources of free legal advice to which to refer LiPs (given Citizens Advice seldom give family law advice). The running of this efficient and caring court was under-pinned by an active PSU but threatened by imminent staff shortages, and the imposition of unfamiliar information technology. The new Family Advice Clinic (open one morning a week) would be able to offer effective advice in family matters, but only to a small number of those in need.

3. A university-based outreach clinic

In this third example we were invited by a DFJ to come and meet the university-based group helping this court to cope with the post-LASPO avalanche of LiPs. CLOCK, or Community Legal Outreach Companions Keele, consists of students, trained in the traditions of community outreach to help all those involved in this spiral of need for legal help: the clients, the lawyers and the court. The activity is part of the law course at the local university, and the costs of supervision, admin-istration, insurance and even the collection and analysis of data on the work done are covered under the university's outreach budget. The judge and court staff have encouraged participation by the group in the local court where students man a help desk on court days, including during vacations, as a number of students live locally. The students sit in pairs at a desk at the entrance to the court with a computer and the court list, and are able to go into court with an anxious unrep-resented party or help sort out papers and make sure everything is there, or even help draft a position statement.

These students have had extensive training from local practitioners and are able to guide a client through court procedure. They all have a file which contains guidance on ethics, conflicts of interest, procedure, forms and more. When the judge is confronted by an anxious client having difficulty in speaking to the court, he is happy to ask the Community Legal Companions (CLCs) to speak, otherwise when in court they act in the way of a 'McKenzie Friend',[30] supporting but not representing a party in a hearing. But additional input arises from the street law outreach ethos of the project in that the CLCs are there to help not only the court staff, the judge and the clients, but also the local practitioners. The students are able to act as a trainee might act for a solicitor, helping to check legal aid eligibility, a lengthy process which solicitors are increasingly unwilling to undertake as time is spent for no recompense. But the students have been able to participate here

---

[30] See pp 113ff.

(without impinging on the borders of the forbidden territory of legal advice) and have even been successful in helping to obtain exceptional funding. They are able to deliver papers, help draft statements and support anxious clients, making sure they have recorded dates correctly and are aware of the next steps in their case, acting almost like the traditional outdoor clerk. Their contribution can even make it possible for a local solicitor to keep prices for fixed term work at a lower level. The university gains in reputation from the higher grades which these students with CLC experience attain, and also from the research activity generated and made possible by the careful collection of statistical data on each case supported. This model has been running for five years at the time of writing, and is being extended to other universities in slightly different formats. The CLCs are skilled helpers, not advisers. They are not there to substitute for lawyers, but to help clients find affordable legal help where possible and to offer skilled support where not.

The local court in this example no longer has a counter service, and values the daily support of volunteers whom they have helped to train. The only tension arises from the wish of the DFJ that the CLCs could do more. There is pressure for the CLCs to speak in court. But the originator of this service is anxious to maintain the objective of the service as seeking legal help for clients whether through supporting legal aid applications or by signposting to other services. The academic outcomes are a bonus but not the primary aim, but they enable the university to justify taking on the financial responsibility. The specialist IT system with data on clients and referral possibilities is open to all other groups wishing to sign up to the CLC ethos of supporting clients, supporting solicitors and enabling them to do more, while also supporting the work of the judiciary. Everyone benefits. This branch of CLOCK saw and helped 124 clients in a five week period early in 2017. 75 of these were children cases. 24 legal aid applications were made. 10 clients were accompanied in court, and eight subsequently signposted to advice agencies for legal help. They also helped in 15 divorce cases, and five domestic violence cases. 64 per cent of their cases were Children Act matters with 10 accompanied to court. 35 per cent of users were signposted to law firms and 32 signposted for legal aid.

The DFJ in this area had not considered setting up a duty lawyer scheme as he found CLOCK met a great part of the need for legal help. It is remarkable for helping not only the parties, the students and the court, but also local practitioners, and in the number of clients seeking and receiving help. The community outreach philosophy makes it possible to think in terms of access to justice for a community, not just specific individuals or a particular professional group.

IV. Conclusions

We have described three different kinds of judicial initiatives for responding to the LiPs crisis. All of these involved considerable investment of time and energy by the Designated Family Judges, at a time of great pressure, and varying degrees of impact on the running of the courts. The first venture began with great enthusiasm, aiming to provide pro bono help from a rota of practitioners, originally mainly from the Bar. But it remained unable to help more than a small number of litigants as a result of being limited by losing key players and problems affecting the court premises. In the second example, the DFJ turned first not to the legal profession but to the volunteers who offered lay support through the PSU rather than legal advice and who would work with a small new Family Legal Advice Clinic one morning a week. But a key resource in this court was the comprehensive and accessible guide written by the judge in person, to enable parties to understand how the court works, what it can and cannot do for them, and how to get the 'best' out of the system. This was the first indication of what became a recurring theme, the need not just to tell the parties what to do next but enabling them to understand the court's viewpoint, which is primarily directed at the paramountcy of the best interests of the children concerned rather than the conflict of claims/rights between the parents. The third example also focused less on trying to achieve a duty practitioner presence in court but on the need for support in court backed up by achieving maximum possible access to legally aided help and supporting the work of legal aid practitioners in the area.

These developments prompt the speculation whether it may no longer be realistic always to expect a parent with a parenting issue to find professional legal help if they lack the necessary financial resources. We may be entering a period when the concept of support supplants that of representation for most of the small group (about 10 per cent of the total number of separating parents) who go to court. Perhaps we should look more carefully at how parties make their original choices and, having chosen, how they are supported in implementing their choices. With this in mind, we move on from looking at the ways in which the legal professions have tried to provide a form of traditional legal service pro bono in the absence of legal aid after LASPO, through the more varied initiatives of the judiciary faced with running a court where working with lawyers used to be part of their job but where they are now often absent, to new forms of lay, but trained, advice and support.

7

Support in Court by Non-Lawyers

So far we have been looking, first, at the ways in which government has attempted to maintain a residual level of legal help for those of limited means with family issues which cannot be resolved without assistance. We then looked at how the legal professions have attempted to provide their traditional services or parts thereof (information, sometimes advice, rarely representation) in a variety of settings, including working with the advice sector and with students. We saw that this was complicated by regulatory issues, such as the restrictions concerning reserved legal activities and whether legal advice as opposed to legal information could be provided, and about insurance cover for the various actors. Lastly we looked at the response of the judiciary, who have been directly affected by the unexpected increase in LiPs, and who have been able to develop a range of ideas and activities, sometimes working with duty lawyers, but also with support from students and lay volunteers. This chapter looks further at the work of non-lawyer volunteers who do not ostensibly provide advice, but offer support for those facing the challenge of litigation without legal help, and the more complex case of McKenzie Friends, who may not hold a professional legal qualification, but who can assist litigants in person in court proceedings in the manner described in detail below.[1]

I. The Personal Support Unit (PSU)

A. Nature and Origins

The PSU was founded in 2001 by Diana Copisarow as a charity based in court buildings, where volunteers provide free support in the civil and family courts for persons with issues including divorce, financial matters and disputes over children. Its units are well signposted at the court's entrance with banners and leaflets stating clearly what they can and cannot do. They proclaim that, if you are coming to court on your own, the PSU volunteers can 'listen to you, and provide information[2] and support, help you find out if you can get free legal advice, discuss

---

[1] See pp 113ff.
[2] This may be intended to refer to general, non-legal, information: see below p 109.

settling issues without going to court, explain how court works, help you fill in the court forms and organise court papers, help you plan what you want to say in court, go into court with you, take notes and help afterwards, and provide details of other specialist agencies', but add: 'please note that we CANNOT give legal advice'. The service offers appointments and drop-in help.[3]

The PSU is well established and growing. There are 733 regular volunteers. The schemes vary locally, some having closer links to local sources of legal advice than others, and some developing a more bureaucratic structure. But the basic principle for service remains constant. PSU provides emotional and practical support, not advice, legal or otherwise. The test is: 'if the client has decided what to do, we can help them to do it ... but we cannot advise on what they should do'. As the Annual Report for the year ending March 2017 states: 'we talk our clients through the legal processes ... we help them understand what will happen in the court room ... in short we aim to help our clients engage with the justice system, and regardless of the outcome of their case, know that they represented themselves to the best of their abilities.'[4]

As noted earlier,[5] it is a partner in the LiP Support Strategy (LiPSS) and in the year ending March 2017, received 41 per cent of its annual funding from government.[6] In 2017 it was working in 20 courts.[7] The PSU routinely collects and analyses demographic data about all clients, and more detailed information from up to 30 per cent of them, through 'Spot' surveys, which are small scale, but help to identify trends and can be considered with due caution alongside other research findings. In the year ending March 2017 it helped people on 56,119 occasions, reaching 5,000 contacts each month by the end of the period. 56 per cent of these were family cases, of which 74 per cent were children cases and 24 per cent divorce cases, a total of nearly 28,000 cases. The client group as a whole had a number of difficulties: 23 per cent had serious health or disability issues, with a further 10 per cent being registered as disabled. 22 per cent did not speak English as their first language and 58 per cent were unemployed.[8]

They ask about how their clients find their way to the PSU, what impact their intervention has, and what other sources of help are being used. In 2016,[9] 60 per cent of clients said that they had had no idea where to start looking for reliable advice or information on legal issues, and that PSU was the first place they

---

[3] A similar service is provided by 'Court Navigators' in the New York Housing Court: https://www.probono.net/oppsguide/organization.186792-Court_Navigator_Program_in_NYC_Housing_Court_and_NYC_Civil_Court_Consumer (last accessed 22 August 2018).

[4] Personal Support Unit, *Annual Report 2016/17*, 3.

[5] See pp 109–12.

[6] In 2016–17, of its budget of £1,325,923, £539,130 was received from the government, the remainder coming from trusts, corporations, friends and individuals and the community: PSU Annual Report for 2016–17, 12.

[7] PSU (n 4) 1.

[8] PSU (n 4) 3–4.

[9] See Personal Support Unit, *Spot Survey Summary Report 2014–16*, May 2016: https://www.thepsu.org/media/1405/spot-survey-summary-report-2014-2016.pdf (last accessed 5 June 2018).

came to for help. The most consistent single source of help reported is Citizens Advice, with 26 per cent of PSU clients seeking advice there. Only 18 per cent of survey respondents had spoken to a solicitor. In the 2014 and 2016 surveys, only 'a few' had used mediation in some form, and 3–4 per cent had been in touch with Cafcass, though the figures are higher for 2015 (22 per cent and 25 per cent respectively). In 2016 fewer than 10 per cent had looked for help online (a fall from 20 per cent in 2014). But 17 per cent had spoken to court staff. After receiving help, almost all were satisfied with the PSU intervention and less anxious, feeling more confident about handling their case and getting a fairer hearing.

We described earlier[10] how in some courts PSU support is provided not only to clients but also to additional services on the same site, through help with the administrative tasks of making appointments for pro bono lawyers who were offering sessions in a legal advice clinic located in the court, and keeping records and copies of redacted orders and judgements and information for signposting to other services. They may also share phonelines, copying, computers and printers etc, and even offer a form of triage for clinics under pressure in court on hearing days. In other courts there has been some rivalry between a PSU and other newly emerging additional help desks, where space is limited. In one court we observed,[11] the Designated Family Judge works closely with the PSU. In others the local judges, while appreciative of the part played by the PSU, are frustrated by the limits on their practice and want them to increase their range of activities. Some PSU volunteers described judges asking them to take parties outside and see if they can find an agreement, effectively expecting the PSU volunteers to mediate. In other courts, members of the judiciary, frustrated and stressed by the pressure of a large LiP population, expressed a wish for a service which *could* offer legal advice, not just emotional support. This was also noted in the 2017 Ministry of Justice Report, *Alleged perpetrators of abuse as Litigants in Person in private family law*, which states that 'it was suggested that some areas of legal advice could be sensibly redefined as legal help; for example, advising on which forms to complete. This would mean HMCTS (the Courts and Tribunals Service) and PSU staff being able to deliver more tailored support whilst enabling litigants and vulnerable witnesses to make better use of free legal advice services offered by other external organisations'.[12] The current guidelines for the role of PSU volunteers accompanying a client in court are that they can make notes on what should be raised and remind the client by pointing to the line, but (unlike McKenzie Friends[13]) cannot ask to speak. They are there only to increase the party's confidence.

---

[10] See pp 66, 70, 98–100.

[11] See pp 101–3.

[12] NE Corbett and A Summerfield, *Alleged perpetrators of abuse as Litigants in Person in private family law* (Ministry of Justice, 2017) 44.

[13] Discussed later: see pp 113–7.

B. Observational Data

How does this work in practice? We were fortunate in being able to observe a day in PSUs in four locations. They were all different, but all shared an air of cheerful competence, the doors were open, the kettle was on, the volunteers knew what they were about and not a moment was wasted. Demand was constant but well managed. Levels of distress varied, and people came in at the end of a case as well as before the beginning, sometimes by appointment, having booked a volunteer to sit with them in court. We were told by the manager of one PSU that, from the volunteers' records, a third of PSU clients were estimated to have been repeat players, a third to have been referred by court staff on the premises, and a third to have come via other sources. Clients may take as much time as they need, and return for further help.

In order to try to make clear what is meant by support in practice, we offer a note on our observations of a PSU in a busy family court. The court service (HMCTS) provides a room and phone line. Computer and printing costs are covered by the PSU, but they are able to offer a limited (five) number of photocopied pages. The amount of support from the court service in providing forms etc varies locally. In this PSU, the court provides copies of the C100 form needed to begin a child arrangements matter. The PSU opened at 10 am, with four volunteers present who work two days a month after training, and a full time manager. One of the volunteers was a barrister on maternity leave, the others included a young BME woman, and an older white man. A law student was shadowing one of the volunteers for the day, not as part of his course but on his own initiative. He was learning how to work and after two days would be able to see clients with supervision over a maximum of three weeks. But students generally were thought to have a high dropout rate.

Two cases were booked in, one for help with forms and another for someone to accompany the litigant to a directions hearing. A third man had returned for additional help with a previous matter. The court ushers are familiar with and supportive of the PSU in this court, and can direct LiPs towards its open door, an important element in the accessibility of the service. An anxious LiP can see into a room of busy people at desks, shelves of papers, and a buzz of purposeful activity. The manager indicated that this PSU has little contact with McKenzie Friends. In the manager's view, the hardest part of the volunteer's work (despite the statement in the PSU handout quoted above) was to NOT give information, by which he seemed to mean 'legal information'. He went on to say that the volunteers cannot even say which form a client would need in order to follow their chosen course of action, but instead show them the government website and scroll through and say: 'how about this one? you choose'! In another PSU visited later, this particular problem was dealt with slightly differently, by taking the client to the counter and asking the counter staff if they could suggest a useful form, which they did, even though the PSU had a shelf with these forms on it at all time.

The first client that morning was a lady (A) with legal bills amounting to over £40,000 which she wanted to settle, and had been sent to the PSU by Citizen's Advice. She wanted to delay her decree absolute until the finance had been settled, and had applied to the Bar Pro Bono Unit (BPBU) for help, but time was short (a three week deadline before a hearing). She needed to write a case summary and was finding it difficult. She was also anxious about getting back to meet her children from school. A began to give her narrative of the case, but the volunteer stopped her, asking if she had any evidence, such as solicitors' letters. When she said 'no', the volunteer advised her to go home and do her best on her own, saying that there was a lot of information but that it was not a complicated story. A asked how much detail to give, and said 'I want some help ... it's cost me £30 to get here'. The volunteer said that he had not done one before and asked his manager for guidance. The manager explained that it was difficult, and pointed out that the BPBU will review her application and may or may not accept it. The manager told A that the BPBU know that the PSU cannot give legal advice;[14] A says she is going round in circles, and is advised to go on asking for help but not to rely on getting it. The manager suggests approaching Barristers Direct who will represent for a reasonable fee, and that the hearing will be just looking at the facts in order to decide what further hearings will be needed. He says: 'just have a bash at the form and then ring here and ask to see the court staff legal advisers or we could try taking you down there now'. The volunteer does this. Half an hour later they return with A very pleased with the advice and help she has been given. She will be able to go home and prepare her case summary. So while PSU avoided giving advice itself, it led A to a source where this was available.

Another volunteer is about to go into court with a client (B) and asks what she can do with the notes she will take in the hearing. She is 'not supposed' to give them to a client, but they can be a very useful record of what happened, especially for a client who is not a native English speaker. Notes could be shown to a friend with good English if there is not enough time at the end of the day to go through and debrief the client, and check that they understand the next steps. (This procedure was also followed at one of the student help desks discussed in chapter eight). There is some discussion among the volunteers about how some PSU services are 'gung ho' about the kind of help they are willing to provide. Similarly, some judges are more relaxed about what might be termed legal advice than others. But some services were considering stamping any notes 'Not legal advice' to prevent problems.

The next case was a lady (C) who had just been issued in another court with an order preventing her from making any further application for contact with her children for a period of two years. She had been unable to get legal aid as she owned a small rental property. English was not her first language, and she was very

---

[14] PSU are not able to 'do' a Form E (a financial statement).

distressed as she felt her children had been 'stolen' from her. The volunteer told her that she needed legal advice and suggested going to Citizens Advice. C replied that she had been there three times about her divorce and they will not give her any more appointments. At present the contact is for three hours four times a year, and she wants to ask for weekly contact. Social services are involved.

A lady wishing to complain about a judge returns, and wants to make an appointment for the following week. A second volunteer is carefully explaining by phone that the PSU cannot give legal advice, saying 'we can sit beside you and explain some things you don't know'. This volunteer is frustrated by the restriction, and says that although they see some disturbed people and need to be careful, a little more could be attempted. But volunteers can access AdviceNow and work through it with a client making sure it is understood. They are also appreciative of the regular usher who is well trained and can do 'anything'! A lady comes in with a query about forms: 'does it mean print three and submit two or three'? The volunteers agree that the drafting of the instructions is not very clear, and suggest she submits two and keeps one. Another lady comes to ask if she can use the PSU computer to call up her divorce petition later and print it.

In the afternoon an East European man (D) dropped in, anxious about his ex-wife taking the children out of the jurisdiction. She had done this the previous year and he had been very worried about their return. He wanted the court to prevent this happening again. His English was limited, and he could not afford a lawyer. The volunteer showed him a number of forms on her computer for making application to the court, and asked him if the Prohibited Steps Order looked like what he had in mind. He agreed, so she could print off the form, and ask him if he needed help filling it in. The answer was 'yes', and this was done. This case is a clear example of the limitations and potential of the PSU in giving what we might term legal help. As D knew what he wanted to achieve but not how to go about it, the help he received in identifying the legal remedy and beginning the process of application was permissible under the PSU's Code of Practice. If he had been a little less legally aware, and had come saying that he had wanted control over where his children could spend the school holidays, it would have been more difficult for the PSU to help him without explaining the scope of joint parental responsibility and the welfare paramountcy principle before getting to the idea of suggesting a Prohibited Steps Order as that would have involved legal information and probably legal advice. The distinction is a hard one for potential clients to understand and may act as a barrier between service and meeting client need.

C. Assessment and Reflections

The PSUs offer a high quality service. They have not so far become involved with student volunteers to any great extent as they do not seek to spend time on supervision and they do not usually include practitioners or academics among their volunteers. Their work is recognised by government through the LiPSS, but ironically the very quality has led to higher expectations. In some courts the judiciary are pressing for the PSU to expand the range of work they do to include more use of legal knowledge to provide more legal help in the post LASPO period. Where there is interest in providing a problem-solving court, with additional services including mediation, supervised contact, financial advice and so on, there is an appetite for the PSU to push out its frontiers. This poses a real dilemma for the PSU which often plays below the strength of its volunteers, and has an effective managerial structure and a vigorous head office. But this policy of caution has worked well so far, and though it must be tempting to push forward in times of such financial stress and increasing need, there is also a case for proceeding with caution and maintaining the confidence of both the public and the judiciary by not moving too far into the field of professional legal advice giving. But even the legal advice given by lawyers with practising certificates in practice can be very similar, comprising giving information about which court to approach, reminding clients to give court staff the up-to-date address for service, reminding people of dates, checking forms, and offering emotional support.

Support services without doubt provide practical and skilled help with paperwork, collecting and collating necessary information, separating emotion from fact, providing practice for speaking in court, and explaining not only what will happen in a court hearing but also explaining afterwards what did in fact happen and what the next steps are. The PSU is highly valued by clients and professionals and the service offered is standard across the current services. There is no confusion about opening hours, eligibility, charging, competence and focus on support (with some information and just possibly advice slipping in here and there).

Help with using family law to resolve a problem is not always totally reliant on in-depth knowledge of black letter law, or even the skills of drafting and advocacy. It may be possible to provide help with a family legal matter where children are involved by drawing on and communicating the child-centred nature of family justice, and its focus on what will be safe and best for the child in question. Other evidence in our study suggests that where clients understand that they are asking for the court's help in keeping their child safe and promoting their welfare, they will have a smoother pathway than if they are demanding that their own rights as parents are protected and enforced. For example, we were told by a Citizens Advice Family Legal Adviser, who is not a lawyer but has an office in the court building and supports clients, that where the client is seeking to protect the child, the court will listen, but where the client is seeking to punish the other parent, they will find it harder to be heard. Similarly the Gingerbread helpline adviser[15] makes it clear to callers what the law seeks and how this usually fits with the caller's needs, but that things will go more smoothly if the problem is presented in a child-focused way.

---

[15] See pp 147–8.

Giving information about the way family legal regulation is structured, its aims and procedures, can be another indirect way of providing advice. And if information is added about how these procedures can most effectively be used, is this still legal information or is it shading into advice, especially if it is given in the context of a specific case? The insurance implications need to be considered. Other groups offering professional information at the point when it is most needed use various ways to avoid possible liability that might be incurred when giving legal advice, either by stating that they are not providing legal advice or excluding liability if they do. The Family Law Panel, mentioned in chapter three, which describes itself as a 'free service for members of the public to access initial professional and independent family law information' does both, stating both that 'information gained from this website is for general guidance on the issues raised and should not be relied or acted upon without taking detailed advice from an appropriately qualified person' and that 'the Family Law Panel will not accept liability for any loss, damage or inconvenience arising as a consequence of any use of, the inability to use, or the reliance upon of any information gained via this website'.

II. McKenzie Friends

There is another support service which has increasing visibility but is not regulated and includes a variety of practitioners and practices where it is less clear what is being offered and what is being charged for: the McKenzie Friends. The term is used to describe an individual who provides reasonable assistance to a LiP. It derives from the case of *McKenzie v McKenzie*[16] where an Australian barrister had been refused permission to represent one of the parties in divorce proceedings, and on appeal the trial judge was found to have been wrong in not allowing Mr McKenzie to have the help of Mr Hangar who was there 'not to take part in the proceedings in any sort of way. He was merely there to prompt and to make suggestions to the husband in the conduct of his case, and perhaps very importantly on the very difficult question of fact in this case to assist him by making suggestions as to the cross examination of the wife and her witnesses'. The term is now used to refer to anyone who assists a litigant in that way, and therefore there is no regulation over who may provide it. They could be members of the LiP's friends or family. In fact, they are often people who have had personal experience in the family courts, a number openly professing a pro fathers' rights agenda.[17]

There is, however, also a Society of (fee-charging) Professional McKenzie Friends which operates a system of self-regulation, requiring that its full members

[16] [1970] 3 WLR 472.
[17] See A Melville, 'Giving Hope to Fathers: Discursive constructions of families and family law by McKenzie Friends' (2017) 31 *International Journal of Law, Policy and the Family* 147.

fulfil one of the following criteria: (1) membership of a professional body which regulates their conduct, for example, as a Solicitor, Barrister, Legal Executive, or Social Worker, or (2) has a law qualification, or 'other qualification relevant to their field of work, which is equivalent to A level or above', or (3) has worked for 20 or more hours a week as a McKenzie Friend for three years. They must hold professional indemnity insurance, and comply with a Code of Conduct. There is now a Civil Justice Council Code of Conduct standard form used in many courts describing a Code of Practice for McKenzies, with which members of the Society of Professional McKenzie Friends must comply, together with the Court Rules.

According to Guidance from the Judiciary, the help provided by a McKenzie Friend may take the form of providing moral support to the LiP, taking notes, helping with case papers and 'quietly giv(ing) advice on any aspect of the conduct of the case'. The court retains the power to refuse to permit this support if it deems that justice and fairness do not require it, and it does not extend to managing the case outside court, 'for example, by signing court documents'.[18] However the Society of Professional McKenzie Friends would expect to prepare for a case before a hearing in the sense of meeting the client outside court, researching the problem, and advising on lines to take. But their presence in court depends on the permission of the court and the court may also allow a McKenzie Friend to address the court, which carries the right to call and examine witnesses. If they address the court they perform a 'reserved legal activity', but they are exempted from the requirements of professional qualification set out in the Legal Services Act 2007[19] if the court grants them the right of audience.[20]

The 2014 Ministry of Justice Study on Litigants in Person, referred to earlier,[21] drawing on some observations of cases in which McKenzie Friends were involved, doubted whether they provided sufficient value for money to justify their increased use. But a Legal Services Consumer Panel report, published slightly earlier, based largely on interviews with 28 McKenzie Friends, while recognising the risks involved, had nevertheless concluded that they added to the range of services available to help separating families, especially following the legal aid cuts of the preceding year, and that fee-charging McKenzie Friends should be recognised as a legitimate feature of the evolving legal services market.[22] A consultation by the

---

[18] See Courts and Tribunals Judiciary, McKenzie Friends Guidance: https://www.judiciary.gov.uk/publications/mckenzie-friends/ (last accessed 6 April 2018) and Lord Chief Justice of England and Wales, *Reforming the Courts Approach to McKenzie Friends, Consultation* (February 2016): https://www.judiciary.gov.uk/wp-content/uploads/2016/02/mf-consultation-paper-feb2016-1.pdf (last accessed 6 April 2018).

[19] See pp 60–1.

[20] Legal Services Act 2007, Sch 3, para 1(2). See Lord Chief Justice of England and Wales, *Reforming the Courts Approach to McKenzie Friends, Consultation* (February 2016), para 2.9.

[21] L Trinder, R Hunter, J Miles, R Moorehead, L Smith, M Sefton, V Hinchley and K Bader, *Litigants in person in private family law cases* (Ministry of Justice Analytical Series, 2014), see p 38.

[22] Legal Services Consumer Panel, *Fee Charging McKenzie Friends* (April 2014): http://www.legal-servicesconsumerpanel.org.uk/publications/research_and_reports/documents/2014%2004%20 17%20MKF_Final.pdf (last accessed 27 September 2018).

Lord Chief Justice in 2016[23] drew attention to the risks of the absence of regulation (such as poor quality or agenda driven advice, lack of insurance and risks of over-charging) and made a number of recommendations which included substituting the appellation 'McKenzie Friend' for a term like 'court supporter', codification of the Guidance to Courts with respect to McKenzie Friends and, most significantly, prohibition of the right of McKenzie Friends to recover fees or charges because this would 'implicitly acknowledge the creation of a new branch of the legal profession' which lacked proper regulation. This, it was held, should be a matter for Parliament. A further Working Group has been established to consider the responses to the consultation.[24]

There has been concern arising from anecdotal accounts of large sums of money being charged for what is advertised as legal advice from non-lawyer McKenzie Friends. A small in-depth study of McKenzie Friends who charge for their services which was supported by the Bar Council identified five types of McKenzie Friends and a number of models of activity, ranging from the business opportunist, who might have some personal experience or incomplete legal training, the redirected specialist seeking to employ their considerable professional experience after LASPO, the good Samaritan, motivated by concern for the needs of low income clients, the Family Justice Crusader following a personal agenda critical of a perceived bias in the Family Justice system against fathers, and finally the Rogue, a small minority charging inordinately high fees for fraudulent conduct and damaging the interests of litigants and the administration of justice.[25] There are accounts of highly inappropriate behaviour.[26] The study notes that such behaviour is rare, but comments that this area of work is particularly vulnerable to exploitative opportunists given that there is no regulatory body, no professional code or scrutiny and potentially no set-up costs.

The term 'McKenzie Model' is used by a number of student pro bono support services, where no charge is made and no advice given without supervision, but effective support can be provided along the lines described earlier[27] which are strongly supported by, for example, Professor Andy Unger from London South Bank University.[28] In 2016 the Master of the Rolls, Sir Terence Etherton, suggested that law graduates could help plug the access to justice gap by representing litigants

---

[23] Lord Chief Justice of England and Wales (n 17).

[24] See http://www.transparencyproject.org.uk/whatever-happened-to-the-judiciarys-mckenzie-friends-consultation/ (last accessed 6 June 2018).

[25] L Smith, E Hitchings and M Sefton, *A study of fee charging McKenzie Friends and their work in private law family cases*, Cardiff University and Bristol University for the Bar Council, 2017.

[26] See eg, M Walters, 'McKenzie Friend "jailed for deceit in family court"', *Law Society Gazette* 17 October 2016: www.lawgazette.co.uk/law/mckenzie-friend-jailed-for-deceit-in-family-court/5058352.article (last accessed 6 June 2018); M Walters, 'New alarm over role of McKenzie advisers' Law Society Gazette, 3 October 2016: www.lawgazette.co.uk/news/new-alarm-over-role-of-mckenzie-advisers/5058028.article (last accessed 6 June 2018).

[27] See above pp 74, 103.

[28] See M Walters, '"McKenzie students" have a role to play – but only under supervision – says professor', *Law Society Gazette* 1 August 2017: www.lawgazette.co.uk/law/mckenzie-students-have-a-role-but-only-under-supervision-says-professor/5062211.article (last accessed 6 June 2016).

in person in court proceedings.[29] In March 2017, students at the University of Westminster and BPP Law School University of Law set up a 'McKenzie Market-Place', suggesting that students could charge LiPs up to £25 for legal advice to LiPS, though this was strongly challenged by the Law Society a year later. In March 2017 it was clearly stated by the MarketPlace that 'no active student would be able to use the (MarketPlace) portal to give advice'.[30] In June 2017 in a judgment handed down in the East London Family Court HH Judge Carol Atkinson took the Law Society view, saying 'there is no such thing as a quasi solicitor', adding: 'you are either a solicitor or you are not'. She stated that the McKenzie Friend who runs a company called 'Maxim Legal' which provides support and services to the legal profession and individuals had a 'fundamental misunderstanding of the limitations of his role'. He had also allegedly asked a witness if he could amend a Core Assessment in a children case before it was handed to the judge, conduct which Judge Atkinson described as 'utterly inconceivable'. She added that: 'If professional McKenzie Friends are to assist parents in such emotionally fraught cases they must be sensitive … and mindful of the dangers of hindering the process rather than giving the assistance courts have been used to in the past'.[31]

The McKenzie Model in student clinics and help desks is not universally accepted either by the judiciary or by law teachers. Farhana Begum has emphasised the differences between student support services and McKenzie Friends, pointing to the facts (among others) that the arrangement between a McKenzie Friend and a LiP is a private arrangement, whereas student services are part of a scheme managed by a project supervisor, that students are supervised and covered by indemnity insurance, whereas McKenzie Friends are not, that McKenzie Friends may be permitted by the court both to address the court and help the LiP in the conduct of litigation, whereas this would not be expected of students. She suggests that the term 'McKenzie students' is an oxymoron.[32]

There is also a small group of former legal aid solicitors who are now unable to work for clients as they were accustomed to do before the LASPO Act, but who wish to continue helping the former legally aided population with family matters. We were able to observe the work of one such solicitor who remained on the Roll but did not retain a practising certificate who provided a client care letter which gave her Roll number, her indemnity insurance details (up to £1million) and her experience as a solicitor but states clearly that she did not run a regulated law practice:

> The service I provide is guidance, support, legal and practical advice to enable you to deal with your family law issue or court case. My primary duty is to assist you to achieve the outcome you seek. I do not manage contested or defended matters for you, you are

---

[29] Cited by M Walters (n 26).

[30] M Walters, 'McKenzie friend entrepreneur backtracks on student portal' *Law Society Gazette* 28 March 2017: www.lawgazette.co.uk/law/mckenzie-friend-entrepreneur-backtracks-on-student-portal/5060442.article (last accessed 6 June 2018).

[31] M Walters, '"No such thing as a quasi-solicitor": judge slaps down paid McKenzie', *Law Society Gazette* 28 June 2017: www.lawgazette.co.uk/law/no-such-thing-as-a-quasi-solicitor-judge-slaps-down-paid-mckenzie/5061767.article (last accessed 6 June 2018).

[32] F Begum, 'McKenzie students – an oxymoron?' (2018) 48 *Family Law* 77.

a litigant in person throughout the proceedings, I can help you write letters, complete court forms, and documents and help you to prepare your case and present it to the court. I cannot sign letters or documents on your behalf. I will not give you advice as to how I think you should decide what to do in your case but I can advise you of your options and what the court might decide to do in deciding your case if you and your partner cannot agree. You are responsible for filing your documents. ... if I attend court with you I can help you negotiate and go into the court with you to quietly advise you on points of law and procedure and issues that you may wish to raise. In some circumstances the court may grant me rights of audience which means I can speak on your behalf as a practising solicitor or barrister would. All documents you give me will be held securely and not communicated to others save when I am ordered by the court or where you give me your consent to disclose or instructed me to negotiate on your behalf ... my time will be charged at £90 an hour, no VAT, pay as you go.

This is a clear description of a supportive but specialist service, offering information and practical support, but also an element of advice, including quiet advice in court and even representation with the leave of the court. This McKenzie Friend is well known in the area where she formerly practised as a legal aid solicitor, and her work is widely appreciated in the current situation. The local judges invite her to speak in court on behalf of her clients, and even to go outside with both parties and try to help them reach agreement and draft the order. She visits clients at home, then helps on their own computers to draft letters and witness statements. She is often approached by the solicitor for the victim in a domestic violence case to act for the alleged perpetrator, so that she should be able to question the alleged victim rather than the accused which would otherwise be the case.

Clearly there is wide variety of forms of service, of charging codes, and of ability and ethical values. The Society of Professional McKenzie Friends argues that its members are able to help LiPs who are conducting their own cases in court because they cannot afford a lawyer's fees, and legal aid is becoming harder to obtain. The need for support is clear, but the quality of that support is difficult for the first time LiP to assess. It may be of great assistance and provided from the best of philanthropic motives. It may be a reasonable business venture in response to unmet need for legal help. But it may also be costly, incompetent and, for the provider, a way of pursuing an old grievance against the family justice system. There are differing views on how these risks might be managed. In the case of the PSU the rigorous self-regulation of the service may frustrate the court in some circumstances, but does provide a degree of certainty about the way in which the volunteers will work and the supervision they receive from their managers. In the case of the McKenzie Friends, the lack of supervision and regulation or accreditation, and the variation in expertise and motivation of the participants leaves a degree of anxiety for clients and courts. The outcome of the 2016 consultation, referred to above, is awaited with interest. The legal services market may be approaching a period of change, in response to increasing unmet need and the withdrawal of public funding. But there is still little consensus on how legal help may be provided safely and affordably outside the regulated professions.

8

The Student Contribution: Clinical Legal Education

We noted in chapter three that over a half of volunteers in LawWorks pro bono clinics are students,[1] in chapter four we gave our observations of students working with practitioners in legal advice centres and providing support to LiPs through court help desks, and in chapter six we described how the CLOCK project at Keele was supporting the work of the Designated Family Judge. In this chapter we will take a closer look at the questions arising around the multiple aims and organisation of student pro bono work, and the range of activities undertaken by different groups of students, before presenting additional examples of our observations of students in action.

I. Aims

Jeff Giddings has described Clinical Legal Education (CLE) as involving 'an intensive small group or solo learning experience in which each student takes responsibility for legal or law related work for a client (whether real or simulated) in collaboration with a supervisor'.[2] It is the defining term for a form of legal education which exposes students to the practical application of the law and puts them in the position of using their legal knowledge to respond to real life issues. When CLE first developed in the US in the 1960s, the focus was slightly different in the context of low public funding for legal help, and the developing university-based clinics tended to be built on to existing services that were already providing help and advice, with a focus originally almost entirely on poverty law. As described earlier in relation to pro bono activity in the US,[3] law schools were under pressure to provide CLE opportunities and there was major philanthropic support. In Australia, CLE was originally based in the existing community legal centres, within a strong service ethic, though the implications for enhancing career prospects are now becoming more prominent. In Canada there is currently debate

---

[1] See pp 57, 58, 118.
[2] J Giddings, *Promoting Justice through Clinical Legal Education* (Melbourne, Justice Press, 2013) 14.
[3] See pp 46–9.

about how much students (and paralegals) should be able to do for those lacking the resources to purchase legal help.[4]

In the UK, CLE has developed in a slightly different way, as, until the LASPO watershed, the need for legal help particularly in family matters was largely met through publicly funded legal aid, and enhancing the employability of students through the acquisition of practical legal skills took priority. These national differences were discussed by the Clinical Legal Education Organisation (CLEO), supported by the Legal Education Foundation, at the International Conference of the Clinical Legal Education Organisation held in Northumbria in 2016 with participants from over 22 countries, including Eastern Europe, Iran, Israel, India, Africa as well as the US, Canada, Australia and Western Europe. The topics discussed focused on the clinician's contribution to curriculum design, best practice in supervision, how clinics can help communities and the contribution of clinic data to research.

The rapid growth in CLE in England and Wales over the last decade has been accompanied by continuing uncertainty about the purpose and potential impact of the activity, which echoes some of the questions raised about the purpose of pro bono work by established legal practitioners. For the practitioners, there were issues about how far the aim was philanthropic, and how far other motivations were influencing practice. This covered the value of pro bono as a marketing strategy, the professional development value of client interaction for young practitioners, especially those in areas of law where this is not common, such as commercial law, and the desirability of enhancing the socially responsible image of legal practice for the profession as a whole. For the students, there is a similar mixture of motives. Are they acting altruistically to improve access to justice after LASPO? Or are they also additionally, or even primarily, concerned with improving their career prospects by learning at an early stage about how the law works in practice, about court procedure, about relating to clients and about new areas of law? How far are these philanthropic and self-interested aims compatible? If they are altruistic volunteers with a mission to promote access to justice, might they seek to take on a more active legal role, providing advice and even representation? Or are they supporting and enabling practitioners through an apprenticeship model by carrying out tasks for a practitioner, under supervision, such as taking the history when a client attends a pro bono clinic and then, still under supervision, observing and writing up the advice given by the practitioners? How far do the differences between these various models lead to conflict about the nature of student pro bono practice? Can they simply be adopted separately by different groups of students? Is there a difference between what first or second year law students can do (mainly support) and what final year students can do (supervised advice) and what trainee solicitors or barristers can offer, which might even include supervised pro bono advocacy?

[4] See pp 118–9.

This set of issues is related to a second question about whether these students are engaged in learning, an academic activity, which will benefit the community in the long term, or undertaking occupational training, which will benefit their own career development and their value to an employer. Are they in part filling the gap left by the reduction in numbers of court staff and thereby helping the judges, and, indirectly the government? This leads us to ask: who is paying for the activity and where should the costs of CLE fall? If the students are primarily learning and the costs fall to the education budget, there will also be some additional benefit to the university through its reputation for social responsibility and also by raising the class of degrees achieved. If a clinical education course is required as part of the law degree course, just as clinical training is required of medical students and placement experience in social work or teacher training, and are subject to some form of academic assessment, then not only the cost but also the responsibility for actions taken will clearly lie with the education sector. Some universities employ staff in academic positions (sometimes known as pracademics), who are solicitors with practising certificates, to organise and supervise such activity. But if the activity is purely philanthropic and largely organised by students, then any cost may appropriately fall at least in part on the third sector organisation with which the students are linked, or be subsidised in kind by the court service who may offer premises or access to wifi or phonelines.

A third form of student pro bono activity sits closer to community outreach work, and has been referred to in chapter six in describing the activities of the CLOCK scheme where the aim is to establish a virtuous circle of activity which benefits clients, students and the university, lawyers and courts, but is not wholly dependent on university funding. Under this scheme the unrepresented clients are supported (but not advised) by the students and helped to access legal advice from local practitioners, while the court is helped to cope with the cuts in counter staff numbers. In addition, the university also benefits from the collection of data on the work done which is of great value for research and future publications. For example the Keele service recorded helping 608 clients with family matters in 2017, of whom 28 per cent were helped to access affordable fixed fee legal services. The students often achieve higher marks, which raises the profile of the law school at a time when demographic changes are making it more difficult for law schools to fill their places. The structure results in the interests of the different players being brought together in cooperation rather than in competition.

Student help is obtained not only from undergraduates as part of their CLE but also from students intending to qualify for entering into the legal profession. Those planning to be solicitors take the Legal Practice Course (LPC) after having completed their academic legal qualification, which is either a qualifying law degree or a degree in a different subject at a UK university plus the Graduate Diploma in Law (GDL) or Common Professional Examination (CPE). The LPC is a two-stage programme, lasting one year (full-time) or two years (part time). Stage 1 covers the three essential practice areas of Business Law and Practice, Property Law and Practice and Litigation, together with Course Skills (Practical Legal Research, Writing,

Drafting, Interviewing and Advising and Advocacy) Professional Conduct and Regulation, Wills and Administration of Estates and Taxation. Stage 2 is made up of three Vocational Electives, one of which could be family law. There is also a requirement of two years of recognised training and completion of a Professional Skills Course, namely, a course normally completed during the training contract, building upon the LPC, providing training in Financial and Business Skills, Advocacy and Communication Skills, and Client Care and Professional Standards. Those wishing to become barristers take the Bar Professional Training Course (BPTC) rather than the LPC. It is designed to ensure that students acquire the skills, knowledge of procedure and evidence, attitudes and competence to prepare them for the more specialised training that comes later in pupillage.

Concerns over the consistency of delivery, costs, and assessment of the current system led the Solicitors' Regulation Authority in 2016 to seek consultation on proposals to revise the process for solicitors, dividing it into two stages: Solicitors' Qualifying Examination (SQE) stage 1 (which would test candidates' ability to use their legal knowledge to address clients' problems or within legal transactions) and stage 2 (which would test the legal skills of analysis, advocacy, interviewing, writing, drafting and research), separated by work-based experience. The contexts listed in which skills would be assessed at stage 2 now notably do not include family law.[5]

II.   Organisation of CLE

In 2015 Orla Drummond and Gráinne McKeevor of Ulster University published a comprehensive account of the aims and organisation of student pro bono activity after LASPO, which they describe as research into 'the place of the university law clinic in the eco-system'.[6] Based on data collected during the previous year, they identified 62 university law clinics and received information from 32. Although their response rate was only just over 50 per cent, they are able to give a general idea of the level of activity. The survey gives the most recent data on student clinic profiles, with family work the third largest category, offered by 21 of the 32 clinics surveyed. Staffing levels were low, on average limited to two academic staff, with support staff often relying on student help and external professional supervisors often working pro bono. University funding was the most important resource, with a diminishing level of support from private donors or charitable trusts. 20 clinics included graduate students on training courses as well as undergraduates. Referrals were mainly received from solicitors and advice agencies, who in turn received

[5] Solicitors' Regulation Authority, *A New Route to Qualification: The Solicitors Qualifying Examination (SQE)* (October 2016), para 62: https://www.sra.org.uk/sra/consultations/solicitors-qualifying-examination.page (last accessed 8 June 2108).
[6] O Drummond and G McKeevor, *Access to Justice through University law Clinics* (Ulster University, supported by LEF. 2015 ISBN 978859232682).

referrals from the clinics when they had done all they could. Case selection was driven by the practical limitations faced by clinics, which included the need to meet the academic needs of the students. Most clinics accepted self referrals. The majority of clinics collected data from clients, partly to improve service but also to meet the academic need of the university for research materials. This has already produced interesting findings, for example on the perceived current barriers to justice. Few collected financial information from clients, but the majority were clear that lack of resources was a key reason for accessing the clinics. Other barriers to justice were also identified, including practical difficulties in knowing how to access relevant documents, lack of confidence, stress, and English language barriers. The clinics expressed multiple objectives: assisting communities, developing professional capacity, improving student employability, meeting unmet legal needs, and delivering access to justice.[7]

All the responding clinics provided 'advice', though this is not defined as general or specific legal advice, but fewer than a third were able to offer both advice and representation.[8] We are not told how many of the clients of each clinic received which level of service. The issue of what is or is not legal advice and who may offer it was present in our earlier discussion of the pro bono work of the professions,[9] the lay supporting services,[10] as well as the students, and it will arise again when we turn to the work of the advice sector. But in our visits to student clinics in 2016–17 we found that what was termed initial advice often consisted of general legal information, but sometimes specific advice was given under the supervision of a practitioner and this was sometimes put into writing as a single letter of advice and checked by the supervising practitioner. The students at one clinic described their experience of writing these letters of advice. One said: 'It's not like writing essays ... we are used to exams where things are black and white. These letters are written for reassurance and confidence ... we mustn't overcomplicate, and we must tell about other kinds of help like mental health services'. This group had clearly understood the supervisor's message, that 'every client is different ... it's not about us, it's about the client'.

Advocacy was offered under supervision by a small number of students on professional advocacy courses.[11] But provision of full legal services with ongoing advice and representation were not observed. The Ulster report found that the average number of clients helped per year by the 32 clinics surveyed (bearing in mind that most student clinics are only active during university terms) was 104 cases. This was limited by the inability to increase staffing from the average of two salaried members. The clinics clearly faced a difficult question when considering what would happen to their clients when their ability to intervene came to

[7] ibid, 8.
[8] ibid, 5.
[9] See eg pp 60–4.
[10] See eg pp 107, 110, 111, 113.
[11] See p 129 below.

an end. The response to the survey indicated that 75 per cent of the 32 clinics described referring client cases to external partners, mainly solicitors, and collaborating with them. They also collaborated with independent advice agencies and barristers through a variety of formal and informal arrangements. Sadly the advice agencies are themselves in difficulty with reduced funding and are often losing the ability to offer specialist advice, which affects their ability to both develop casework and deliver general legal advice in a specific area such as family law.

The data in the Ulster study is particularly helpful in addressing the complex issue of priorities. The responding clinics expressed giving clear priority to 'the objectives of improving student employability and developing professional capacity in law over assisting local communities and delivering access to justice'. The view was expressed that, although the university clinics do provide access to justice, they should prioritise education, which is their primary task, that they do not have the resources to be access to justice providers, and that it is the role of the state to take responsibility for access to justice. This echoes the view of the legal profession described earlier regarding pro bono work. But while the role of the clinics as providers is limited, Drummond and McKeevor comment that they are also a unique environment in which to test and develop innovative solutions to legal problems, drawing on expertise in related areas within universities (such as psychology, philosophy, communications and IT) and suggest that funding bodies should support research in these areas.

The Ulster study gives us an idea of the quantity of student pro bono help. If each of the 21 responding clinics helps 100 clients with advice each year and one third with advice and representation, this could mean over 2,100 clients helped, and 700 given advice and representation, though we are not sure whether the levels of support are standard across the areas of law covered. The report is helpful and informative, but we are left with a degree of uncertainty about exactly what kind of service is being offered, and how the provision of help by students and their supervision by practitioners is organised and regulated. The two elements are interlinked, as clinic organisers need to present the student activity to the university, to potential clients and to the justice system as competent, reliable and trustworthy.

III. Regulating CLE

CLE practice can take place under a series of possible scenarios: (1) students may be offering non-legal support, which may involve helping to explain what will happen in court, accompanying a LiP into court but not speaking, and taking a note of what happened and the next steps; and (2) the non-legal support or advice can come closer to legal advice if the students are assisting with intake at an advice clinic by taking a history, offering advice on and help with form filling and court procedure, helping with preparing a position statement and giving the information sometimes known as initial advice, which may be put into the form of a letter of advice sent later with the approval of a practitioner. Solicitors are involved as supervisors for student activity at clinic sessions and in particular for checking and signing letters of advice before they are sent. But they may also hold academic appointments and be responsible for a clinical education component of the law course, including teaching in preparation for student participation, and assessing performance. They may or may not hold a practising certificate.

The details concerning the accreditation of solicitors were discussed in chapter three[12] in relation to their pro bono work and this becomes more complex in the case of employment by a university with respect to their non-teaching activities and also with regard to the work of the students. If they hold a Practising Certificate, their work will be regulated by the SRA, which requires appropriate insurance cover.[13] But the university's insurance may not include work of an employee carried out as a solicitor. One student clinic organiser described how she had sought clarification from the SRA on her multiple roles as teacher and lawyer, ie holding an academic position but also a solicitor on the Roll with a current practising certificate running a student help desk in court and also a university legal advice centre with an in-house solicitor. Her questions were answered by the SRA as follows (August 2017): as an in-house solicitor she would be able to provide legal services under Practice Framework Rule 4.16[14] provided that the conditions under that rule are met and also that there should not be an issue with carrying out reserved legal activities such as conduct of litigation. As we have seen,[15] this is not a straightforward matter. It may be that she could undertake reserved legal activities pro bono in a personal capacity if this was not considered to be part of her employer's (the University's) business. It might be different if this was considered to be part of the university's business. She was further advised that she would not have to apply to become an ABS (Alternative Business Structure) if she satisfied Rule 4.16. This advice was followed immediately by a waiver stating that the guidance should not be treated as a formal ruling on the matter in hand and is not binding on solicitors, their clients, the SRA, the Legal Ombudsman or the Courts.

Our respondent took the view that giving advice within litigation is not a reserved activity but on-going legal advice could be reserved, which might explain the insistence by some clinics that they give only initial advice which might also be seen as information. Different rules can apply to two pro bono CLE activities within the same university. A student help desk offering only support might be seen as part of the university's educational activity, not involving either initial or ongoing advice, and therefore supervised by the organiser in her academic capacity covered by the university's insurance. The legal advice clinic on the other hand could be seen as employing an in-house solicitor who could therefore give general legal advice, sign off advice letters under Rule 4.16 of the SRA Practice Framework

[12] See pp 60–2.
[13] See pp 52, 61.
[14] See p 61.
[15] See p 1.

Rules 2011, provided this was protected by the University's insurance as required by Rule 4.16(d).[16]

The organiser told us she was worried about being in breach of the conflict of interest rules where the help desk was supporting both parties, even though as organiser she did not see the clients in person and the students on the help desk were offering information about procedure, not legal advice. The SRA replied that they did not see a problem, as the students were not giving advice and the supervisor was not seeing clients. They said that the job included two roles, one as a solicitor when working in the separate legal advice clinic, but that when supervising students at court, the organiser was working as a teacher. The organiser commented that it would be much easier to offer the service if it were not regulated at all. This could come about under the SRA proposals allowing solicitors to offer non-reserved advice *as solicitors* outside the SRA regulation framework.[17] As it was, she would prefer to give up her practising certificate because the clinic was not conducting litigation but the presence of solicitors in the university advice services gives 'credibility' with both students and public and the court.

A second CLE organiser told us of her need for clarification from the SRA about regulation. She too held an academic appointment, and was a qualified solicitor with a practising certificate. However, because the advice desk she had set up sometimes supported both parties at court, she was worried about being in breach of the conflict of interest rules, even though as organiser she did not see the clients in person and the students on the help desk were offering information about procedure, not legal advice. The SRA replied that they did not see a problem, as the students were not giving advice and the supervisor was not seeing clients. They said that the job included two roles, one as a solicitor when working in the legal advice clinic, but that when supervising students at court, the organiser was working as a teacher. The organiser commented that it would be much easier to offer the service if it were not regulated at all. She would prefer to give up her practising certificate because the clinic was not conducting litigation but the presence of solicitors in the university advice services gives 'credibility' with both students and public and the court.

So with these complexities it is hardly surprising that some universities are cautious about entering this field of activity. Are comparable issues found in more established forms of practice involving placements, such as medicine, social work and school education? In all three settings supervision in the educational sense is very much a part of the process both during training and later in employment. In teaching placements there is always obvious supervision, and a well-defined code of practice for working with young people. The comparatively recent development of CLE perhaps contributes to the anxiety of providers to have 'real' lawyers in evidence, to establish the credentials of the activity and protect clients, students

---

[16] See p 61.
[17] See pp 60–2.

and the university in case of client dissatisfaction. Insurance issues are mainly relevant to accreditation in the case of employed solicitors rather than to potential liability in practice, and the references to reserved activities are mostly irrelevant with respect to student activity as students rarely go beyond personal support and general information or once-off legal advice, and never to advocacy or conduct of litigation. Legal trainees are in a different position as members of the firms where they hold their training contract, with a defined supervision structure, and are covered by the firm with respect to insurance. Indeed, if they undertake a placement in a voluntary advice clinic they may be doubly covered both by their own and the clinic's insurance. And they may be able to undertake reserved activities including advocacy if permitted by the court.

IV. CLE Training and Student Preparation for Family Work: Observational Data

First and second year law undergraduates may be interested in taking part in CLE, in which case they may be directed towards support work, possibly in a court help desk. Second and third year students may move on to participating in a pro bono advice legal clinic where solicitors are giving advice, and they may help with intake and writing the advice given to be sent to the client after checking by the supervisor. In some clinics (such as CLOCK) students are supervised to give or refer for advice. Finally there are trainee lawyers on professional practice courses who may be able to offer representation under supervision. And, moving beyond educational institutions, there is also some training, supported, for example, by LawWorks, in specific areas of work for practising solicitors wishing to offer pro bono help outside their own area of practice. We set out in some detail four examples of the approach taken in preparing students for entry into to pro bono work through support work in a university court help desk.[18]

We start with a description of the training for participating in a court help desk offering support: The Family Court Project. This consisted of a two hour session for first or second year students interested in participating, of whom perhaps half would be selected to do so. The 'pracademic' began the training sessions by introducing the students to the project, to the role of a supporter, to the nature of the cases they would be helping, and to the relevant terminology. The students are able to help on the days when a FHDRA (First Hearing Dispute Resolution Appointment) in children cases is heard, as for these the procedure is designed to be accessible without legal representation, and the aim is to encourage parents to reach agreement about the care of their children under the watchful eye of the Cafcass welfare officer and judge or magistrate. Next, the students were asked to

---

[18] We are most grateful to the clinic organisers who shared their teaching notes with us, as this provides the clearest indication of how aims and activities are explained and planned.

'begin thinking about the needs of LiPs at the cases they would be supporting and how they can support them WITHOUT GIVING ADVICE' and to think about their motivation. They were reminded that the experience will look good on a CV, that it will be exciting to work with real people and that practical work helps with understanding the academic courses. The welfare presumption in the Children Act 1989, what a child arrangements order is, the concept of safeguarding and the necessary legal terms are all explained. The students are then given a practical exercise. They are asked to think about what the different parties might want from the hearing. For example, the mother may want to explain her fears, the father may want a contact order now, the judge to know what the issues are, and Cafcass to ensure safeguarding. Then the group discusses how to manage a LiP's expectations, such as by helping them to understand that they may not get a decision on the day, but will know that the court wants what is best for the child. They learn how to help the clients prepare what they want to say to the judge. Finally the lecturer/pracademic checks that the students understand the difference between advising on the merits of the case and giving practical support. This will need to be revisited 'every time they go to court because as they get more confident they are more likely to want to advise'.

The students are then tested on the terms, and those selected for the project (only half of those applying to take part are usually accepted) are given a handbook. This covers the tasks to be undertaken, the first being for students to explain to a client that they are being offered free and confidential support to LiPs at a FHDRA. The handbook sets out the kinds of orders which can be made: A Child Arrangement Order concerning who will be the primary carer, and who will have contact; a Prohibited Steps Order and a Specific Issue Order. The FHDRA will be followed if necessary by a Dispute Resolution Appointment (DRA) and a Final Hearing (FH).The students are advised to check that the clients have a MIAM, as legally required, with some exceptions.

By the time of the hearing the court should have the forms C100 and C1A, if relevant, Notice of the Hearing, C7 and C1A Response if relevant, Position Statements, and a Cafcass Safeguarding letter. The FHDRA will consider safeguarding by looking to the contents of the Cafcass letter and deciding whether to disclose this to the parties. If it has not been received there will be an adjournment. There may be a Finding of Fact hearing, risk identification and active case management with a Practice Direction, MIAM, a Consent Order, a Wishes and Feelings report, Case Management Allocation, and CAP02, the Order itself.

A dress code is given (chewing gum is forbidden) and directions given on how to get to the court. At court a lead student will identify LiPs and offer the service information leaflet, making clear that it is a free and confidential service. Students must tell their client that they can explain court process, help plan what to say to the judge, make sure parties have sent the correct forms to court, wait with them until called into court, take notes in the courtroom, provide a written summary of what has happened and the next steps, and explain that the service is free and confidential. They must then explain court procedure. If LiPs are in court for the first time, the service can assist greatly by explaining terminology, which will have a positive effect on the litigant. The student will need to confirm which court to go to, explain how this hearing is to provide an opportunity for parties to be helped to an understanding of the issues which divide them and to reach agreement if possible, and that if an agreement is reached, the court will make an order, and will assist parties so far as it is able to put it into effect in a cooperative way. If no agreement is reached, the student must explain that the court will explore the next steps to take, explain the role of Cafcass, say where to sit, say that the applicant will be spoken to first, then the respondent, and advise that, if they want to speak, they should interject politely: 'excuse me sir/madam ...'.

The lead students go first to the Family Court Project's room, check the leaflets are available, and work with the usher to identify LiPs, allocating a team member as required, and checking with the university supervisor. If the student is placed with a litigant, they should wait with them, complete the Family Court Project form, whereby a LiP accepts the service, check they have all the documents, and check that there is a position statement, or if not, prepare what to say. They then go in and help the LiP to be seated, explain at the end of the hearing what happened, quickly check with the supervisor, and give the leaflet with their written reminder of what the court has ordered, and introduce the LiP to the university Legal Advice Centre if necessary. They MUST NOT share a confidential order, or tweet – it may be a criminal offence. The student must get the litigant to sign the disclosure section on the FHDRA checklist otherwise they cannot support them, and must not leave a section of the checklist incomplete. If the LiP will not fill it in, the student must write that the LiP declined to provide information. Students are told not to leave the LiP alone too long, and not to give out the service leaflet without being checked by the supervisor. This concentrated preparation is reinforced with discussion with students at each session they attend and in feedback on their preparation of case summaries for parties in the leaflets completed at each session.

Other longer forms of preparation for second and third year students were described to us. They would enable a student to make a contribution in a legal advice clinic as well as a court help desk. A broader training is offered to CLOCK students[19] to become Community Legal Companions, aimed at enabling the student not only to help individual clients but to contribute to access to justice in the local community. This included a full day of training with local family practitioners on taking a history, checking for legal aid eligibility, helping with form filling and being given a file which contains not only copies of forms but also clear instruction on conflict of interest and confidentiality issues and client care. A further training day with local court staff enabled the students to offer skilled support to LiPs when they get to court, where they are much appreciated by the judiciary.[20] Careful recording of information about the client and the progress of

---

[19] See above pp 103–4.
[20] Ibid.

the case enables the university to contribute to research on legal need and access to justice.[21] But again there is continuing emphasis on the tasks which can be undertaken, and their boundaries. The key tasks are headed 'assistance' (not 'advice') with application forms, arranging paperwork, accompanying in formal proceedings and attending to take notes. CLOCK students are prepared for working with solicitors on intake, listening to advice being given, discussing and writing up what has been said, but are again continually reminded about not giving unsupervised advice. Each student is given information about the local CLOCK partner services provided by legal aid and fixed fee specialists, mediation services, charitable services for help with housing, family relationships, domestic abuse, asylum and refugee support, mental health issues, and also public services including the courts and police.

Other services are more clinic based, but in a university service calling itself a Legal Advice Centre, the client care information sheet states:

> The University Legal Advice Centre has been established to enable students studying at the University to obtain practical legal experience. Our students are studying degree level law: once they have completed their degree they will normally go on to undertake a further professional course and then undertake practical training for 1 to 2 years before qualifying. Our students are not professionally qualified and they will be working under the supervision of fully qualified lawyers. All our lawyers are fully qualified and are either university staff or volunteers living or working in the local community. The Centre's aim is to provide a high standard of service similar to that offered by any solicitors' practice. The Centre offers an advice only service. This means we cannot represent you in court or at any other hearing. However whenever possible we will refer you to an appropriate body or organisation. We do not offer assistance beyond initial advice, for example letter writing or form filling. We usually offer clients the chance to return for up to one further appointment. After this appointment we refer ALL clients to other sources of help.

A form accepting these terms must be signed by the client before help is given.

A small number of courts are helped by students in the postgraduate final stages of their professional law training. Trainee solicitors are able to offer an advocacy service, with practitioner supervision, as part of the 12 week Dispute Resolution Elective on their Legal Practice Course. Students on the Professional Skills Course which forms the final part of LPC training for solicitors may choose a Family Law elective which includes advocacy and practice and are also able to take part. The trainees are prepared and supervised for this short course by their University tutors. Students taking the family finance and advocacy option as part of the Bar Professional Training Course may take part in pro bono cases under their local Legal Advice Centre Full Representation Service.

In addition, for newly qualified solicitors, there is also some training by practitioners outside the formal education system, known as secondary specialisation

---

[21] See, eg, B Waters and J Ashton, 'Situated Learning through the CLOCK Community Legal Companion Scheme', Paper given to the ALT Conference at the University of Portsmouth, April 2017.

training. This will enable them to carry out pro bono work in an area of law where the need for pro bono work has expanded, particularly family law, but which lies outside their usual area of practice, which may be commercial or property law. Again, mixed motives are present, in that a law firm may want to develop the young lawyers' client handling skills as well as enhance the socially responsible profile of a large city firm, while the young lawyers value the additional training and experience as well embracing the pro bono ethic. This form of secondary specialisation training is offered free to participants through LawWorks, carried out by experienced specialist practitioners and is able to equip a practitioner with the necessary skills after a single intensive session. High quality reference materials are provided, plus access to LexisNexis Library which enables a practitioner affiliated to LawWorks to access the materials needed for practice in a new area, including recent cases, template letters and orders and relevant recent judgments. For family work, LawWorks offers three sessions a year in Private Law Proceedings. We were able to observe one evening session covering Child Arrangements Orders, Prohibited Steps Orders, MIAMs and exemptions, Specific Issue Orders, and the new forms being used known as the Tick Boxes. During the second half of the evening we observed training on domestic abuse issues, conducting fact finding, DRA and final hearing, then discussion of three key cases on contact.

V. Conclusions on Student Pro Bono Activity

We have at several points in this book described the role of students in pro bono activity,[22] drawing on interviews and observations with practitioners and students. We in this chapter so far focused on its nature, organisation and extent of effectiveness in filling the shortfall in access to justice in family matters after LASPO. We conclude by reflecting on its potential value for the students themselves, and give some final examples of its potential benefit for LiPs.

The value for students is that, in addition to traditional legal study, it confers a taste of what it is actually like to practise in this area of law, including interaction with client groups. For example, the strength of the CLOCK scheme described in chapter six lies in its community outreach orientation. Students enjoy seeing how law works in the real world. We met students seen earlier in the day playing football in their jeans later in the afternoon sitting at the court desk in their suits, asking 'do we look like solicitors?' They not only looked like lawyers, but, with their extensive training in practice from local practitioners, they were able to be helpful as quasi outdoor clerks to local practitioners, even contributing to successful applications for legal aid on human rights grounds, and standing as CLCs beside anxious parties both before, during and after court involvement, trusted by court

---

[22] See eg pp 70–7, 102, 115–6.

staff, sliding their laptops out of the locked cupboards in the court lobby ready to work with parties.

We saw students arriving for an evening advice clinic, setting up tables, setting out the forms, looking after a nervous client for an hour until the solicitor finally arrived, taking the history and then offering supportive comments to the client at the end of the solicitor's fast and highly technical and specific advice session. Afterwards they discussed with the solicitor the advice he had given in preparation for writing up a letter of advice to be sent by the solicitor. At another university we spoke to a group of grandmothers with Special Guardianship Orders who were caring for grandchildren whose parents (their children) had serious problems, often mental health or substance abuse issues, and who had asked if any students might help them with the repeated issues arising over applications for more contact, and how to deal with autism and attention deficit. The ladies said that the students were just observing: 'they can't do anything, but they can sit with us in court', and one said:

> I prefer it to a free half hour with a law firm because the students are learning as well … the solicitor can tell us what might happen, what we should be saying to social services and what we shouldn't, it's a struggle, the stress … but the clinic, they put us on the right road. Now we help teach the social work students and we wrote a book.

At a third university clinic we saw a well-funded service in lavish premises, setting up a new link with local health services as their main source of referrals, following ideas about the links between stress and health developed earlier in Australia. But sadly the family practitioner had left, and the co-located general medical practice was not making referrals as expected with the result that there were few clients. The two students present were working on data for the evaluation project.

We also observed a young trainee solicitor from a large corporate city firm who was nearing the end of his final advocacy placement prior to taking up a position abroad in finance in the Middle East. He was very professional in appearance, and could easily be mistaken for a young barrister. After checking with the supervising solicitor from his course, he quickly made contact with a very nervous Asian mother in a contact case, where the father, who had shown little interest in the child since leaving the marriage soon after the birth, was now asking for contact 12 years later. The mother's view was that he was doing this because of a problem with his leave to stay in the country. Without any preparation, the trainee quickly gained his client's confidence. The father had not yet arrived at court, some hours after the appointed time of the hearing. When he finally arrived, the hearing began. The Cafcass officer acknowledged the child's need to be involved with both parents but wished to assess the father's parenting capacity. Questions had been raised about the father's mental state. There were drug issues and some domestic abuse allegations. The trainee carried out excellent advocacy, with tight and effective cross-examination about a possibly falsified letter attributed by the father to the mother in support of his residence application problem. A date was set for a further hearing when the Cafcass report would be in and both parents would have had time to respond. Without this advocacy, the mother's position would have been extremely difficult. However, the problem of continuity of help arose as the trainee will have left the country before the next hearing date. But the supervisor arranged for the mother to call and make an appointment before the next hearing.

These brief examples offer an idea of the variety and difficulty of the people being supported and represented by students and trainees. Although the numbers helped in full are small, the motives of the students and their institutions are mixed, and the organisational and regulatory structures for this pro bono help are labyrinthine, it is clear that a contribution to access to justice is being made, though it is possible that the greater benefit may lie in the learning process.

We end with a comment on the most successful scheme, in our view, for both students and clients. This clinic combined pro bono professional legal advice with student support in court. The organiser was in an academic university post dedicated to CLE and held a practising certificate as a family solicitor. He had established a close working relationship with the local court, had a group of enthusiastic and well trained students with whom he spend two hours week in small groups, workshopping the experience. On FHDRA days students were able to identify LiPS, take their history, offer a meeting with the lawyer before their hearing, and take them into a side room in court for legal advice from the solicitor. The student would stay and hear the advice, which often covered the client's aims and strategy for the hearing, but also stressed the need to remember that the court is interested in the welfare of the child, not the misdemeanours of either parent, and to speak to the judge, not to the other party. Sometimes more complex and technical legal advice was needed and given, but this basic message, delivered with authority and kindness was highly effective. The service as a whole could support 8 to 10 cases per day.

The FHDRA day is of course designed to be accessible to lay participants, and contained within a single hearing. This facilitates effective use of CLE time and resources. The other outstanding service we observed, CLOCK, had a broader remit, working with local practitioners and the court over the length of a case. The outcome for extended activity is harder to measure. But the data currently being collected will mean that a great deal can be learned about the needs of these clients and what can help them. The current proposals from the Solicitors' Regulation Authority[23] to unify and extend the route to qualification as a solicitor, to be known as the Solicitors Qualifying Examination, with an increased emphasis on practical experience, is likely to enhance the place of CLE in the qualification process.

---

[23] See above p 121.

9

The Third Sector

I. Introduction

The activities described in previous chapters have all made a valuable contribution to attempts to 'close the gap' in support for access to family justice after LASPO. But their combined efforts cannot resolve the acute continuing problem of unmet need set out in the evidence referred to in chapter one and referred to in the Memorandum submitted by the Ministry of Justice to Parliament's Justice Committee as the first stage in the post-implementation review of the Act.[1] This leaves unaddressed the call made in 2017 in the Final Report of the Commission[2] chaired by Lord Bach, former Minister in the Ministry of Justice with responsibility for legal aid, to bring some areas of civil law, including family law, back into the scope of legal aid, with a focus on early legal help in order to prevent problems developing down the track,[3] and for a Right to Justice Act to be monitored and enforced by a new independent commission.

Similarly, the Low Commission, which confined itself to the impact of LASPO on social welfare law, in a first report published in 2014,[4] called for a 'fresh approach, which involves measures to reduce the need for advice and legal support in the first place, while developing more cost-effective approaches to service provision, both centrally and locally drawing on a wider range of funding sources than hitherto'. In a second report, published in March 2015,[5] the Low Commission raised questions about the impact of the LASPO on the non-profit advice sector, including the availability of specialist advice, and re-iterated its earlier suggestion that there should be a National Strategy for Advice and Legal Support, supported by a ten-year National Advice and Legal Support Fund to be administered by the Big Lottery Fund and (among other things) that local authorities should work with

---

[1] See pp 1–2.
[2] Bach Commission, *The Right to Justice: Final Report of the Bach Commission*, Fabian Society, London, September 2017.
[3] ibid, Recommendations 11 and 12.
[4] Low Commission, *Tackling the Advice Deficit: A strategy for access to advice and legal support on social welfare law in England and Wales* (Legal Action group, 2014) https://www.lowcommission.org.uk/dyn/1389221772932/Low-Commission-Report-FINAL-VERSION.pdf (last accessed 9 June 2018).
[5] Low Commission, *GETTING IT RIGHT IN SOCIAL WELFARE LAW: The Low Commission's follow-up report* (Legal Action Group, 2015) http://www.lowcommission.org.uk/dyn/1435772523695/Getting_it_Right_Report_web.pdf (last accessed 9 June 2018).

their local advice sector to co-produce ten-year local advice and legal support plans to ensure the provision of a basic level of information and advice, including some face-to-face and some legal support, through a combination of local funding and support from the National Advice and Legal Support Fund. A similar approach has been advocated for Scotland.[6]

This emphasis on advice and the role of the non-profit sector leads us to turn to that sector (known as the Third Sector) as the final potential source of legal help in family matters. This territory lies between state and market, linked with both but controlled by neither. The contribution of voluntary organisations to the provision of legal advice has formed a longstanding and valued part of the complex web of provision of information, advice and support across many areas of social need. But concerns have been raised about changing policy attitudes to this contribution in recent years. A recent report from the Third Sector European Policy Network at the University of Kent, where Dr Jeremy Kendall has carried out a number of comparative studies measuring third sector impact across Europe,[7] describes a change in England and Wales towards linking political interest in the Big Society under the Cameron administration with promoting voluntary activity as an alternative to state intervention, rather than following their historical role of identifying new needs, developing new services and supporting policy development. Where third sector organisations are still involved in giving legal advice, such as at law centres, this is primarily aimed at poverty-related problems, such as benefit entitlement, debt, homelessness, and employment, seldom touching on family matters.[8]

Given the relatively generous scope and provision of public funding for family legal help from the setting up of the legal aid scheme after World War II up to 2012, it is not surprising that the third sector, though developing legal expertise, had remained focused on the primary issue of immediate material needs. A variety of charities operate in this sector, and in the aftermath of LASPO, the Ministry of Justice set out to describe third sector activity which offered legal advice by commissioning a *Survey of Not for Profit Legal Advice Providers in England and Wales* by Ipsos Mori which was published in 2015.[9] The study used a number of public listings to identify 1,462 providers of legal advice, of which 718 (almost one half) took part in the study. They broke down into: 186 (26 per cent) Citizens Advice, 149 (21 per cent) Advice UK, 76 (11 per cent) Age Concern,

[6] M Evans, *Re-thinking Legal Aid: An Independent Strategic Review (of Legal Aid in Scotland)* (February 2018).

[7] See E Hogg, J Kendall and B Breeze, 'Knitting together? the third sector and the state in England' (2015) *Sociologia e Politiche Sociali* 27.

[8] See P Alcock, 'A Strategic Unity: Defining the Third Sector in the UK' (2010) 1(1) *Voluntary Sector Review* 5.

[9] A Ames, W Dawes and J Hitchcock, *Survey of Not for Profit Legal Advice Providers in England and Wales* (Ipsos Mori for Ministry of Justice, 2015). https://assets.publishing.service.gov.uk/government/uploads/system/uploads/attachment_data/file/485636/not-for-profit-la-providers-survey.pdf (last accessed 11 June 2018).

37 (5 per cent) Youth Access, 24 (3 per cent) Law Centres and 56 (8 per cent) Other and 190 (26 per cent) None. While this was an achieved rather than representative sample, it is probable that similar proportions would be found for the country as a whole. Significantly for our purposes, less than a quarter (24 per cent) of all the agencies studied were able to offer advice with family problems at that time, which was immediately after LASPO. Only 9 of the 62 Law Centres listed as members of the Law Centres Network in 2017[10] were able to offer family advice as law centres share the advice sector traditional focus on poverty: debt, access to benefits, homelessness and employment issues.[11]

94 per cent of the agencies responding to the Ipsos Mori researchers reported having professional indemnity insurance and were accredited as reaching the Advice Quality Standard of the Advice Services Alliance[12] or Citizens Advice Membership. But the anxieties referred to earlier about professional indemnity insurance when giving pro bono legal advice or assistance in court appear to be less troubling in the advice sector, which exists to give advice, and has a robust attitude to how it is to be defined and how quality can be assured. The study defined advice as the provision of information which identifies options and may include giving some help towards the next steps for the client, such as by helping to fill in forms. This is based on the Advice Services Alliance definition that 'any advice which involves interpreting how the law applies to a client's particular problem or set of circumstances is legal advice'. A distinction is drawn in the study between advice and casework, whereby the latter involves action on behalf of the client in carrying out negotiation or advocacy. The final element in what is sometimes called by members of the legal profession 'full legal service', that is, legal representation, is defined as acting as a representative for the client in a court or tribunal. This is rarely available in the third sector for family matters.

The third sector agencies which were providing legal advice were long established (the majority for over 10 years) but were expecting change as a result of LASPO. Some expected to limit their activity: 10 per cent expected to close in the coming year, 13 per cent to merge, and 25 per cent to reduce their activities. On the other hand, others were planning to try to respond to increased demand: 42 per cent described expanding their geographical area of activity and 15 per cent

---

[10] See http://www.lawcentres.org.uk/about-law-centres (last accessed 11 June 2018). Julie Bishop, Director of LCF, gave 2 as the number of Law Centres offering family legal advice (personal communication, July 2018).

[11] See M Mayo, G Koessel, M Scott and I Slater, *Access to Justice for Disadvantaged Communities* (Policy Press, Bristol University, 2015) which describes the Law Centre movement as seeing access to law as the way to access all rights, and top heavy with lawyers, while funders had expected more to be done by lower cost paralegals. Attempts at collaboration by lawyers have not often been successful, as the problems of CLACs and CLANs noted earlier showed. Law Centres share the political agenda of the welfare rights movement which drives so many not-for-profit organisations, but at the same time retains some of the traditional (elitist?) working practices of the traditional law firm with a focus on the individual expertise of the professional.

[12] An umbrella body of national networks of not-for-profit organisations that provide advice and help on the law, access to services and related issues.

expected to enter new areas of law. Some had been assisted under the government's contribution of £33 million to the National Lottery's Advice Services Transition Fund available over the first two years after LASPO.[13] But the ability to respond to increased need for legal help after LASPO was constrained for these agencies by the ongoing impact of a long period of austerity, with cuts in local government funding and in the funds available from the larger charitable foundations on which most of them were relying. This impact is clearly demonstrated by the fact that, by the time of the survey, half were sharing premises with another agency, and three quarters had made formal referral agreements with other agencies as their ability to advise directly became reduced. It appears that it is the medium sized agencies which are hit hardest, with the large and small organisations faring better.[14]

The advice agencies were clearly already in a vulnerable position when LASPO presented the challenge of adding family justice, a new large and complex additional area of work, to their list of activities at a time when they were severely stressed. As a result of cuts to core funding, many were moving unhappily from regular grant income for core activities from a local authority to short-term contracting for specific projects where evidence of meeting the targets pre-set by the funder are used as the key measure of successful outcomes, and can unduly influence the work done, limiting flexibility and development of new ideas. And where an agency could do no more than refer family matters to others better able to help, even the work of referring family justice matters was problematic as it was likely that cuts were also being made in the agencies to whom they might wish to refer.

The strength of the advice sector, however, lies in its expertise in the specific task of giving advice, not necessarily in an area in which its practitioners personally have high levels of specialist knowledge, but where they have the materials they need in order to look for and make good use of helpful information. A trained advice worker will elicit the nature of the problem, collect the relevant information and give appropriate advice about the client's options and the next steps to take, recording the circumstances described and the actions taken, much like a solicitor taking an attendance note. They are less likely to agonise over whether their insurance will cover the matter, or whether their own area of expertise is sufficient to enable them to help. Their experience of battling for the vulnerable individual in need of help against the larger forces of state, local authority, employer and others against the odds, may provide a more robust starting point for offering advice than the personal anxieties of a legal professional working pro bono in an area beyond his or her competence. An advice agency usually assumes that advice will be given face-to-face, assisted by access to websites, together with reliance on colleagues for support. Effective use of links with high quality Public Legal Education materials

---

[13] See p 30.
[14] Personal communication from Lindsay Poole, CEO of the Advice Services Alliance.

and the support of volunteers with administration, has created a determined workforce, committed to action, with impact not only for individual clients but for the wider community they serve.

II. Observational Data

In our attempts to understand the contribution of the third sector, we spoke with and observed the work of a number of organisations. We begin with a description of the Child Poverty Action Group (CPAG), which offers policy analysis to stimulate governmental awareness of the issues but does not conduct casework. We then look at Citizens Advice (CA), starting with our observations at their headquarters, where staff are working to develop the online material needed by their local franchised individual CAs and to contribute to the policy debate, and then give an account of a CA funded project supporting a family legal adviser in a court in a north-eastern urban area. We then describe the work of a local independent advice centre in a very disadvantaged community trying to add family legal support to its work on poverty and immigration in a Midland city. After that, we describe the work of a specialist pressure-group charity working to improve understanding of the legal needs of a growing group of lone parents with family justice issues, using a helpline, information sheets and secondary legal support. Finally, we describe an energetic self-help group, the Liverpool Nans, who provide support for members who are caring for grandchildren under SGOs and involved in court cases, helped by a local university-based advice service.

We also spoke to Rights of Women, a high profile group who, among other things (eg training and policy work, sometimes involving litigation[15]) offer advice and information relating to the legal rights of women in difficulty, mostly in family and immigration matters. Initial telephone advice is provided by qualified lawyers, and inquirers are referred on where necessary, and legal aid may be available in domestic violence cases. However, the lines are open only for limited periods and there is lack of information about how many calls cannot be answered. The choice between quantity and quality of provision remains unsolved.

A. The Child Poverty Action Group (CPAG)

We begin with the central concern of the traditional advice sector, the alleviation of poverty, and in particular, child poverty, through the traditional social policy process of identifying a social need and asking government to respond. The starting point has always been the need to support the individual against the state both in achieving access to existing benefits and also improving the level of provision

---

[15] See eg *R (Rights of Women) v Secretary of State for Justice* [2016] EWCA Civ 91.

on a national level. But the welfare rights movement was not traditionally involved in the private disputes between individuals which characterise family matters. For them, family matters are a new and difficult area, where, instead of supporting the vulnerable individual against the greater power of the state, the employer or the landlord, they are brought into disputes between two individuals, where it is not clear whether they should support both and risk a conflict of interest, or just one or neither.

The CPAG does not provide individual advice, and has lost its legal aid contract for second tier social security tribunal work. But it remains a powerful voice in presenting the facts and raising awareness of child poverty. The CPAG *Cost of a Child 2017* Report demonstrates that, while benefits will have risen by 3 per cent between 2012 and 2019, prices will have risen by 12 per cent. Benefit entitlement and access is the cornerstone of their work. But when the cost of a child became the subject of policy debate during the development of the Child Support legislation,[16] CPAG was able to provide information on the costs of single parenting, and has increased awareness of what they call 'family change issues' in the onset of child poverty. The recent report from CPAG with the Trussell Trust and others on the use of food banks identified 'Family Change and Bereavement' as a 'significant life shock which played a key role on triggering food bank referral'.[17] Examples in the report included a woman left by an abusive partner without income, a woman in her 50s separating from her husband who was a farmer thus losing home and income, as well as young mothers leaving abusive relationships. The report concludes that 'change in relationship status is fundamentally disruptive, affecting housing, finances and social support networks … the resulting upheaval can have a negative knock-on effect on physical and mental health and personal resilience, particularly where the relationship breakdown has involved domestic violence'. But they add 'many of the practical arrangements can be assisted by constructive steps', including advice. Sadly, many of these food bank users had not had formal advice but had relied on family and friends.

The researchers had expected to find emergency situations, such as repossession, to be the immediate cause of food bank use, a key measure of extreme poverty, but this was not the case. The main causes were delays in benefit receipt, sanctions, the Department of Work and Pensions' 'hollowing out' of job centres, relying on hot phones and digital interaction, scripted help lines, lack of local knowledge, and the chaos associated with the introduction of Universal Credit. CPAG has now added family change to their list of major causes of child poverty, and, while not giving individual advice, remains a high profile and reliable provider of second-tier advice to advisers through their *Welfare and Benefits and Tax Credits Handbook 2017–2018* (available in hard copy or on line for £61) and

---

[16] See above p 20–3.

[17] J Perry, M Williams, T Sefton and M Hadda, *Emergency Use Only: Understanding and reducing the use of food banks in the UK* (Child Poverty Action Group with the Church of England, OXFAM GB, and the Trussell Trust, London, 2014) 33: https://www.trusselltrust.org/wp-content/uploads/sites/2/2016/01/foodbank-report.pdf (last accessed 11 June 2018).

Universal Credit: What you need to know (4th edition, £15), advertised as easy to use, jargon free and including useful examples.[18]

Current activities include employing a solicitor to develop ASK CPAG, an advice tree, and to work on cases where the personal liabilities of cohabitants on joint loans can be established, and other personal finance issues linked to separation and family change. Sadly, though CPAG had expected greater demand for help with family law related financial issues, the demand has instead fallen as the agencies who used to refer cases to them are 'going under' and those remaining are less able to refer to specialists for advice and the quality of advice is falling. However, organisations helping with benefit claims are better able than other forms of intervention to demonstrate their effectiveness. For example, by using two workers in two food banks, CPAG advisers were able to demonstrate that they had assisted users in accessing £8,000 due to them.[19]

B. Citizens Advice (CA) Headquarters

If we turn from the work of policy and campaigning alone to combining this function with offering individual advice, the organisation most frequently represented in the Ministry of Justice Survey of Not-for-Profit Legal Advice Providers was Citizens Advice. The organisation was set up in 1939 in order to help the population cope with the impact of wartime bombing raids, and included mobile units. By 1979 there were more than 800 independent CA Bureaux, each a separately registered charity. The numbers are now much reduced, to just over 300. The Survey included 149 of the 307 bureaux, which formed 24 per cent of the total sample. Again, as we find across the advice sector, the top five issues for the organisation were benefits, debt, consumer issues, housing and employment. But according to its Annual Report for 2016–17, the fifth largest subject accessed is now 'relationships', with 6.2 million contacts over the previous year.[20]

This is not surprising for those working in family justice who are familiar with the rapid and direct impact of relationship breakdown, especially where children are involved, on where you live, your income needs, your mental as well as physical health, your ability to hold down a job, and more. CA is becoming increasingly aware of the links between the needs they traditionally addressed and the importance of being able to help those who need support with the legal implications of family issues. For example, following a divorce, is liability for various debts joint or several or joint and several? Is a house in joint names an asset to be shared or does it belong to the person who put down the deposit and pays the mortgage? When does a separating partner cease to be a member of the household for tax credit or

---

[18] Also available from CAPG 30 Micawber Street London N1 7TB.

[19] Hogg, Kendall and Breeze (n 7).

[20] Citizens Advice, *Annual Report 2016/7*, 7: https://www.citizensadvice.org.uk/Global/Citizens Advice/citizens%20advice%20annual%20report.pdf (last accessed 10 June 2018).

universal credit purposes?[21] How might child arrangements affect these issues? These are in practice family justice issues.

Like CPAG, CA is both an effective campaigning organisation and a major direct service provider. As an organisation where all 307 CA services are separate charities in a franchised relationship with Headquarters, it is not easy to see how the pattern of service provision is developing across the service as a whole. But the legal adviser at Head Office has noted the increase in requests for help with family matters since LASPO. There is a recognition that not all these new requests for help can be handled face-to-face at a local CA, and nor can referral to a specialist always be arranged. CA advisers have always used centrally designed websites in order to give information and advice across their key areas, even when face-to-face advice was more available. But since 2013 it has been imperative to work on developing the family justice content of the CA websites, both the Advisernet used by staff and made available for a fee to other advice agencies (£590 to voluntary organisations, £1,500 to Advice Services) and also the outward facing guidance accessible to the public via https://www.citizensadvice.org.uk/. The 2016–17 Annual Report records 43 million visits to online advice, but only 1.8 million face-to-face and 1.6 million telephone contacts.[22] Headquarters reported a 50 per cent increase in hits to the website on family matters in the second quarter of 2016, with 65,000 hits.

Because there is little choice as public services continue to decline, they are working hard on developing digital advice technology for resource reasons, even though they are aware that their users have a higher rate of low IT competence than the general population. They say that 'it's not us or lawyers for our people, it's us or nothing …'. But they also emphasise that the CAs can offer more than just legal advice. They offer 'wrap around content' on family issues, a more holistic approach to the problems associated with family change (CPAG said this too when describing how relationship breakdown could lead to mental and physical health problems as well as the need to visit a food bank, and as CLACs and CLANs had hoped to do.[23]) They are hoping to improve on the information services currently in use in courts and offer a generic digital tool to help those presenting with the main family issue reported by their tracker system, that of ending a marriage.

The courts, however, are thought to take differing views on encouraging litigants to seek advice, some expressing concern if one side gets advice and the other does not. But CA is interested in trying to join up aspects of advice, trying to offer advice which reaches outside the current silo presentation of, for example, a website service for divorce, and a separate service for fee exemption. For probate, a digital service works well as there is a small and scattered population of users whom it would be difficult to meet face to face. Divorce, however, is more difficult as more than one party is involved. CA is always unhappy about advising two people who are in conflict. They give individual advice, not alternative

[21] Samuel Kirwan, personal communication, July 2018.
[22] ibid, 6.
[23] See above pp 29–30.

dispute resolution/mediation. For example, if both parties want a divorce but are in dispute about responsibility for debts and an adviser giving debt advice to one party recommended bankruptcy, this would drastically affect the other party's freedom of action. 'There is complexity in how you support people … if you stop one party going to court there may be equality issues as women are usually disadvantaged by divorce … even human rights issues'. CA have therefore been more interested in developing digital tools directed at a specific family problem, such as the CourtNav website for making application for divorce developed at the RCJCA,[24] always bearing in mind that there are levels of vulnerability and need for assistance with digital process.

At the level of policy development, rather than concentrating on specialists, CA would like to develop more general advice outside the regulated areas. They do not support the direction they believe the Solicitors Regulation Authority is taking towards greater regulation of the 'Rolls Royce' sector of professional accredited and regulated legal work, while ignoring the unregulated sector, particularly 'McKenzie Friends'. For general family law work in the CA the level of skill required is thought by Headquarters to be no higher than that required from a standard, experienced, CA adviser who needs to be able to identify the vulnerable in every area of their work. So there is thought to be no need of specialist legal training. Instead, the CA policy is to expect that bureaux should rely on solicitor backup built into the system either electronically (as in CourtNav) or in person.

Policy development at CA Headquarters is backed up by a research team who have produced high quality research reports by Katherine Vaughan, Imogen Parker and Laura Blunt. One entitled *Standing Alone* is about going to the family court without a lawyer,[25] and another, entitled *Responsive Justice*, is about how citizens experience the justice system.[26] The former gives a clear picture of the impact of LASPO in private family law through a small in-depth study of 16 LiPs, together with data from the Citizens Advice Network Panel which surveys over 600 staff and volunteers monthly across the country. The researchers report clear links between the experience of being a LiP and both physical and mental health issues, and 79 per cent of advisers had seen an increase in the number of people choosing not to follow up their issue, which they attribute to the complexity of the system and the lack of clear information and direction. Even those who were able to see a lawyer, particularly vulnerable clients (including victims of domestic abuse) need more information to make effective use of legal help. CA online information on

---

[24] See above pp 79–80.

[25] Citizens Advice, *Standing Alone: Going to the Family Court without a Lawyer* (2014) https://www.citizensadvice.org.uk/Global/CitizensAdvice/Crime%20and%20Justice%20Publications/Crime%20and%20Justice%20consultation%20responses/StandingAloneGoingtothefamilycourtwithoutalawyer finalversion.pdf (last accessed 11 June 2018).

[26] Citizens Advice, *Responsive Justice: How citizens experience the justice system* (2015) https://www.citizensadvice.org.uk/Global/CitizensAdvice/Crime%20and%20Justice%20Publications/Responsive justice.pdf (last accessed 11 June 2018).

family issues[27] is already of a high standard, clear and detailed, and also refers the user to AdviceNow materials and the Money Advice Service (MAS) with a link to the forms for help with court fees.[28] But in their campaigning role CA continue to present strong arguments, including those in this report, for improvements in the information and guidance provided by the court service (HMCTS).

C. Citizens Advice Local Project

We referred above to the franchising of the various independent members of Citizens Advice. The individual seeking advice on a family matter may find himself or herself at a busy office, shared by the CA with perhaps a Law Centre, neither of whom offer help with family matters.[29] But they will be referred to the nearest advice centre which can offer help with family matters. As a result of their dependence on local authority funding, CAs usually only helps those living within their local authority area. Kentish Town CA were able to refer to the specialist CA at the Central Family Court, but the advice centre referred to will not necessarily be a CA, but may be a university law clinic. At the other end of the spectrum there are CAs with special projects in the family area where, in the face of what they termed 'huge unmet need', and having past experience as a CLAC, in one case the CA succeeded in attracting funding of £20,000 from Access to Justice to appoint a Family Adviser for two days a week to run a Family Law Advice Clinic at the Combined Court, who will, according to the advertised job description, 'provide free and independent legal advice, practical support and guidance to vulnerable people involved in application to the Family Court Service'.[30] The project would run for eight months in the first instance with the possibility of renewal depending on evaluation. The help offered by the Clinic is described in the CA flyer as: (1) support through the court process; (2) help to fill in forms; (3) advice and information. They add: 'Our advice is always free, confidential[31] and independent and we always work in your best interest.'

The advertisement for the position did not specify that the post was to be held by a lawyer. In fact the person appointed came from the advice sector with an interest in family justice, but was not a member of either of the regulated

---

[27] See   https://www.citizensadvice.org.uk/family/ending-a-relationship/how-to-separate/deciding-what-to-do-when-you-separate/ (last accessed 11 June 2018) for access to advice on children and young people, ending a relationship, young people and family, child maintenance, child arrangements and family breakdown problems.

[28] https://www.gov.uk/get-help-with-court-fees (last accessed 11 June 2018). The MAS however is likely to be restructured with additional funding from the Financial Levy under the Single Finance Guidance Body.

[29] See above pp 134–5.

[30] As advertised in CHARITY JOB April 2017.

[31] As an impartial and independent charity, the term 'confidential' is used rather than 'client privilege' as they are not part of the court process, just using a room to give advice.

branches of the legal profession or a law graduate. The help offered resembles that provided by lay support services such as PSU or a student court help desk. The difference, however, lies in the promise and expectation of advice giving. This is not described on the form as legal advice, but in the context of an adviser working in a Family Law Advice Clinic based in the court and approved by the local judiciary, it might well be interpreted by a potential client that they could expect legal advice. The adviser attends for two long mornings each week, and by the time of our visit had dealt with 60 clients in the first six weeks of operation. Clients had been helped with a variety of issues, many concerning filling in forms (32 C100 forms, one interim relief application, and two C8 confidentiality forms). Over half of the clients had been helped to apply for help with court fees, one with public funding not covered by legal aid, and one with the cost of a transcript of previous proceedings needed in a subsequent hearing. 14 had been helped with the paperwork associated with child arrangements, four with variations of an order, three with Prohibited Steps Orders, two with parental responsibility applications, 12 with matters additional to ongoing proceedings, 10 concerning allegations of harm, and three with enforcement proceedings. There were also eight clients who needed help with a divorce petition, 12 who needed an explanation of mediation, and three of a SPIP course. Two had forms returned for correction, and many needed general support concerning court hearings or the role of Cafcass and social services, and help with contact centre forms.

The adviser calculated that the help with form filling she had provided as an adviser to families who could not afford a lawyer would have cost £17,000 if carried out by a local solicitor: a clear indication of effectiveness. She had been trained by court staff and found this experience-based contribution more helpful than the website format, Advisernet. Her help with LiPs was appreciated by the judiciary. During a morning spent observing the adviser's meetings with clients, she described her work as keeping people calm, enabling them to negotiate, dealing with the Local Authority and legal representatives for both parties and helping a client talk to their own barrister as a solicitor would have done. She was confident that her early intervention was helping people get to mediation, and that she was doing the things which court staff could not do. While she worried about the lack of interpreters in public law cases, she thought many private law cases don't really need the court. She had interesting ideas for working with local solicitors to set up a voluntary 'Future Court' which would consider a possible family solution prior to going to court. She hoped that, if a group of local solicitors put in a small contribution, perhaps £3,000 a year, it could happen. This could, however, raise issues about the application of an 'alternative' system of justice, similar to those that arise in the context of arbitration.[32]

She stressed the importance of getting information to the client to manage expectations and keep them calm. That morning she had seen an

[32] See p 179.

East European/English couple who had been together happily for 12 years, but were now both so homesick that they wanted to live in their home countries, but it would cost £500 to divorce. The next client had been a grandmother with parental responsibility who needed an early hearing to renew a child's passport but could not find the mother. Two clients came by appointment. The first was a mother wanting a Consent Order as her daughter wanted to stop seeing her father, saying she was scared of him (five years after the separation). She had been sharing the children 50/50 but had been to court to ask for 80/20 as this child was so upset. But the school had brought in social services, and the court had sent the child to the father pending a second hearing in a few days' time while seeking an independent psychiatric report on the mother, who now only saw her child once a week. The adviser said to her that she could make a position statement saying why she was not going to be able to get the report, but that she would have to ask her own doctor to write what he could for her. An independent psychologist's report on underlying personality could cost £2,000. Her new partner was present and supportive. The mother asked the adviser: 'will you help me? I'm dyslexic'. The adviser said: 'dictate it to me, then take it home and think about it and come back to me, you have the phone number'. She also suggested a McKenzie.[33] The couple left, agreeing to come back with the position statement at the end of the week. After they left, the adviser commented that the she was not sure how well it was understood in court that now, after LASPO, in the absence of legal aid, the mother would have to pay for this kind of report herself.

The second client was a young Asian girl, with a toddler, whose former partner was seeking increased contact. The father had moved away, and not shown interest in the child until recently when he had a problem with his residence status. The adviser told her how to apply for legal aid and ask for a Child Arrangements Order. The young mum said she would ask the Sharia council about it and then said: 'Shall I tell you what the Sharia council tells me and then I can make sure with you?' The adviser answered firmly: 'I can't advise you. Try legal aid first.' So, in a Family Law Advice Clinic situated in the court and run by Citizens Advice with a flyer in court stating: 'Our advice is always free confidential and independent', the Family Adviser needed to end a meeting in which she helped a woman with an urgent problem to manage her difficult relationship with the court by saying 'I can't advise you' and advising legal aid on a matter in which legal aid was unlikely to be available.

D. An Independent Local Community Advice Centre

We turn now to an independent local community advice centre in a very disadvantaged area of a prosperous city in the West Midlands which was established

---

[33] See above pp 113–7.

40 years ago and has a paid staff of a manager and five trained advisers. They prefer not to use student helpers as in their view it is not worth the time and effort training them. The local council provides the premises at a nominal rent. Over the year 2016–17, the centre had managed client debt of over £2.5 million, and achieved £1.5 million worth of financial gain for clients. Their aims are to ensure best practice in the delivery of free, independent and confidential advice by maximising income through welfare benefit take up; encouraging long-term sustainable plans to tackle debt; enabling people to remain in their own homes and empowering people within their own community.

General advice, which the manager describes as 'substantial advice', is offered as a drop-in service, while appointments are needed for specialist advice. A free legal advice session clinic is provided 'courtesy of' a local firm of solicitors where a solicitor (often a trainee) comes to the Centre once a fortnight for the afternoon. They also refer to the free clinic at a local law firm where a lawyer gives a free 30 minute session once a week on areas of law the staff do not cover themselves, and they refer legally aided cases to a local firm. Six per cent of issues are recorded as 'family'. There is also a trainee solicitor working part time in the centre. The centre is funded by the local authority together with a consortium of housing associations (who benefit when rents become payable again). Unlike CAs which rely on volunteers doing intake and paid caseworkers on specific tasks, this Centre has paid caseworkers/advisers delivering the bulk of the service, which is casework, not just giving information and advice. Some volunteers with the relevant skills and training are able to do casework. But for the Centre to reach the Advice Quality Standard (AQS) for casework in benefits, debt and housing it has to show that the advisers carried out work in these areas for a minimum number of hours a week and in sufficient depth. The AQS attaches to the agency not to the individual worker, unlike the CA who have their own membership audit.[34] The manager emphasised that the quality of advice inevitably varies, but the emphasis is on monitoring the quality of the advice given, not who gives it. 'But the pro bono lawyers who come to our office to see our clients sit outside this. Their firm is responsible for the quality of their advice, and they are covered by their own PII. Similarly with solicitors when we refer client to them.'

The centre's advisers will undertake family work (70 cases in the past year, of which 20 went on to the pro bono solicitor) but do not see enough cases of sufficient variety to build up the expertise to reach the Advice Quality Standard. There were two domestic violence cases, but the remainder were mainly queries about divorce or child contact. A small number of housing issues are related to shared

---

[34] The AQS is an independently audited quality standard awarded to services delivering social welfare legal advice, held by 700 local services in England and Wales in 2017. It has requirements about how case files are kept and about experience and competence of advisers, and agencies are required to operate an internal file review procedure. Family related issues include domestic violence, child protection, contact, support issues, relationship breakdown and divorce, property rights and disposal of joint property after sale, housing after relationship breakdown or domestic violence, marriage and residence.

parenting issues. There are also issues around the payment of child maintenance. The advisers have access to Advisernet, which is comprehensive, with detailed guidance structured in a manner which relates directly to the way clients present their problems. It is not difficult to use, but does take time to go through all the steps, writing notes, and quoting paragraph numbers for reference. For example, the relationship breakdown section begins not with the word 'divorce' or 'lawyer' but says: 'if a couple no longer want to live together and are thinking of ending their relationship before making a decision they need to consider the following: any domestic violence issues, the type of relationship they have (married, cohabiting, civil partnership), whether a short term solution is required immediately, whether one partner needs to leave temporarily, whether they can discuss issues and reach agreement … if there are children, who will they live with, does the client have any money to live on if the partner leaves, will it be necessary to seek the help of the courts, how will family and friends react (ie will there be any support?)'. Information follows on mediation and arbitration. Then at paragraph 8.5 the practical matters to sort out are listed: income? is a solicitor needed? any specific religious or cultural considerations?

The website is underpinned by law but framed in a way that relates to client perceptions: it is cast within a sound legal framework but is user friendly. It is then made clear that the adviser may act on the client's behalf, may assist the client to act in person, may refer to another professional adviser, such as Gingerbread, and if a solicitor is needed, the client is asked to think what the solicitor will do for them, and advised to check accreditation if considering McKenzie Friends or PSU (but it is unclear how this could be done). The following sections address money issues, care of children, benefits, and who to inform of separation. At para 23 practical ways of ending the relationship are clearly set out: the client staying in the home? Or separating, but with both staying? Or, if the client is thinking of leaving, protecting the right to return, or staying with friends? Or applying as homeless? Only at this stage are the words 'separation', 'divorce', 'child support' and 'contact disputes' used. The approach is client centred, holistic and practical.

The centre staff reported that LASPO has had a major impact on their debt-related work, but that there has been less family work than expected because fewer people in this community marry, and if they do, they do not own property or have jobs, and a single mother with children is more likely to be avoided by the father(s) of her children in case child support is asked for, than pressed to give greater access to any children. The population served is in effect below the threshold for private family law.

E. Gingerbread

We move now from a local professionally staffed advice service willing to find and share legal information and provide both advice and casework, but with low demand for family legal help, to a high profile not-for-profit organisation known specifically for its support to single parents to see what can be done by a small but specialised pressure and support group, serving people from a wider socio-economic background, but focused specifically on lone parents. Gingerbread was founded in 1918 as The National Council for the Unmarried Mother and her Child. This title was shortened to One Parent Families, but the role of a top down policy and pressure group remained unchanged. The most recent change of name to Gingerbread indicates the move to more of a membership organisation, with emphasis on community-based mutual help and support while continuing to research and press for policy change.

Gingerbread campaigns for, researches about and helps single parents. They offer a telephone help line which provides support and expert advice on anything from dealing with a breakup to going back to work or sorting out child maintenance. For Gingerbread, LASPO has been followed by a major increase in the family legal calls received, and these are coming at a later and more complex stage in the problem when a lawyer is needed. They do not have a solicitor in house, but do have access to advice on difficult issues pro bono from a family barrister for the kind of secondary level consultation described by Ab Currie in Canada,[35] and can also refer callers to the Family Law Panel (FLP), a small group formed by practising solicitors and mediators who offer 30 minutes of free advice under this umbrella.[36] This is, however, subject to a comprehensive waiver set out in the Terms and Conditions referred to earlier.[37] Few clients are able to stay with the practitioner as paying clients. One solicitor quoted her rate of £400 per hour, but deals with about 30 cases a year through the FLP and finds that she is listening to what the caller says and then trying to interpret this in legal terms, often spilling over into housing or debt advice, and can refer on. But the FLP also run a Reduced Fees Scheme which aims to offer a more affordable legal advice service for people with an annual income of less than £20,000 and having less than 20,000 of accessible savings.

The Gingerbread website states: 'Our friendly advisers will talk through your option and send you useful information: your call is free and confidential'. Lines are open for at least half of every working day, manned by staff trained in advice giving but not legally trained or qualified. The section headed 'Getting legal help' begins: '[there are some situations when it is important to get legal help. Some examples could be if you are separating and need to sort out finances, if you could lose your home through repossession or eviction, or if either you or your child is in danger or at risk of being harmed.' It goes on: 'If you need legal advice it should always be given by a qualified person who has professional liability insurance, but it can be difficult to know how to find this help. Some services are free and some will charge … it has become more difficult to get legal aid, it only covers some kinds of

---

[35] See p 84.
[36] See p 63.
[37] Ibid.

legal problems and you need to be on a low income to qualify … The Gingerbread helpline cannot give legal advice, but this fact sheet gives you details of organisations that can give you legal advice or help you find it.' The list includes McKenzies, PSU, AdviceNow CA, Child Law Advice (operated by the Coram Children's Legal Centre), the Family Law Panel and others. The website also gives access to the various fact sheets which cover, for example, 'Parental responsibility … and Making Arrangements for your Children'.

The helpline adviser gave examples of calls received, describing her role as being legal, tactical and emotional, and saying how hard it is to reply without knowing about the other side of the story. In a conflict situation callers want support, saying: 'do you think what I'm doing is right?', which is what a lawyer can tell them, but the helpline cannot. The adviser said: 'they need advice and confidence, so we signpost to the FLP (Family Law Panel)'. But the helpline adviser was able to do something more important in securing a better outcome, in our view, which was to help callers understand what the law can and cannot do and why, and, in particular, to make clear that family law is about protecting and promoting the best interests of children rather than making adults into winners and losers in a dispute. The adviser said: 'When a woman says "He's got rights" I try to get them away from that power dynamic, where she thinks "I have to have his permission". The old terms are still in the callers' minds … they will google custody when they should say should say access and residence or parenting arrangements; they google the wrong terms.'

This seemed to be the kind of intervention which would help to keep people away from engaging in unproductive disputes in courts, and enable them to access the help of experienced specialists in finding the best possible outcome for their children. The helpline does not collect information on how callers find their way to Gingerbread. The advisers have no special legal training and do not mention legal aid, nor do they offer help with divorce petitions. But they do have Citizens Advice training and are not overly worried that they may be giving legal advice. The adviser said: 'We have Advisernet. And I refer to the fact sheets. They will call back and say "how do I make him give me a Consent Order?"; they don't understand it cannot be forced on someone. Sometimes they think it is one thing and it is another. They don't understand the information or what we can do … they want us to make him nice and normal'.

The helpline adviser's frustration is understandable, but having observed a range of interventions, this was the clearest attempt we observed to start from where the client is, to check for any need for immediate action, to listen to the story and to indicate what part the law can and cannot play, and where to go for further help. While we saw no undue anxiety about giving information and advice about legal events, they drew the line at predicting the outcome in a specific case. The adviser observed that: 'We can't give legal advice, that is, an opinion on what a court would do in a case. We can give principles, guidance, we don't want to mislead about possible outcomes. But we can help with the next step'. She would not wish to work with the PSU definition of support as helping the client to do what he or she has decided to do,[38] saying: 'What if she has decided the wrong thing? But I can do things like explain that if he is saying he will send a solicitor's letter it doesn't mean anything, it's just intimidation'.

We were able to listen to redacted anonymised tapes, where this well-informed, helpful common sense approach was clear. For example, a young mother, separated from her partner, who she described as not a bad man, but with a terrible temper, called to ask how she could make him give her a letter to prove that he had been seeing the counsellor about his temper, which he had promised to do before she agreed he should see their child. The adviser carefully explained that she had no right to that information, BUT 'it is about making sure your child is safe. Contact is about trust. If he is willing to give you the appointment letter saying he has seen the counsellor, that's fine; if you think your child is safe, that's fine; BUT if you are thinking about the way your child can be safe, you might look at supervised contact. The child would be safe and you would not be involved. The family law process starts with mediation, then you go to court for a Child Arrangements Order by consent if you agree. The court can impose seeing a counsellor, but you can't. You want to look at contact in a different way; would he?' And the conversation developed from there. There was a clear identification of the issue and a possible solution framed in a way that fits the Children Act welfare paramountcy test, and not as a fight between two adults, which fits well with Ministry of Justice's attempts to reduce conflict and keep people out of court.

Another caller said that she had been given the number by her local Citizens Advice, and wanted to know urgently how she could stop her ex-husband taking the children out of the country on holiday. They had managed to share care amicably for some years, but the husband had health problems which she thought put the children at risk if they travelled alone with him to a holiday out of the country. When she objected, he said he was going for custody and would get a C100 and stop paying child support. The adviser gently indicated that, as they share parental responsibility, neither can override the other, and if necessary she can go to court for a Prohibited Steps Order, but mediation comes first: 'the law is there to protect the children'. The caller described a change in the father recently after forming a new relationship, saying that they had been friends and 'everything was for the children … and now it isn't'. The adviser gently steered her towards mediation with a view to seeking a court order if necessary, making it clear that maintenance is separate from care, and that the court will look only at the interests of the children.

III. 'Advice' in the Third Sector

What we seemed to be seeing here was well-informed, authoritative and practical advice, at a pre-legal stage, supported by legal professionals in the background.

[38] See p 67.

This is a very promising route, but it must be difficult to be told 'we give you advice but we don't give you advice'. In a recent study of the work of Citizens Advice[39] as part of a four-year research programme, *New sites of legal consciousness: a case study of UK advice agencies* at the University of Bristol, Samuel Kirwan describes asking a group of CA advisers whether or not they gave legal advice. He describes some lack of clarity, but could see two groups. The first said they did not give advice and were noting the limits of what can be advised on, stopping at the Advisernet warning triangle which indicates when a legal issue has arisen. Others said that they *were* giving legal advice, as they saw advice work as communicating information derived from legal frameworks, saying, for example: 'when you say legal advice, people think solicitors, barristers, wigs and gowns, and formal letters. They don't realise that what they are coming to see is actual legal advice'. Others were less certain: 'it is advice on the law but not so much … we can only really advise them on how the law relates to the issue we've got, as opposed to delving into bits of law I don't understand'.[40]

The advisers were clear that giving advice does not mean telling people what to do. It is the provision of accurate and appropriate information in a language clients can understand, oriented towards enabling the client to make an informed decision. One worker put it is thus: 'we give them their options and we help them with the implications of pursuing those options, saying for example: "you are within your rights to do this, but this is the other side, what they can do to you … go away and think very carefully"'.[41] Kirwan has described the 'relational' work of advice in terms of 'constructing clarity' and 'constructing ownership': the former involves explaining legal concepts in everyday language and relating them to the problem at hand, allowing clients to 'move problems that arouse anxiety and distress to the abstract and impersonal field of options, procedures and consequences'; the latter 're-shapes' the client's emotions so that while regulations and responsibilities are drawn upon, attention is focused back on the client on what the might happen to them and what they can do about it: 'this is what could happen to you, rather than this is how the law defines your problem'.[42] Rather than taking an authoritative stance saying to the client 'just tell me your problems and I will give you the answer', the relational approach is harder, but more introspection will make it more possible to find a way through the difficulty. For example, in debt cases, the adviser cannot balance the budget, but can help the client by making it clear that creditors are not always as powerful as they think.

[39] S Kirwan, '"Advice on the law buy legal advice not so much": weaving law and life into debt advice' in S Kirwan (ed), *Advising in austerity: Reflections on challenging times for advice agencies* (Bristol, Policy Press, 2016).
[40] ibid, 149–50.
[41] ibid, 152.
[42] S Kirwan, 'The UK Citizens Advice service and the plurality of actors and practices that shape "legal consciousness"' (2016) 48 *The Journal of Legal Pluralism and Unofficial Law* 461.

As part of the same project, Morag McDermont and Eleanor Kirk[43] looked at the work of Citizens Advice in the area of employment disputes, which was then one of the top four fields of inquiry for Citizens Advice (the others being housing, debt and benefits), considering how volunteer advisers who in the most part do not have legal qualifications, or are at the margins of the legal profession, intervene in this highly legalised field. They noted that advisers 'were made to understand that it was not so much a matter of in-depth legal knowledge, but of using relational skills developed in other fields which enabled them to speak on behalf of clients, negotiating with those (the Council, employers) who frightened, frustrated or excluded their clients'. What was needed was the expertise of an *adviser*, not necessarily a lawyer. Once trained up the employment team became more interventionist, contacting employers to try to negotiate on their client's behalf:

> Our early involvement with cases has transformed the outcomes (…) two cases (…) got as far as a tribunal hearing. All the other cases we've taken on have settled. And in most instances it's helped to get the employer on board and it seems our involvement, far from being a negative, it's been an extremely strong positive (…). I think we brought in about £42,000 of compensation since the beginning of this calendar year. (Richard, Advice Service Manager)

This work moved away from the *specifics of law* to advice-giving as a skill developed in one field that could be translated into another. They were to become brokers, who could use the authority that the title 'CAB adviser' suggested, to negotiate settlements.[44] But there were difficulties and limitations. The work required time, skill and some degree of legal familiarity. Moreover, they point out that 'brokering only works if the employer is willing to communicate', or as one adviser put it, 'it takes two to tango, and if the employer doesn't dance, there's only one option'. If negotiation proved impossible, engaging with law's technicalities became essential.[45] That could be an important limitation in family disputes. Nevertheless, the scope for advisers who are not legal professionals to engage in a negotiation process on behalf of their client, using legal knowledge and undeterred by an imaginary 'red line' between providing information and advice, may be significant. The technique is currently being piloted with immigration and benefit overpayment cases which are both often interrelated to family matters.

---

[43] M McDermont and E Kirk 'Working in Law's Borderlands: Translation and the Work of an Advice Office' (2017) 7(7) *Oñati Socio-legal Series* [online] 1445–64. Available from: http://ssrn.com/abstract=3067359 (last accessed 12 June 2018).

[44] ibid, 1453–54.

[45] ibid, 1461.

10

Public Legal Education – Legal Capability and the Boundaries of Law

We have looked at the expanding role of clinical legal education in developing awareness of legal needs among those studying to become legal professionals who are already able to offer some support to the unrepresented and also at the world of welfare advisers in the voluntary sector where there is willingness to advise but resources to provide help with family matters are dangerously overstretched. We turn now to the activity known as Public Legal Education (PLE), which brings education and advice-giving together in the form of legal education which aims to enhance public legal capability, always of importance in a liberal democracy but essential in a post liberal state where public support is diminished, as now, after the Act.

The development of PLE, with its emphasis on teaching the public about legal rights and enhancing their ability to access them through developing greater legal capability, carries the risk, as the movement recognises, of a perverse outcome by increasing juridification of personal life, thus increasing demand for legal services while failing to increase their supply. An alternative strategy therefore is to 'decentre' the role of law, and develop other ways of solving the problems which become disputes and then require resolution.[1] The latter approach appears to fit well alongside government's simple need to reduce court use in order to save money, and hence give priority to policies designed to keep people out of the hands of lawyers and courts, both for financial reasons and consistent with the recently prevailing neoliberal context of increasing personal responsibility.[2] As we have seen, these policies rely on removing access to affordable legal help for the majority of the population, while expanding the provision of information and interactive court and out of court dispute resolution, including the move towards Digital Justice.

We will consider both strategies in our concluding chapter.

---

[1] L Wintersteiger and T Mulqueen, 'Decentering law through PLE' (2017) 7(7) *Onati socio-legal series* 1557–80. Available from: http://ssrn.com/abstract=3058991 (last accessed 12 June 2018).
[2] See above pp 23–5.

I. The Legal Education Foundation

The PLE movement began to bring together the work of various fragmented but like-minded agencies under the auspices of the Public Legal Education and Support Task Force (PLEAS) convened in 2006 by Dame Hazel Genn whose report highlighted the concept of legal capability.[3] The availability of considerable initial financial support for PLE can be traced back to the merger in 1962 of the Law Society's law college with the tutorial firm Gibson and Weldon (founded in the 1870s) to form the College of Law, with branches in Guildford and London. The College was officially registered as a charity in 1976 'to promote the advancement of legal education and the study of law in all its branches' and by 2012 was in the top 100 of UK charities ranked by their expenditure.

Following a strategic review in 2012, the College of Law carried out a major restructuring and decided to sell the education and training business, and the College split off from the parent charity and was sold for £200 million, subsequently becoming the University of Law. The proceeds of sale went to the parent charity which was endowed as a Foundation, changing its name to the Legal Education Foundation (LEF) and remained under Royal Charter, officially launched in July 2013 with the announcement of its first six grants. The original endowment was invested and the income yielded is being used to support a number of projects designed to increase accessibility to legal services or to increase public understanding of the law.

Within the first four years, the Foundation had made grants of over £10 million to over 185 projects to advance training and practice in legal education and services, to ensure legal needs are met, and to increase access to employment in the legal profession, in particular advancing social mobility and diversity. LEF initiated the Justice First fellowship programme which supports trainee solicitors who wish to work in the field of social welfare. LEF also works with other charities, including the Sutton Trust, on the Pathways to Law programme, and with the Baring Foundation on widening public access to legal advice. Details can be found on the official website.[4] In addition, LEF seeks to develop a robust evidence base of needs and ways of meeting these needs, and in particular to understand the role of technology in achieving these objectives. For example, on 8 March 2016 LEF issued a press release welcoming the proposals from Lord Briggs for a Civil Courts Structure Review for legal disputes over money to be settled online, but at the same time warned that adjudication is a judicial function which may not be properly delegated to someone without the independence to be expected of a judge.[5]

---

[3] Public Legal Education, *Developing Capable Citizens: The Role of the Public Legal Education, Report of the PLEAS Task Force* (July 2007) www.pleas.org.uk/uploads/PLEAS%20Task%20Force%20Report.pdf (last accessed 16 May 2018).

[4] The official website is https://www.thelegaleducationfoundation.org/.

[5] https://www.thelegaleducationfoundation.org/articles/press-release-legal-education-charity-welcomes-plans-for-digital-courts (last accessed 15 May 2018).

II. Law for Life

The LEF, together with the Baring Foundation, the Ministry of Justice, and others, support the most visible and accessible source of public legal information, the charity *Law for Life: The Foundation for Public Legal Education*. The objectives of the charity are listed as being 'to ensure that citizens are equipped with the knowledge, the confidence and skills needed to deal with the law related issues they are likely to encounter in the course of their lives'. It aims to secure legal capability for all, recognition of the value of public legal education, excellence in the delivery of PLE and to maintain its position as an international centre for PLE.[6] Its activities are listed as being education through information and guidance, research, policy and consultancy, and, through education and training, to work to build the capacity of other organisations to enable them to deliver effective public legal education, aiming to ensure that PLE is embedded in the work of many professionals,[7] including educators, lawyers, advisers, and youth and community workers. This work extends well beyond the legal profession, and, looking beyond concerns about definitions of legal advice, focuses instead on the next steps to take. It is currently chaired by Amanda Finlay (formerly of the Ministry of Justice) and is fortunate in having Lisa Wintersteiger as CEO. The sources of funding listed in the Trustees' Report and Financial Statement in March 2017 are as follows: *Income 2016–17*: Advice Services Alliance – £21,398, Baring Foundation – £20,000, Esmee Fairbairn – £25,000, LEF – £25,000, Access to Justice Foundation projects – £7,532, Ministry of Justice – £91,848, John Ellerman Foundation – £17,502, Trust for London – £1,050, others – £24,949.[8]

Law for Life carries out research in parallel with academic researchers, particularly in the report published in 2015 entitled *Legal Needs, Legal Capability and the Role of Public Legal Education*.[9] This report analyses some of the findings of the 2010 and 2012 English and Welsh Civil and Social Justice Panel Survey alongside underlying policy contexts for PLE and Information (PLEI) and reveals 'on-going significant gaps in legal knowledge and capability amongst the UK population creating substantial barriers to access to justice and undermining the rule of law'.[10] Knowledge of legal rights in relation to family problems was found to be worryingly low, at just below 40 per cent.[11] Most people handle their legal problems without

---

[6] eg, in 2016–17 LawforLife provided Legal Empowerment Courses at the Central European University in Budapest to over 60 participants from 25 countries.

[7] A clinical module is taught to law students at Birkbeck, University of London.

[8] LawforLife: The Foundation for Public Legal Education Report of the Trustees and Financial Statements for the Year ended 20 March 2017.

[9] L Wintersteiger, *Legal Needs, Legal Capability and the Role of Public Legal Education, A Report for Law for life: the Foundation for Public Legal Education* (2016), produced in parallel with P Pleasence, N Balmer and C Denvir, *How People Understand and Interact with the Law* (2015), funded with the support of the Legal Education Foundation.

[10] Report, n 9 above, 1.

[11] ibid, para 3.12.

a lawyer, and lawyer use declined from 27 per cent in 1997 to 6 per cent in 2012,[12] while the incidence of legal problems remained the same. A quarter of those with legal problems now use the internet to solve legal problems, but do so in different ways. The most effective form of use is in seeking contact information concerning advisers.[13] But 'in the search for information online the requisite understanding of the legal dimensions of an issue impinged on the complexity of finding the right key word to accurately seek information'.[14] Finding out about legal rights was only partially successful. The report observes that the then widely admired *Rechtwijser* in the Netherlands produced little lasting increase in confidence and most users expressed a wish for third party review of agreements reached through the platform, but there was a degree of working towards an integrated system together with the legal aid counters (help desks) and legal assistance.[15]

The report argues that understanding of law and legal process is shaped by pre-existing attitudes and beliefs, and social and family setting. Lack of confidence affects the ability to act effectively, and justice policy is found to lag behind advances in health and consumer education where innovative teaching, together with practical help, has enabled individuals to see the value of education and information. Difficulties are compounded by the fact that it is people with low levels of legal capability who are most likely to encounter legal problems. The report recommends integrating PLEI into wider health and social assistance programmes, recognising PLEI as a vital tool in early intervention, preventing problems from escalating later on, and argues that measures of outcomes in the justice sector which look at timely, fair and lasting resolution to legal problems need to incorporate the element of legal capability as fundamental to access to justice and the rule of law.

The Foundation therefore seeks to spread awareness of legal procedures, to help individual exercise their legal rights, to foster self help, to counteract relations of dependency between lawyers and clients and to demystify the law, using the twin tools Information and Education. Techniques have been largely informal, but are now recognising the value of web-based solutions to information needs and online dispute resolution opportunities. These developments proceeded alongside the policy move towards increased marketisation of legal services, which requires greater consumer competence to make choices.[16]

---

[12] ibid, para 3.18, citing P Pleasence, N Balmer and R Sandefur, *Paths to Justice: a past, present and future roadmap* (Centre for Empirical Legal Studies, 2013).

[13] ibid, para 3.34.

[14] ibid. para 3.11.

[15] ibid, para 3.39. 38% of the Dutch population are eligible for legal aid and 31% hold legal insurance. See further, pp 31, 35–6.

[16] Note that the Legal Services Board regulates only the reserved activities of the legal profession, while the provision of legal information and education falls outside the regulator's ambit.

III. AdviceNow

Law for Life hosts the AdviceNow website (originally developed by the Legal Services Commission). If the twin strategies of PLE are empowerment and enhancing legal capability through information and education, how does the key activity, the AdviceNow website, with its excellent for family sections, fit into the picture? To quote the website, 'Law for Life's AdviceNow website translates the law into accessible and engaging information which not only explains the law but empowers you to use it.' By 2016–17 the website was able to offer accessible and helpful information and support to over a million users. AdviceNow's advice on how to write legal information demonstrates their expertise and experience: to be clear what you are trying to achieve: to include only what your audience needs to know: to address the realities of their situation, test it out and signpost accurately. Action guides on *How to apply for parental responsibility without the help of a lawyer, A Survival guide for to Using Family Mediation after a breakup, Applying for a financial order without the help of a lawyer* and *Applying for a court order about the arrangements for your children without the help of a lawyer* can be found on the website.[17]

The Mediation guide emphasises in clear straightforward terms that mediators do not give you legal advice, so it is usually wise to see a solicitor as well, and states that another option is to get a family solicitor to negotiate with your ex on your behalf, while acknowledging that some people cannot agree even with help and have to take the issue to court so that the court can decide.

The Arrangements for Children guide is described as explaining 'how to apply for a court order about the arrangements for your child, who they will live with, and who they will spend time and when'. The guide is described as 'for you if you are a parent and you disagree with the other parent or other family members about where your child lives, how often they see the parent they do not live with and who else they should see'. It is also for people supporting others in this situation, such as PSU volunteers, CAB advice workers and court staff, as well as relatives and friends. The first section is called simply 'things to understand', for example, 'that courts expect a parent to see their children … that court is not the first place to come to, mediation first'. Legal aid is described, followed by what a court takes into account in making a decision (the welfare check list) and finally explains the requirement to attend a MIAM. A pictorial route map sets out a story. Then the guide turns to going to court and answers the questions: which court? how long will it take? It gives information about forms, costs and fees, court rules, applying for an order, urgency, action in case of domestic violence issues, who do I have to tell, what is Cafcass, what a respondent should do, the FHDRA (described in a short film), Consent Orders who can come to a hearing (eg McKenzies or PSU), Dispute Resolution Appointments and Final Hearings. Various terms are explained, for example 'telling your story is called giving evidence … promising to tell the truth is called taking an oath or affirming'. Users are informed that questions will be asked, and 'if you don't turn up the hearing will go ahead without you'.

There is a checklist of how to prepare for a hearing, with Top Tips: to use plain English, to ask a question if you do not understand what is going on, to remember that the judge is not for or against you, to take notes, to listen carefully when someone asks you a question, and making clear that you can take someone with you to take notes and write down what the order says, and that you can ask the Judge what the order means if you do not understand. Information is given about who you may talk to about the case. Examples are given of statements, and Top Tips include advice not to 'go on about what a poor parent your ex is … focus on the child's welfare'. The guide ends with more help and advice tips, and a glossary of terms.

In the guide *How to apply for a financial order without the help of a lawyer* the technical legal elements here are more prominent and much more complex. The guide warns on the first page that it will be of only limited value if the case is what lawyers call a 'high value' case, involving lots of money and property and possibly extensive business interests also, and also that this guide is only for those who are divorcing, not for separating cohabitants or those who have not yet started divorce proceedings. But it lists the kinds of decision which have to be made on divorce about whether to sell the family home, and how to divide up savings and possessions and other property and pensions. The guide warns that it is long, but 'you don't have to read it all at once. You can start by looking at the process in pictures to get an overview of what a typical case might look like, and then use the contents page to find the sections that are relevant to the stage your case has reached'. There is a jargon buster at the end. Readers are told: 'We do not explain what to do if you need financial help from your partner but have not started divorce proceedings yet, or what to do to stop your ex hiding money to avoid having to share with you. If you think you are in this situation get legal help quickly … see More Help on p 63'.

The structure of the guide is similar to the Child Arrangements Guide, starting with 'things to understand', what the court takes into account, what kind of orders the court can make, sorting things out by negotiation and agreement, and a story in pictures. The structure of the process and the forms used are explained: Form A for the application for a financial order, then the notice of the first appointment, Form E setting out financial information, Form G to indicate readiness to negotiate at first appointment, a statement of issues and chronology: the first appointment, then a date set for a Financial Dispute Resolution confidential meeting, where the judge will make a suggestion for the way forward. If both parties accept, a Consent Order can be made. If not, a final hearing may be needed before a different judge.

There are three stages and agreement may be reached at any stage: at the first appointment, at a financial dispute resolution appointment (FDRA), or at a final hearing, where a judge can make the decision if necessary. The process can take a year, and can cost a great deal if lawyers argue every point. The guide advises care in looking for legal advice, describing the possibility of low cost telephone advice, or a fixed fee package, and states that a solicitor must give an estimate of costs before starting work. In addition, there is a detailed guide on how to fill in Form E, and information which defines and explains equity and insurance terms like 'maturity date'. It also provides links to the forms, to Wikivorce, and to the Money Advice Service Divorce and Money Calculator.[18] There is a checklist for financial requirements, a short film about the first 30 minute appointment, and detailed descriptions of how to prepare an indexed bundle for a final hearing and to fill in Form 81 and the statement of information from both parties when seeking a Consent Order in relation to a financial remedy. Both guides end with a Jargon Buster, and information on where to find further advice.

The Law for Life Annual Review 2017 records that in 2016–17 the website 'provided information and support' in 1,064,000 sessions and was used by 806,776 people. 60 per cent of their survey respondents were women, and 46 per cent recorded some disability.[19] 10 per cent of users are acting for others, but are not an adviser, and another 10 per cent are in the advice sector or are lawyers.[20] Lisa Wintersteiger[21] described their current focus as moving forward from providing information and increasing levels of confidence to dealing with the 'pinch points' where there is still a need for legal expertise, for example, in trying to understand whether a judgment is fair. She is also concerned about the step from knowledge to action, especially the need not to feel isolated. Law for Life and AdviceNow have had significant success with their programme designed to assist persons with respect to Personal Independence Payments (state benefits for people aged 16 to 64 with a disability or health condition)[22] supported by the relationship with health professionals. Wintersteiger stressed the need for 'trusted intermediaries' (in Canadian terminology) or 'barefoot' lawyers (a term deriving from a Chinese practice where activists do not need a full professional qualification but have acquired a specific expertise). According to her there is a view that people do not use lawyers not just because they cannot afford it but because they do not trust the legal professions.

[18] Money Advice Service is being restructured as part of the Single Financial Guidance Body established in 2018 as an Non-Departmental Public Body responsible to the Department of Work and Pensions, which will not have a public interface but instead a funding role for other bodies.

[19] http://www.lawforlife.org.uk/wp-content/uploads/LfL_AR2017_proof6_FINAL.pdf (last accessed 16 May 2018) at 7–9.

[20] Lisa Wintersteiger, Personal communication, February 2018.

[21] Personal communication, February 2018.

[22] This is also the focus of Horizon, a special group founded by paralegals helped by DLA: see p 59.

Despite its name, does AdviceNow provide information rather than advice? We have referred at various places to this distinction.[23] If a broad view is taken that it extends to information with legal implications, such as help with form filling by PSU, this would also clearly include sections of the AdviceNow guides, especially when material is referred to as 'suggestions' or 'tips' or 'warnings', such as that in the Finance Guide about the impact of remarriage on ending spousal support, and the need to sort out finance before entering a new marriage or civil partnership as an order cannot be applied for afterwards. If that is so, the significance of the distinction between advice and information is further undermined. We will return to this in the concluding chapter.[24]

IV. Reflections on PLE

Lisa Wintersteiger has described PLE as part of the continuum of legal help 'not merely as concern for the social welfare needs of the most vulnerable but also as a locus for the meaningful engagement of citizens with the state'.[25] But the process is problematic in a number of ways. Wintersteiger acknowledges the conundrum that, on the one hand, PLE may become a panacea for replacing the absence of urgently needed advice and representation in primary areas of law with an alternative means of accessing justice, while on the other hand it risks falling into the narrative that if only people were more capable they could resolve their own legal problems outside the court and pull themselves up by their own bootstraps.[26] A third possibility however (not raised by Wintersteiger) is that in the short term PLE might increase awareness of possible legal solutions to family problems when access to the professional help needed to achieve such outcomes is unavailable, thus increasing frustration and conflict rather than solving problems. Despite this danger, given the widening gap between the need for legal help as family structures change and conflicts arise, and the diminishing availability of affordable professional help, the recent and rapid development of PLE has become an increasingly important part of the response to a situation where, as Christian Fleck, managing director of Lexis Nexis UK put it at the Civil Justice Forum 2017 'problems are so multifaceted (and) the market so fragmented that I have a struggle to map the provision ... it is doing my head in'.

Law for Life is led by radical thinkers who have some sympathy with the view that the legal profession is contributing to its own demise by protectionism.

---

[23] See pp 17–18, 31, 40, 42, 63, 64, 67, 71, 102, 103, 106, 111, 112–3, 122, 123–5, 135, 143, 144, 147, 148, 150–1.

[24] See pp 172–3.

[25] L Wintersteiger, 'Legal Exclusion in a post-LASPO era' in L Foster, A Brinon, C Deeming, and T Haux (eds), *In Defence of Welfare 2*. Policy Press Bristol (2015) 68.

[26] ibid, 70.

This underlies their interest in self help and legal capability supported by 'barefoot' lawyers[27] as a means to achieving more active citizenship and a more active democratic society. Such intermediaries are hard to find in our present justice system, but there are developments here, for example the group led by Laura Goodwin which is active in regard to land rights in Kenya and Bangladesh. This critical view of lawyers from the radical elements in the PLE movement thinks legal aid was not a golden age, that there is a long history of commodification, market failure and help only in extremis. The attack on legal aid is thought to have been received in silence by the lawyers, in contrast to the response of the medical profession to the attacks on the NHS. Lawyers need a voice in the system. Even law making is thought by these radicals to be simply serving the establishment, as they consider that there is a need for other ways of managing conflict in a plural society. We will revert to these issues in our concluding chapter.

This kind of interpretation of recent developments helps us with the problem associated with the development of PLE identified by Wintersteiger mentioned above where she fears a policy response emerging which might expect people to simply 'raise themselves by their bootstraps'. Wintersteiger and Mulqueen have argued[28] that the division between education and advice is a false dichotomy, arising from the emphasis on legal need which makes the law appear to be the only way of framing social relations. They refer to a widening in the concept of 'legal need' from 'those actively seeking a resolution to a legal problem' to include 'events that raise legal issues that may never reach the formal justice system'.[29] They argue that this emphasis on 'legal need' not only reinforces the proliferation of law (which they call 'juridification') but can obscure the value of other ways of understanding and addressing human conflicts and that PLE can 'develop an awareness of how law could be used as one among a range of ways of dealing with the increasing presence of law in everyday life'.[30] PLE need not only increase awareness of legal procedures, it can also counteract relations of dependency between lawyers and clients, demystify the law and support the autonomy of groups to pursue other forms of political and social action.

Wintersteiger and Mulqueen remind us that it is odd to imagine that people need something (law) that is so highly professionalised and exclusive. They give examples of how problems might be approached (eg, where a landlord is reluctant to undertake repairs) where simple insistence on legal rights is likely to be ineffective.[31] But, taking an even broader view, they explain how 'juridification' of problems can obscure law's essentially political nature. For example framing a problem as bad luck may deprive the person of legal redress, but it may also be an

---

[27] See p 158.
[28] L Wintersteiger and T Mulqueen, 'Decentering Law through Public Legal Education', (2017) 7 (7) *Onati Socio Legal Series* 1557–78.
[29] ibid, 1564.
[30] ibid, 1561.
[31] ibid, 1569.

accurate reflection of the weakness of existing rights. 'A legally enabled citizen is one who can not only gain redress through the courts but also possesses the necessary capabilities for taking an active part in democratic life.'[32]

However, useful as this approach to PLE can be in raising general awareness of the political nature of much of the law, in the case of a person faced with an immediate problem or dispute with legal dimensions, would the legally enabled citizen be better able to handle it independently, or would increased legal awareness increase demand for legal help with legal process? There has been a parallel debate in the field of health education, where it was hoped that increased access to health related information would lead to wiser behaviour with respect to smoking, alcohol, obesity and so on. Sadly there is little evidence that this has been the case. And any attempt to make access to legal rights for those with legal needs conditional on legal knowledge would appear to contravene any formulation of human rights, European or otherwise. If we again draw the comparison with access to medical services, while there has been discussion of sanctions to be applied against those who engage in unhealthy behaviour, there has been none so far for taking them against those without knowledge of medical science. While these arguments give little guidance on how to deal with the current changes to the structure of the legal system which exacerbate the very issues they cover, they take us into new territory, raising important questions about the future role of law and lawyers in society, which we will address in our final chapter.

[32] ibid, 1572. See also B Garth, *The Radical Promise of Legal Education* (Centre for Public Legal Education, Alberta, Canada, 1980); C Menkel Meadow, 'Dispute resolution: Raising the Bar and Enlarging the Canon' (2004) 54 *Journal of Legal Education* 54(1).

11

A Post-Legal World for Family Disputes?

This book arose from our concern about the withdrawal of public funding for legal help with most private law family issues in LASPO effective in 2013. The prevailing message from government clearly set out in the policy paper preceding the Act[1] was that legal help with problems arising from personal decisions should not be the responsibility of the state. We therefore began by looking carefully at the evidence regarding the need for such help[2] and began to explore published reports, interview key people and directly observe the services provided as we tried to map the initiatives developing after the changes effected by the Act. We aimed to describe who is doing what, and comment on what seems to work. The range of activities surprised us, from residual support from government for various bodies and initiatives to pro bono work by the legal professions, the activities of students and the work of the advice sector. But we were left with a number of unanswered questions which we set out here, followed by our thoughts on where they might take us.

I. The Initiatives Summarised

In chapter one we described what we term 'the collapse of the supportive state' as it affects access to family justice, and the continuing need for family legal help. We began by presenting the evidence of the prevalence of such need. In the questions asked in the early surveys, Hazel Genn[3] used the term 'justiciable event' rather than 'legal need'. She was interested in the prevalence of problems for which there could be a justiciable outcome, with a view to raising awareness of what the law can offer, before going on to ask questions about what kind of help had been sought, ranging from talking to friends and family, through general advice, to the active partisan help of a lawyer. The problems included under the label 'family' in these early surveys are not always independent of each other; they may overlap, and there are

---

[1] Ministry of Justice, *Proposals for the Reform of Legal Aid in England and Wales*, CP 12.10, Cm 7967 (2010).
[2] H Genn, *Paths to Justice*, (Oxford, Hart Publishing, 1999).
[3] ibid.

differences of overall definition in the various surveys, such as whether to include domestic violence and children's schooling issues. However defined, family issues have been found to be linked to other difficulties with health, debt, housing and employment.[4] But there is no evidence that a lawyer is the only person who can help, or that various combinations of intervention cannot be effective.

Chapter one also traced the development of legal aid for family matters from the acceptance of government responsibility to help service men and women after World War II, acknowledging the need for help in re-establishing post-war stable family life in a heavily legalised divorce system, to a comprehensive and generous level of support. But after the cost began to rise in the 1980s, legal aid was given a fixed budget, and tightly controlled contracting began in the attempt to secure value for money. As economies of scale were sought, many small firms were no longer able to offer family legal aid services. The government had failed to realise that the rising costs were due not so much to lawyer-driven increases in litigation, but rather to the rising number of divorces, more complex legislation on finance, more wealth to divide derived from more home ownership, and more willingness to contest children issues. A more holistic community-based approach to providing legal help, together with advice services, was attempted during the 1990s, bringing together local sources of advice in CLACs and CLANs, but the different cultures and funding mechanisms of the various agencies made cooperation in seeking a legal aid contract too difficult to sustain at the time. But these relatively recent attempts indicate that the present post-LASPO approach is by no means the only way to work. The Scots have managed to avoid cuts to provision while experiencing similar cuts in funding, and innovative work is developing in other jurisdictions.

Given the failure of government attempts so far to discourage use of courts in family matters by removing access to lawyers, and given the major cuts in expenditure as part of 'austerity' policies across government departments, we were pleasantly surprised by the extent of support to the litigants in person who now populate the family courts, which we describe in chapter two. This is no longer in the form of direct subsidy for using a lawyer, but instead resources are directed to advice and support organisations through the LiPs support strategy (LiPSS) and the aims of the modernisation of courts programme to achieve effective use of IT to simplify process and provide information for users. Following the failure of ADR (Alternative Dispute Resolution, in effect, mediation), the policy focus has turned to ODR (On Line Dispute Resolution). This line of development slowed down as the Dutch leading brand, the *Rechtwijzer*, proved to be both unpopular and unprofitable despite government support. Government here is now more focused on providing information, and is making progress. But research confirms that, while information can be obtained from a website, the step of making decisions

---

[4] See eg P Pleasence, A Buck, NJ Balmer, A O'Grady and H Genn, 'Multiple Justiciable Problems: Common Clusters and their Social and Demographic Indicators' (2004) 1(1) *Journal of Empirical Legal Studies* 301.

about what to do next requires the support of what the Canadians call a 'trusted intermediary'. There are encouraging developments: government departments are now contractually required to set up digital support when taking a service out of direct provision and offering it online, and work on the Alternative Digital Pathway (alternative to court) continues in a more nuanced form with close reference to client needs, and is now complemented by pilot schemes where trusted expert intermediaries (Cafcass) help parties settle children cases even after issuing an application to the court.[5]

Having looked at the role of government, we then considered the activity of the professions (chapters three to six). Pro bono activity is clearly increasing through the Law Society and LawWorks with their organisation of member clinics, and the Bar Pro Bono Unit. Motivations are complex. They include not only philanthropy but the wish to support the reputation of the profession as being socially responsible, or to give young lawyers in city firms experience with clients who are not otherwise available in corporate work, or young barristers the chance to handle complex cases before high profile judges. There is no direct government support as in Australia, where Public Interest Insurance for in house lawyers doing pro bono work is covered by government. (There appear to have been no claims so far in the 10 years of the scheme.) The profession also has anxieties about letting government off the hook by doing too much pro bono work.

The impact of pro bono work on potential clients is limited by the number of hours available, problems of matching expertise to client need, and the general culture/pattern of working pro bono, which is more often a set number of hours rather than full end-to-end casework. It is particularly difficult for members of the Bar to offer firm diary slots. There is no tradition of pro bono work being undertaken by recently retired lawyers, as in the US. The profession is also working to offer more affordable services, such as through free initial advice, use of unbundling and IT and cutting down on administrative costs. Even so, it is increasingly difficult for former legal aid practitioners outside the large firms to stay in business under the combined impact of fewer eligible clients and lower rates of legal aid remuneration. And the quantity of pro bono work done, though representing a considerable commitment and cleverly organised by groups of firms or individuals, remains far from filling the LASPO gap. And if it ever did fill the gap, there is every chance that government would feel able to move the goalposts.

We have illustrated that pro bono legal work by solicitors is currently provided in an extraordinarily confusing range of settings with different criteria for access and levels of help offered. The situation for members of the Bar is even more difficult. The Bar Pro Bono Unit had helped only 470 family cases in 2016–17, less than half of those referred to the Unit by solicitors or MPs. A number of schemes

---

[5] See *Piloting child impact analysis and Positive Parenting Programme*: https://www.cafcass.gov.uk/ 2018/02/01/piloting-child-impact-analysis-positive-parenting-programme/ (last accessed 5 September 2018).

run by barristers had foundered, as being simply too difficult to organise timing and appropriate specialism, with the added stress of direct access. But the judiciary, having taken due notice of the impending LASPO changes, had in some cases made preparations. Although the cuts were intended to reduce the number of cases coming to the family courts, they were followed, after an initial dip, by increases in applications and a large increase in the number of self-representing litigants. Some of the judges needed to deal with cross examination by alleged perpetrators in domestic violence cases, others had cases with a need for translation in care proceedings, or simply with litigants who did not understand what a court could or could not do. A number of Designated Family Judges had set up duty solicitor schemes in their courts, which varied in scope, strategy and level of success. It seems that vision alone is not enough, and that practical and reliable support services matter.

In chapters seven to ten of this exploratory study, we moved from the work of the professions to look at lay support. Chapter seven reports on two examples of unregulated non-professional activity related to legal needs of unrepresented persons appearing in family courts, the Personal Support Unit (PSU) and McKenzie Friends. The PSU, now active in 20 courts, offers a court-based support service for LiPs, drop in or by appointment, with no limit on visits. After LASPO, over half their work consists of family cases. The volunteers are carefully trained *not* to give legal advice. They come from a range of backgrounds, including retired judges, and run a reliable and efficient service. They do not speak in court, though some judges would like them to, but can sit with a LiP in support. There are pressures for PSU to do more, with volunteers reporting that the judiciary would like them to help parties reach agreement, perhaps through some form of negotiation or mediation. The distinction between providing information and giving advice, however, remains difficult. Their line is that if someone knows what they want to do, they can help them to do it. If they do not know, they cannot advise them what to do, but we observed how difficult this approach can be in practice. In the view of some key lawyers, PSU goes too far towards giving advice, such as in help with filling in forms which have a legal implication. People are using terms like 'legal help' or 'divorce coaching' to avoid the issue. But at present PSU is holding firmly to the distinction, however frustrating this may be for volunteers and clients. This secures the confidence of the judiciary and avoids further criticism from the profession and possibly avoids concerns over insurance.

The second non-professional activity discussed in chapter seven was the work of McKenzie Friends, who are not qualified lawyers, but who may sit with the client and speak if asked to do so by the court. They can certainly be seen as offering advice to clients in the conduct of the case in court, but not as 'conducting litigation' on the client's behalf outside the court (such as signing documents, which is a regulated activity) or addressing the court (which is also regulated), but they may do this with the permission of the judge. There is a Society of (fee charging) Professional McKenzie Friends, but there is fear that recognising these as a professional group risks creating a new branch of the legal profession which falls outside the regulatory system. Discussion about attempts to regulate this group remain ongoing, as there are concerns about the commitment of some to a particular view (such as fathers' rights in children cases) and the provision of legal information and advice which is not always accurate or appropriate. In some settings students are represented as following the McKenzie model, though this has been criticised as being inappropriate. So, as with the pro bono practitioners' services, it is hard for a potential client to understand the range of lay support that is on offer in court.

Chapter eight widens the survey of the variety of forms of assistance that may be available (though by no means everywhere). Sitting between professional and lay support are the students engaging in pro bono legal activity. The numbers taking part are impressive. Over half of the LawWorks clinics are university led and funded. But the numbers of clients helped is not so exciting. Bearing in mind that most clinics are only open in term time, and not during exam periods, and that students are not able to give advice without supervision from a practising solicitor, it would be surprising if large number of clients were receiving significant support. Full legal service is rare. We observed a light footfall in a number of clinics offering legal advice, as opposed to high rates of use of court-based Help Desks in family work manned by students. Again, as in pro bono, there were mixed motives. Are the students mainly interested in improving their CV? Is the university mainly interested in improving its degree results, or obtaining data for research? Is anyone primarily interested in helping as many clients as possible?

We describe in detail the CLOCK virtuous circle process, by which students, trained by local lawyers, court staff and their tutors, can help both solicitors and the court, and benefit the client. The model began in Keele but is rapidly spreading to other institutions and requires particular outreach skills from the organiser. We describe another effective scheme where the court help desk is combined with the provision of legal advice by the pracademic in charge.

Having looked at ways in which legal practitioners, either by themselves or along with others, can work with others outside court settings, and the kinds of help available in court settings, the next step is to ask what we can learn from what is being achieved outside the legal system entirely but within the advice sector (the Third Sector). In chapter nine we note that there was no tradition of family work in that sector before LASPO, as family legal aid had been relatively comprehensive in scope. In addition, the advice sector tradition involved supporting the vulnerable individual against more powerful social actors, such as the state, or landlords, employers or creditors. But as we have noted above, power relations also exist within family settings. Yet in the prolonged period of austerity after LASPO it was difficult for advice agencies to consider responding to additional requests for help while existing funds were under threat, and in 2015 less than a quarter offered legal advice for family issues.[6]

---

[6] A Ames, W Dawes and J Hitchcock, *Survey of Not for Profit Legal Advice Providers in England and Wales* (Ipsos Mori for Ministry of Justice, 2015), Figure 3.3.

So the constraints under which this sector operates are real. Nevertheless, the advice sector has many strengths. It is more accustomed to giving advice than defining it, so does not agonise so much over the distinction between advice and information, or insurance cover (although even here an adviser was found disclaiming the power to advise). Skill in giving advice is the essential element of the work. When dealing with benefit claims or debt enforcement, you often just need the guide book, and the training to look up the rules and help the client apply them. It is easy to quantify success in terms of money recovered. Success in family matters is harder to evaluate, in that family law is mainly about the future, not past facts, and the legal framework contains considerable areas of discretion in money matters and focuses on a third party in children cases.

Citizens Advice (CA) contributes to the post-LASPO gap in a number of ways. One is CourtNav the interactive website for making divorce applications, described in chapter four,[7] and project funding through the local CA has supported a court family adviser in one city for a year. The aim was not to appoint a lawyer but an advice worker. But, as described in chapter nine, there were confused messages about whether advice can or cannot be given. The work is getting harder, particularly to find a specialist adviser or to refer on. But the skills of identifying the issues, discovering the appropriate next step and moving towards it are of great value. The advice worker will always record what advice was given, and will be insured to do this work. Perhaps this is not so different from legal practice. We also described[8] secondary legal consultation by Gingerbread, the national organisation for lone parents, where a non-lawyer helpline advice worker could translate for the caller what the law is about (eg, the child's best interests and not judging unpleasant behaviour by the other parent) and give practical advice or refer to a panel of pro bono family lawyers. But the advice worker could also talk regularly with a specialist family barrister for advice on issues affecting a number of cases. The Canadians call this secondary consultation, and it provides another example of effective use of time, and effective co-working between lawyer and advice worker.

II. Impact Evaluation

What do we know of the impact of these activities? As we noted in chapter two, government is pressing forward with its programme to modernise the courts and for that purpose to digitise the process, including applying for a divorce online,[9] enabling courts to accept applications and other documents online, and even requiring bundles of documents to be submitted online though they may have to be scanned into the system. There was initial anxiety about whether the court staff,

---

[7] See pp 79–80.
[8] See pp 146–9.
[9] https://www.gov.uk/apply-for-divorce.

reduced in numbers, and not necessarily sufficiently experienced, would be able to cope, but the changes appear to be progressing relatively smoothly. Evaluation of this kind of change tends to consist of measuring targets reached and the completion of a process. But IT is also being used by government, as well as independent providers, to give information and guidance about how to take steps to resolve a family matter.

In this regard, government plans have been affected by the failure of the *Rechtwijzer* in the Netherlands, as described in chapter two, so an element of caution can now be observed in moving to digital services, aiming at user-led design, and it is now a requirement across government that when any service becomes digital rather than face-to-face, there must be a contract to provide support for users. Government has published a Digital Service Manual,[10] and the Ministry of Justice has a contract with the Good Things Foundation, based in Australia, to provide a digital assistance service for family matters. Under the heading 'Our UK work in numbers', the Foundation claims to have supported 2 million people to gain digital skills, of whom 84 per cent were socially excluded.[11] Nevertheless, it remains obscure as to how outcomes can be measured, and it is notable that the successor to *Rechtwijzer* in the Netherlands, 'Justice 42', which declares that 'Instead of the tournament model where two lawyers fight for their clients, the clients themselves are led through a guided mediation process that seek the best solution for the couple and their children', makes no mention of law or legal advice. Such websites, like the Parent Guide Family Wizard,[12] an online diary designed to help members of separated families organise their lives, may be very useful in avoiding conflict, but what does it have to do with law? It may be an aid to the functioning of the justice system, by helping parents to comply with an agreement reached either through the courts or privately. But it may equally help to sustain a totally unfair and even harmful agreement reached privately or without reference to the legal position under the Children Act 1989.

As regards the legal profession, in chapters three and five we noted the constraints under which solicitors and (particularly) the Bar operate, which limit the extent to which they can replace the legal services lost after LASPO. In chapter three we referred to the extent of LawWorks clinics (223) and client surveys in Wales which revealed that, after attendance at a clinic, 81 per cent felt less stressed, 67 per cent felt their physical or mental health had improved and 44 per cent felt that (where applicable in their case) they had avoided going to court. This work is now being carried out on a national basis.[13] Similarly the PSU's 'Spot' surveys, referred to in chapter seven,[14] record high levels of customer satisfaction, thus

---

[10] https://www.gov.uk/service-manual (last accessed 5 September 2018).

[11] https://www.goodthingsfoundation.org.au/home (last accessed 5 September 2018).

[12] See OurFamilyWizard.com.

[13] See J Sandbach and M Gregor, 'Hearing the Client's Voice in Pro Bono – What helps and What gets in the Way?', Paper given at the Access to Justice and Legal Services Conference (University College, London, June 2018).

[14] See p 107.

supporting the case for funding. CLOCK, Community Legal Outreach Keele, the university based support programme described in chapter eight, also collects and records a great deal of information which it analyses with care both to improve services and also to provide potential research data to the university which supports the project financially. Finally, in the private sector, where fundraising is not an issue (although providing a good service with due client care is an important consideration), DLA Piper (whose work is discussed in chapter three) recently reviewed various aspects of their pro bono work. One of the areas reviewed was the comparative international research undertaken for NGOs to support legislative reform. They found that although the comparative research often took up to three years to have an impact, it was achieving it, and was valued by the users. They also undertook a review of one-off, face-to-face advice clinics. This review found that the local single advice session, usually with a young lawyer with support but working outside his or her area of special expertise did not lead to high levels of client satisfaction, and so the firm made a decision to transition its clinics away from one-off face-to-face advice towards specialist clinics which offer end to end casework for individuals in specific areas of identified legal need. Because the new clinics provide advice and representation in just one discreet area of law, the lawyers can be trained to a higher standard. Various forms of service are therefore attempting data collection, and there is a variety of motivations at work, with varying degrees of success.

However, a 'pure' examination with a statistically robust sample of what kinds of intervention are most effective for different kinds of client or different kinds of problem at different states of resolution, is hard to find. Indeed this is generally difficult in family matters where there are many additional factors involving new partners, new children, new jobs or a new house. It may take time to see the outcome, and assessment of success may vary between parties and professionals. For example, the Manchester Cafcass pilot was designed to reduce applications to court. This can be measured. But it is not possible to see whether the absence of a court hearing and possibly of an order resulted in a resolution of the problems over the long term, or whether the situation deteriorated further.

The difficulty of assessing the quality of legal aid work is not new. It became acute when the need arose to select which law firms might receive a legal aid contract from the Legal Services Commission. Client feedback was not thought to be sufficiently rigorous, and so a process for selecting samples of case files and subjecting them to peer review was developed.[15] This method is well established now in many jurisdictions, but cannot be applied in the advice sector, which does not typically create case files. For example, while it appears to be the case that the PSU can be of great assistance to the court and clients when working with and supporting another pro bono activity where professionals are pressed for time and need administrative backup,[16] the outcomes for the individuals involved are

[15] See A Sherr, R Moorhead and A Paterson, *Lawyers: The Quality Agenda vol. 1 Assessing and developing competence and quality in legal aid; the report of the Birmingham Franchising Pilot* (HMSO, 1994).
[16] See pp 98–100, 108.

hard to evaluate. And in the case of PLE, with its aim of improving public legal capability and developing websites, in particular, AdviceNow, widely regarded as the most successful of the various independent sites, it is difficult to carry out evaluation as there are so many factors affecting the outcome of any family matter and it is not practicable to attempt a randomised controlled trial. It may not be possible to gather more than a simple customer satisfaction rating.[17] This is often frustrating for those coming from the advice sector, where it has been possible to quantify the monetary gains that benefits or debt advice has achieved for clients.

III. Which Way Forward?

We can see that information-giving about family matters is developing fast. There is more concern to provide support for those who find digital process difficult. While some digital sources, such as AdviceNow, are excellent and may be all that some individuals need, there is still a way to go in recognising that knowledge is a large step beyond information, and a trusted intermediary may be essential for many individuals in enabling them to decide how to use this information and move towards solving a problem or resolving a dispute. This role requires some specific expertise, such as regarding court process, the framework and orientation of the law, and on the limits of what a court might accept.

A. Is a Fully Qualified Lawyer Always Needed?

However, this may not necessarily require a fully qualified lawyer. Our discussion of the advice sector suggested the potential for specific supplementary training for advice workers, not unlike secondary specialism training for young LawWorks pro bono practitioners.[18] But equally, the adviser needs to be able to detect if the issue requires a further level of legal expertise, or if the dispute is too entrenched to be resolved. In that case, the adviser needs to be able to make the appropriate onward reference. If proceedings in court are necessary, it may be sufficient in relatively straightforward cases (such as uncontested applications for certain orders) for a party or parties to represent themselves with the kinds of support offered by the PSU. We might also learn from the work of the pro bono group (Horizon), discussed in chapter three, where trainee paralegals had decided to specialise in an area where they felt there was not too much law to learn, nor barriers to representation, namely, Personal Injury Payment applications and appeals to DWP tribunals. In this way they were helping the maximum number of clients while developing their career prospects. They had an 85 per cent success rate in terms of awards made and appeals succeeding.

---

[17] A Sherr, R Moorhead and A Paterson, 'Transition Criteria: Back to the Future' (1993) 7 *Legal Action* 7.
[18] See pp 150–1.

So rather than thinking only about *lawyers*, we need also to think about changing professional boundaries and look outside the legal professions, and learn for
example how things which used to be done by medical doctors are now being
done by nurses or pharmacists with specific extra training. We see clinical assistants in general practice who have had a year less of medical training but make a
strong contribution. And in medicine more is expected of the patients. They need
to give a good history to take part in the treatment decision making, and to comply
with the agreed regime proposed ('stop smoking!) In the world of teaching, the
role of teaching assistants and Newly Qualified Teachers (NQTs)[19] is expanding.
Access to the highest levels of expertise is being more appropriately allocated. Not
everyone with a minor infection expects to see a hospital consultant. The pharma-
cist is becoming a much more widely used source of medical advice.[20]

We can observe the same process in the creation of 'Limited License Legal Tech-
nicians' (LLLTs) in Washington State. LLLTs acquire qualification after three years
of training (which is considerably shorter, and cheaper, than for a full legal qualification), may give legal advice (presently confined to family law matters) and own
law firms.[21] While we believe that private family law issues should not be kept
out of the scope of legal aid as it now is, we believe that many of the matters dealt
with by lawyers under the previous legal aid system could be treated in a different
way by advisers with enhanced training as described above. Pro bono activity, law
schools clinics and volunteer activity all have a role to play, but alone cannot fill the
LASPO gap. They also serve other purposes. But, together with those activities, a
significant contribution could be made to filling the gap by developing the advice
sector, whether through Citizens Advice or other settings. As was stated in the
Evans Review of Legal Aid in Scotland: 'Advice services provide a critical service
to facilitate early and effective resolution to problems, preventing these escalating,
and avoiding court action. The positive impact on lives can be considerable and
the economic gain significant'.[22]

We are of course aware of the financial constraints affecting that sector. But in
addressing both the personal and social costs of the absence of early legal advice,
it is necessary to take into account all reasonable options. That still leaves the issue
of availability of legal expertise for those without the necessary financial means
in cases which cannot be resolved through the adviser or where a fully legally
qualified professional is needed for court proceedings. We believe that in appropriate cases this could be provided on a publicly funded basis, in the same way as

---

[19] These are qualified teachers who have not yet completed their year's induction period.

[20] See https://nhs.uk/NHSEngland/AboutNHSservices/pharmacists (last accessed June 20 2018).
See Harvard Law School, Center on the Legal Profession, 'Addressing the Supply Problem: how medicine made space for physician assistants' *The Practice*, 4 July 2018: https://thepractice.law.harvard.edu/
(last accessed 21 August 2018).

[21] https://www.wsba.org/for-legal-professionals/join-the-legal-profession-in-wa/limited-license-
legal-technicians (last accessed 21 August 2018).

[22] M Evans, *Re-thinking Legal Aid: An Independent Strategic Review (of Legal Aid in Scotland)*
(February 2018) 56.

mediation is presently publicly funded, by a fully qualified lawyer advising clients together in what we have elsewhere called 'lawyer-assisted family mediation'.[23] In cases where this is not appropriate, such as where the parties are too conflicted, adequate legally aided advice and representation should be available. The overall result would be in essence what has been described as a 'mixed model', recommended in Scotland on the basis that 'any local advice service receiving an enquiry about legal assistance would be required to at least signpost and, better still, refer the client where that service was not able to help. To be effective, an accurate database of local service and referral protocols would have to be developed with responsibility for the oversight of publicly-funded legal assistance and for assessing local action plans resting with a central body, with powers to monitor the delivery of the service'.[24]

B. Information and/or Advice?

It may therefore be time to stop thinking in terms of provision solely by lawyers or by non-lawyers, but of a system in which both legal practitioners and others contribute in an integrated way. It also may be necessary to be less fixated on the boundary between information giving and advising. There is a distinction between them, but also considerable overlap and uncertainty with regard to their provision. One only has to think of a label on a tree describing its species and a notice on a post saying 'Risk of electrocution'. Both convey information, but the latter also advises action. This ambiguity has led to many attempts to refine the distinction: for example, the Lord Chancellor's Department 1999 Consultation Paper on Community Legal Services[25] described 'Information' as being where the customer 'wants to know the rights or obligations he or she has in a particular situation and what his or her options might be' so that what is needed is information 'specific to a category of problem ... but not specifically targeted at the customer's individual circumstances'. 'Advice' however referred to when the customer wants to 'take action, or is being threatened with action' and wants to know exactly what his or her options are, and how to set about taking them, so what is needed is 'detailed information that is directly applicable to the customer's individual circumstance, including suggestions for action ...'.

However, the individual may wish to 'take action' in either case; and, given that both cases arise from a 'particular situation' it may be very difficult to distinguish between information that is 'specific to a category' and that which is 'directly applicable'. In both cases it is said that the customer wants to know what their options are. In its response to the Consultation, the Advice Services Alliance retained the

---

[23] M Maclean and J Eekelaar, *Lawyers and Mediators: The Brave New World of Services for Separating Families* (Hart Publishing, 2016) 129–30.
[24] Evans (n 22) 62–3.
[25] Lord Chancellor's Department, *Consultation Paper on Community Legal Services* (1999) at 39.

definition of information as being 'not specifically tailored to the circumstances of individual clients' but added a further distinction between 'general' and 'specific' advice. The former was 'basic advice as it applies to the circumstances of individual clients, but not offering detailed help or a full range of services in relation to complex legal problems' often involving explaining legal rights and responsibilities 'in broad terms' but also 'setting out possible options'. The latter covered 'services providing assistance on complex legal problems (entailing) detailed advice, negotiation and advocacy ... and representation at courts and tribunals'.[26] Once again, it may not always be easy to differentiate between 'basic' advice that 'applies to the circumstances of individual clients' and the Lord Chancellor's Department's definition[27] of 'information' as being where the customer 'wants to know the rights or obligations he or she has in a particular situation and what his or her options might be' so that what is needed is information 'specific to a category of problem'. The sharper distinction may in fact arise between 'basic' and 'specialist' advice.

Whatever view may be taken of these matters, it is important to understand what turns on such distinctions. Because giving legal advice is not a regulated activity except in the context of 'reserved legal activities', this may be given by someone who is not a qualified member of the legal profession, though of course they should not claim to be acting as such.[28] The true constraint is their training and competence, and in this regard the distinction between general and specialist advice is crucial. At a certain point a matter may need to be handled by a qualified lawyer, even if the matter is not a 'reserved legal activity'. We therefore believe that there should be no constraint upon properly trained non-lawyers from providing 'general' advice, whether legal or otherwise, and that an important part of that training must be to know when the matter should be referred to specialist lawyers. This corresponds to the views and practices of the second group of employment advisers detected by Samuel Kirwan, one of whom said that 'when you say legal advice, people think solicitors, barristers, wigs and gowns, and formal letters. They don't realise that what they are coming to see is actual legal advice'.[29] This seems to accept that what the adviser was giving could be seen as 'general' legal advice (although not recognised as such by clients) which only became 'legal' advice when specialists were required.

C. Only Resolving Disputes?

Understandably, in the context of discussions about legal provision, government tends to frame the issues as concerning the resolution of *disputes*. We speak of

---

[26] Advice Services Alliance, *Response to the LCD's Consultation Paper*, 1999, paras 3.38–9.
[27] See n 25.
[28] See above pp 12, 60.
[29] See p 150.

'alternative *dispute* resolution', of which mediation is a prime example. The government's goal has been to find a cheap, quick way of resolving disputes. However, as we observed in our study of lawyers and mediators, 'it is possible for people to fail to agree, yet not be in dispute'[30] and we noted that those attending mediation may often be seeking advice as to how their problems might be resolved rather than the resolution of a dispute between them. Therefore, the issue can often be presented as one of problem solving rather than dispute resolution.[31] We have noted above how in many cases this advice, even if legal, may be suitably provided by non-legal professionals. But we should go even further, and observe that the advice needed may not only be regarding legal matters, but concern wider ranging problems one or both of the parties are facing.

We observed earlier[32] the evidence that family problems frequently present themselves in clusters: a relationship breakdown can lead to financial and housing difficulties, and these in turn to health issues: or the causal chain may run the opposite way. Without information and support that addresses these matters, disputes may well arise. This understanding underlays the proposals for CLACS and CLANS, which failed for organisational reasons in this jurisdiction, although the approach taken in Scotland has been more successful.[33]

In this respect, also, advisers with a broader remit than that of professional lawyers may be able to find ways to resolve or mitigate the wider problems, thus reducing the risks of subsequent dispute between the parties. This does not mean that legal issues too may not arise at an early stage which need to be understood as part of an early solution. We have referred to the evidence of the impact of early legal advice.[34] The advice services are well aware of the need to translate a problem into a legal issue where necessary.

IV. The Place of Law in Family Matters

A. The Challenge to Law

We conclude by offering some general observations on the place of law in family matters. In a challenging appraisal of the issue, Jana Singer[35] has argued, with respect to parenting disputes, that, just as the move away from fault-based

---

[30] M Maclean and J Eekelaar, *Lawyers and Mediators* (2016) 82.

[31] See T Tyler, 'The influence of citizen experiences on trust and confidence in the courts', Paper given at the Conference on the Future of Justice, UCL London (May 2018).

[32] See pp 13, 28–9, 100, 163.

[33] See p 30.

[34] See pp 19–20.

[35] JB Singer, 'Bargaining in the Shadow of the Best-Interests Standard: the Close Connection between Substance and Process in resolving Divorce-related Parenting Disputes' (2014) 77 *Law and Contemporary Problems* 177. See also JC Murphy, JB Singer, *Divorced from Reality: Rethinking Family Dispute Resolution* (New York University Press, 2015).

decisions and backward-looking grounds of adjudication encouraged a shift away from adjudication to ADR (because adjudication is ill-suited to forward-looking decisions), so also that shift has undermined the place of both lawyers and legal norms in the process. 'The shift from adversary to non-adversary processes has also reduced the primacy of lawyers and legal norms in resolving divorce-related parenting disputes'.[36] In particular, in the case of parental planning, the 'shift from judgment to planning also changes the nature of the question courts and disputants are being asked to resolve. No longer is that question, Which, among a predetermined set of custody outcomes, would be right or best for this family according to some external set of criteria? Rather the expectation is that the process itself will generate the options and the disputants will evaluate those options according to their own interests and values'.[37]

While Singer's remarks are focused on 'parenting' issues, they could equally be applied to related financial and property matters. Wintersteiger and Mulqueen[38] go even further, arguing that excessive focus on 'legal need' risks over-juridification of the issues, leading to frustration and too ready an acceptance of the legal status quo, and that seeking solutions through law can obscure the need to challenge the power structures created by the law. Our own observations on the importance of addressing problems wider than those that concern the application of law could also be seen to contribute to a general de-emphasis on the role of the law in these matters, perhaps even leading to its confinement to a very narrow and exceptional role.

This movement was of course very evident in the government's severe curtailment of legal aid in private law family matters in LASPO, as demonstrated in the Consultation Paper of 2010 which stated that 'cases which can very often result from a litigant's own decisions in their personal life' were less likely to be considered as 'issues of the highest importance'.[39] It might also be illustrated by the change over time in the three straplines used for Family Law, later known as Family Justice, over the last 30 years by the Lord Chancellor's Department, later known as the Department for Constitutional Affairs, and now the Ministry of Justice. In 1989 the Strapline for Family Law was 'supporting the vulnerable', which appears alongside legislation to promote the best interests of children, in a context of relatively generous legal aid, and an indication that family law was seen as an instrument to help people made vulnerable by their personal relationships. In 2012, the Strapline changed to 'Promoting fair and informed settlement', adopted immediately before the Norgrove Review of Family Justice, reflecting the concern with process and making a justice system more cost effective and efficient and reducing

---

[36] ibid, 190.

[37] ibid, 187.

[38] See p 160.

[39] Ministry of Justice, *Proposals for the Reform of Legal Aid in England and Wales*, CP 12.10, Cm 7967; see J Eekelaar, 'Not of the Highest Importance: Family Justice under Threat' (2011) 33 *Journal of Social Welfare and Family Law* 311.

overall costs. The current strapline in 2018 promises 'Protecting and advancing the principles of justice', which indicates a more abstract purpose, not unlike the ubiquitous puff, 'promoting excellence', with little indication of what these principles might be or where they come from, but presumably including the implementation of legislation, including LASPO. 'Protecting vulnerability' is still retained as a qualification to the legal aid reforms, but is given a very narrow definition, with no appreciation that potentially everyone could be 'vulnerable' to imbalances of power in cases of relationship breakdown.

B. The Role of the Law

However, we believe that the presence of legal norms in this area remains important. Of course it is well understood, not least by family lawyers, that the law alone does not hold the answer to all the problems that can arise in personal relationships. Behaving responsibly, demonstrating empathy and awareness of the practicalities are essential ingredients. As one of the solicitors we interviewed said: 'I have to explain that law can't make people nice, and a lot of things which are unfair are not illegal.' Furthermore, while Wintersteiger and Mulqueen's concern about concentration on law could risk failing to challenge power structures, this may be less of an issue in family law, for while it was certainly true that in the (not so distant) past, family law did uphold social and gender power structures, it can now better be seen as attempting (albeit imperfectly) to provide those vulnerable to the exercise of personal power (often women and children) with a countervailing source of power in their legal rights. As Tony Honoré has observed, while societies 'threaten and coerce' through their laws, people are also 'protected and guaranteed' through law, and that in some ways 'law is more valuable in an oppressive than a benign environment'. Indeed, it could be said that, while law can be a helpful instrument for the exercise of power, it is not a necessary one, whereas it is necessary for protection against it.[40]

Yet it may still be thought that family issues are different; that these are best resolved by the parties themselves. A new divorce procedure effective in France from 1 January 2017[41] might seem to support this view. If the parties agree to divorce and follow the stipulated procedure the marriage will be dissolved without obtaining a court decree and agreements about financial and other consequences will be enforceable as contracts. Yet the law is very much present. They must each appoint a lawyer to take care of their interests; a list of items is specified upon which agreement must be reached, and the result must be checked by and filed

---

[40] See generally, J Eekelaar, *Family Law and Personal Life* (2017), chs 1 and 2.
[41] Law No. 2016-1547, 18 November 2016, Art 50, supplementing Code Civil, Art 229. This account is taken from Frédérique Ferrand, 'Non-Judicial Divorce in France: Progress or a Mess?' in G Douglas, M Murch and V Stephens (eds), *International and National Perspectives on Child and Family Law: Essays in Honour of Nigel Lowe* (Intersentia, 2018) 193–204.

with a notary public. Furthermore, either spouse may apply for free legal advice, and it has been doubted whether this will reduce costs to the parties or the state compared to judicial divorce.[42]

So what then is the role of legal norms in the areas of family law with which this book has been concerned?

i. They Indicate the Scope of Options in Making Arrangements

This includes, for example, the kind of property arrangements possible (both in fact and potentially available through court order), including regarding the home; the types of financial order that may be made, including child support and in some cases issues regarding pensions. Similarly, the norms could indicate how certainty and enforceability might be achieved in regard to such matters and also respecting child arrangements

ii. They Promote a More Inclusive Consideration of Relevant Interests

Singer[43] summarises the expectation of the non-legal process as being that 'the process itself will generate the options and the disputants will evaluate those options according to their own interests and values'. Our evidence indeed supports the view that parties often become fixated on what they think of their own or the other party's interests and 'rights', but these may be very different from those contemplated by the relevant family law. Therefore knowledge of and respect for the principle in section 1 of the Children Act 1989 which requires the best interests of the child to be paramount in regard to child arrangements, and also of the direction to courts that 'unless the contrary is shown' the involvement of each parent in the life of the child concerned will further the child's welfare and that 'involvement means involvement of some kind, either direct or indirect, but not any particular division of a child's time' could point the parties towards, or away from, certain outcomes they might otherwise agree. As regards financial and property matters, appreciation of the well-established legal principle that, despite an assumption that equal sharing of marital assets is fair, financial and property arrangements must as far as possible meet the needs of those involved, especially the children, could be very important in affecting the substance of any agreement reached.

iii. They Provide Standards by which Fairness and Safety may be Evaluated

Discussion of these standards falls outside the scope of this book. But we are concerned with how they do or do not come to bear when people seek solutions

---

[42] Ferrand, ibid, 200.
[43] See n 35.

to their specific problems. This will of course happen if a matter reaches adjudication, or even before that in the preliminary stages of the adjudicative process, where judges can become involved in 'facilitating' an agreed outcome.[44] It may also happen where agreed outcomes are subject to judicial scrutiny, as when a draft Consent Order is presented for approval and conversion to an order of the court. In practice a court is unlikely to delve too deeply into financial agreements especially those made with legal advice,[45] but paragraph 6 of the Practice Direction 12J (December 2017) states that:

> In all cases it is for the court to decide whether a child arrangements order accords with Section 1(1) of the Children Act 1989; any proposed child arrangements order, whether to be made by agreement between the parties or otherwise must be carefully scrutinised by the court accordingly. The court must not make a child arrangements order by consent or give permission for an application for a child arrangements order to be withdrawn, unless the parties are present in court, all initial safeguarding checks have been obtained by the court, and an officer of Cafcass or CAFCASS Cymru has spoken to the parties separately, except where it is satisfied that there is no risk of harm to the child and/or the other parent in so doing.

If parents reach agreement on arrangements for the children before coming to court, and submit these as a draft Consent Order, this will be subject to safeguarding checks by Cafcass before the judge decides whether to convert the draft into an order of the court. This involves checking records to see whether the arrangements raise any concerns concerning the children's safety. However, this only happens if the parents want the arrangements incorporated into a court order, which they may do to make enforcement more secure. There is no requirement that they do this. At one time, before a divorce could be granted, any arrangements for children had to be submitted to the court for certification that they were 'satisfactory or the best that could be devised in the circumstances'.[46] But the court's role was later reduced to a duty to consider only whether the proposed arrangements called for a court order,[47] and was eventually removed completely,[48] so there is now no requirement that arrangements made for the children need be presented to the court at all when divorce is sought.

In this respect, while the new French divorce procedure mentioned above allows a divorce to be obtained without going to court, it does *require* the participation of two lawyers, one for each party, and the lawyers are expected to remind them of the importance of the children's interests. Additionally, the parents must inform the child that the child has a right to be heard by a family judge and they can

[44] See J Eekelaar and M Maclean, *Family Justice: The Work of Family Judges in Uncertain Times* (Oxford, Hart Publishing, 2013) 82, where our data suggested that nearly 30% of activities of family judges could be described as 'facilitating an agreed outcome' and 'providing information'.
[45] *B-T v B-T (Divorce: Procedure)* [1990] 2 FLR 1.
[46] Matrimonial Proceedings (Children) Act 1958; subsequently Matrimonial Causes Act 1973, s 41.
[47] Children Act 1989, Sch 12, para 31.
[48] Children and Families Act 2014, s 17.

proceed without this only if the child certifies that he or she does not wish to make use of the opportunity. As this is unsupervised, it seems the parents are in a strong position to control the outcome. As Ferrand observes,[49] this 'does not replace a preliminary check of the compatibility of the agreed divorce consequences with the children's best interests', and the child's certification whether he or she wishes to be heard by a judge could place a heavy burden on the child. It remains to be seen how far this procedure sustains the place of legal norms in the process.

iv. *Transparency Issues*

There are other risks attached to moving decision-making and enforcement outside the court system and into a diverse market place. Apart from issues of regulation and quality assurance, in civil justice there is widespread concern about the lack of cases coming to trial, where justice can be seen to be done and the shadow of the law can reach out and support private agreements. In family law, private ordering makes it difficult to see whether the vulnerable are protected, whether fair and informed settlement is reached, and on what basis outcomes are reached. As Lucinda Ferguson observed regarding family arbitration, 'the very idea of confidential family arbitration makes supervision and development in accordance with public policy concerns difficult' and she warned that the growth of such 'private' determinations risked the development of a two-tier system of default family justice norms.[50] The first tier would be that set by legislation and the courts, and the second would comprise the norms applied by arbitrators for wealthy individuals wanting matters to be resolved privately and the norms that may influence outcomes for less well-off individuals unable to access the law whose issues undergo informal processes.

All this underlines the importance of having a legal framework within which unique arrangements can be made. But the fact that the parties may disregard it, or one might be overborne by the other, shows that support as well as knowledge may be necessary. This support need not necessarily be provided by professional lawyers. In very many circumstances, trained non-lawyers, who can also assist in other matters (whether relationship issues or concerning other practical matters) should be able to do this. Sometimes mere online information may suffice, but we should be aware of the limitations of that.

v. *The Rule of Law*

It will not be possible to eliminate such risks where issues are settled out of court. But they can be reduced. This requires that it is not only accepted that legal norms

---

[49] Ferrand, n 41, 203.
[50] L Ferguson, 'Arbitration in financial dispute resolution: the final step to reconstructing the default(s) and exception(s)?' (2013) 35 *Journal of Social Welfare and Family Law*, 115, 137.

have relevance in those contexts, but that parties should have access to them. It is for this reason that the fundamental approach underlying the severe restrictions on legal aid (and therefore access to law for many) must be unacceptable. In *R (on the application of UNISON) (Appellant) v Lord Chancellor (Respondent)*,[51] the Supreme Court gave a strong constitutional reason for objecting to this when it held that exorbitant government-imposed fees that deterred the use of Employment Tribunals were unlawful. The Court explained:

> 68. At the heart of the concept of the rule of law is the idea that society is governed by law. Parliament exists primarily in order to make laws for society in this country. Democratic procedures exist primarily in order to ensure that the Parliament which makes those laws includes Members of Parliament who are chosen by the people of this country and are accountable to them. Courts exist in order to ensure that the laws made by Parliament, and the common law created by the courts themselves, are applied and enforced. That role includes ensuring that the executive branch of government carries out its functions in accordance with the law. In order for the courts to perform that role, people must in principle have unimpeded access to them. Without such access, laws are liable to become a dead letter, the work done by Parliament may be rendered nugatory, and the democratic election of Members of Parliament may become a meaningless charade. That is why the courts do not merely provide a public service like any other.

Further, the law sets standards of behaviour for the whole community and, while it is perfectly reasonable to expect the burden of the costs of its application to fall more heavily on those who can bear it better, those less able to do this are equally entitled to its protection. Frederick Wilmot-Smith has articulated an elaborate set of arguments for the importance of 'equal justice', which requires equal access to legal resources. He maintains that public expenditure on the legal system should not be seen as in competition with demands for other welfare benefits, but rather as foundational to securing those other benefits by underpinning them through a functioning and accessible legal system which ensures equality of *status* between individuals, irrespective of their de facto power or wealth.[52]

This applies to family relationships as much as it does to dealings between people, whether within the private or public sphere, outside them. It cannot be rational to exclude from this issues resulting from a person's 'own decisions in their personal life'. Some of the most far-reaching consequences in people's lives (and those of others, such as their children) follow from such decisions, and for that reason are subject to a degree of legal regulation. Moreover, unlike some major commercial decisions, which are usually made by people of financial means, people of all levels of wealth take decisions in their personal life, and can be seriously adversely affected if they go wrong. In any event, problems in people's personal lives are often caused by the behaviour of other people, including their partner. As we remarked earlier when the provisions retaining legal aid in cases of violent and

---

[51] [2017] UKSC 51.
[52] F Wilmot-Smith, *Just Justice* (Harvard University Press, 2019).

coercive behaviour were discussed, power imbalances exist in most relationships, and these can become particularly acute when the parties are in conflict. It is therefore precisely in respect to such matters that the community interest in ensuring protection of the law for all becomes of the highest importance.

These remarks, however, only establish the importance of a legal framework within which these issues can be resolved. They do not mandate its use in every case, or demand the use of legal institutions, or even of lawyers, for the process. It is possible that the needs of those with family matters may be better addressed through welfare services, as is often the case in Germany and Scandinavia, or by enhanced advice services in the way we have suggested. It should be possible for such services and advice to be legally informed and provided by appropriately trained personnel, who may not necessarily be lawyers, but would have sufficient knowledge of the law to know when professional legal assistance is needed. This need may occur at a late stage in the process, but may be even more effective earlier at the stage where a problem has not yet become an entrenched conflict.

BIBLIOGRAPHY

Abel, RL, 'State, Market, Philanthropy and Self-Help as Legal Delivery Mechanisms' in R Granfield and L Mather (eds), *Private Lawyers and the Public Interest: The Evolving Role of Pro Bono in the Legal Profession* (New York, Oxford University Press, 2009)

Adcock, C, 'Shaped by Educational, Professional and Social Crises: The History of Law School Pro Bono Services' in R Granfield, R and L Mather (eds), *Private Lawyers and the Public Interest: The Evolving Role of Pro Bono in the Legal Profession* (New York, Oxford University Press, 2009) ch 2

Advice Services Alliance, *Response to the LCD's Consultation Paper* (1999)

Albeson, J, 'The Sorting out Separation Web App: Fit for Purpose?' (2014) 44 *Family Law* 878

Alcock, P, 'A Strategic Unity: Defining the Third Sector in the UK' (2010) 1 (1) *Voluntary Sector Review* 5

Ames, A, Dawes, W and Hitchcock, J, *Survey of Not for Profit Legal Advice Providers in England and Wales* (Ipsos Mori for Ministry of Justice, 2015)

Bach Commission, *The Right to Justice: Final Report of the Bach Commission* (The Fabian Society, September 2017)

Balmer, N, *English and Welsh Civil and Social Justice Panel Survey, Wave 2* (Legal Services Commission, 2013)

Balmer, N, *The English and Welsh Civil and Social Justice Panel Survey, Wave 2* (LSC, 2013), Table 27; *Legal Needs Survey* (Law Society and Ipsos Mori, 2015)

Bar Pro Bono Unit, *Joint Protocol for Pro Bono Legal Work*: https://www.barprobono.org.uk/pro_bono_protocol.html

Bar Pro Bono Unit, *Justifying Justice, Annual Review 2015*: https://barprobono.org.uk/public/downloads/guf-3/Bar%20Pro%20Bono%20Unit%20annual%20review%202015.pdf

Bar Standards Handbook (February 2018): https://www.barstandardsboard.org.uk/media/1918141/bsb_handbook_1_february_2018.pdf

Barendrecht, M, 'Rechtwijzer: Why Online Supported Dispute Resolution Is Hard to Implement': http://www.hiil.org/insight/rechtwijzer-why-online-supporte-dispute-resolution-is-hard-to-implement https://www-mr-online.nl/echtscheidingsplan-online

Barlow, A, Hunter, R, Smithson, J and Ewing, J, *Mapping Paths to Family Justice: Resolving Family Disputes in Neoliberal Times* (Palgrave, 2017)

Barnett, A, '"Greater than the mere sum of its parts": coercive control and the question of proof' (2017) 29 *Child & Family Law Quarterly* 379

Barry, MM, 'Accessing Justice: Are Pro Se Clinics a Reasonable Response to the Lack of Pro Bono Legal Services and Should Law School Clinics Conduct Them?' (1999) 67 *Fordham Law Review* 1879

Bastard, B, Delvaux, D, Mouhanna, C and Schoenares, F, 'Controlling Time? Speeding up divorce proceedings in France and Belgium' in M Maclean, J Eekelaar, and B Bastard (eds), *Delivering Family Justice in the 21st Century* (Hart, 2015)

Begum, F, 'McKenzie students – an oxymoron?' (2018) 48 *Family Law* 77

Bindman, D, 'Pioneering ODR platform to rein in ambitions after commercial setback' Legal Futures Blog 3 April: http://www.legalfutures.co.uk/latest-news/pioneering-odr-platform-to-rein-in-ambitions-after-commercial-setback

Bindman, D, 'BSB-regulated entities reach 32, with pro bono and solicitor-run start-ups': http://www.legalfutures.co.uk/latest-news/bsb-regulated-entities-reach-32-with-pro-bono-and-solicitor-run-start-ups

Birchall, J and Choudhry, S, *Domestic Abuse, Human Rights and the Family Courts* (Women's Aid Federation of England and Wales, 2018)

Bonkalo, Justice Annemarie, *Family Legal Services Review, Report submitted to the Attorney General of Ontario by Justice Annemarie Bonkalo*, December 2016: https://www.attorneygeneral.jus.gov.on.ca/english/about/pubs/family_legal_services_review/

Bryson, C, Skipp, A, Albeson, J, Poole, E, Ireland, E and Marsh, V, *Kids aren't free: The child maintenance arrangements of single parents on benefit 2012* (Nuffield Foundation)

Buck, A, Sidaway, J and Scanlan, L, *Piecing it together: exploring one stop shop legal service delivery in CLACS* (Legal Services Commission, 2010)

Byrom, N, 'Cuts to Civil Legal Aid and the Identity Crisis in Lawyering: Lessons from the Experience of England and Wales' in A Flynn and J Hodgson (eds), *Access to Justice and Legal Aid: Comparative Perspectives on Unmet Legal Need* (Hart Publishing, 2017)

Cape, E and Moorhead, R, *Demand Induced supply? Report to the Legal Services Commission* (Legal Services Commission, 2005)

Carter of Coles, Lord, *Legal aid: a market-based approach to reform* (2006)

Chang, Yu Shan, *The Mechanisms and Rationale for Integrated Publicly Funded Legal Services: a comparative study of England and Wales, Australia and Taiwan* (Doctoral Thesis, University College, London, 2016)

Citizens Advice, *Annual Report 2016/7*: https://www.citizensadvice.org.uk/Global/CitizensAdvice/citizens%20advice%20annual%20report.pdf

Citizens Advice, *Responsive Justice: How citizens experience the justice system* (2015): https://www.citizensadvice.org.uk/Global/CitizensAdvice/Crime%20and%20Justice%20Publications/Responsivejustice.pdf

Citizens Advice, *Standing Alone: Going to the Family Court without a Lawyer* (2014): https://www.citizensadvice.org.uk/Global/CitizensAdvice/Crime%20and%20Justice%20Publications/Crime%20and%20Justice%20consultation%20responses/StandingAloneGoingtothefamilycourtwithoutalawyerfinalversion.pdf

Civil Judicial Statistics 1988, Cm 745

Clementi, D, *Review of the Regulatory Framework for Legal Services in England and Wales, Final Report* (December 2004)

Cohn, EJ, 'Legal Aid to the Poor and the Rushcliffe Report' (1946) 9 *Modern Law Review* 58

Collier, J, 'The Dashing of a "Liberal Dream": the Information Meeting, the "New Family" and the Limits of Law' (1999) 11 *Child & Family Law Quarterly* 257

Cookson, G, 'Analysing the Economic justification for the Reform to Social Welfare and Family Law Legal Aid' (2013) 34 *Journal of Social Welfare and Family Law* 21

Corbett, NE and Summerfield, A, *Alleged perpetrators of abuse as Litigants in Person in private family law* (Ministry of Justice, 2017)

Courts and Tribunals Judiciary, *McKenzie Friends Guidance*: https://www.judiciary.gov.uk/publications/mckenzie-friends/

Cretney, S, *Family Law in the Twentieth Century: A History* (Oxford University Press, 2003)

Davis, G, *Partisans and Mediators* (Oxford University Press, 1988)

Davis, G, 'Reflections in the aftermath of the family mediation pilot' (2011) 13 *Child & Family Law Quarterly* 371

Davis, G, Cretney, SM and Collins, JG, *Simple Quarrels* (Oxford University Press, 1994) 40

de Bruijn, S, Poortman, A-R and van der Lippe, T, 'Do Parenting Plans work? The Effect of Parenting Plans on Procedural, Family and Child Outcomes' (2018) 32(3) *International Journal of Law, Policy and the Family* 394

Denvir, C, 'Online Courts and Access to Justice: Providing Support for the Digitally Defaulted', Paper given at the Access to Justice and Legal Services Conference, University College, London (June 2018)

Department of Work and Pensions, *Child Maintenance Service 2012 Scheme – Experimental Statistics August 2013–May 2016*

Drummond, O and McKeevor, G, *Access to Justice through University Law Clinics*, Ulster University 2015)

Eekelaar, J, 'Not of the Highest Importance: Family Justice under Threat' (2011) 33 *Journal of Social Welfare and Family Law* 311

Eekelaar, J, *Family Law and Personal Life* (Oxford University Press, 2017)

Eekelaar, J, 'Access to Justice' (A Case-Note on *R (on the application of UNISON) (Appellant) v Lord Chancellor (Respondent)* [2017] UKSC 51) (2018) 40 *Journal of Social Welfare and Family Law* 101

Eekelaar, J and Clive, E, *Custody after Divorce* (SSRC Centre for Socio-Legal Studies, 1977)

Eekelaar, J and Maclean, M, *Family Justice: The Work of Family Judges in Uncertain Times* (Hart Publishing, 2013)

Eekelaar, J, Maclean, M and Beinart, S, *Family Lawyers: The Divorce Work of Solicitors* (Hart Publishing, 2000)

Evans, M, *Re-thinking Legal Aid: An Independent Strategic Review (of Legal Aid in Scotland)* (February 2018)

Feathers, C, 'Bar Politics and Pro Bono Definitions: the New York Experience' in R Granfield and L Mather (eds), *Private Lawyers and the Public Interest: The Evolving Role of Pro Bono in the Legal Profession* (New York, Oxford University Press 2009)

Ferguson, L, 'Arbitration in financial dispute resolution: the final step to reconstructing the default(s) and exception(s)?' (2013) 35 *Journal of Social Welfare and Family Law* 115

Ferrand, F, 'Non-Judicial Divorce in France: Progress or a Mess? In G Douglas, M Murch and V Stephens (eds), *International and National Perspectives on Child and Family Law: Essays in Honour of Nigel Lowe* (Intersentia, 2018) 193–204.

Final Report of the Committee on Legal Aid for the Poor (Finlay Committee) Cmd 3016, 1928)

Flood, J, *The transformation of access to law and justice in England and Wales*, https://www.ces.uc.pt/projectos/mutacoes/media/pdf/THE_TRANSFORMATION_OF_ACCESS_TO_LAW_AND_JUSTICE_IN_ENGLAND_AND_WALES_2.pdf

Fox, C, Moorhead, R, Sefton, M and Wong, K, 'Community legal advice centres and networks: process evaluation' (2011) *Civil Justice Quarterly* 91

Flynn, A and Hodgson, J (eds), *Access to Justice and Legal Aid: Comparative Perspectives on Unmet Legal Need* (Hart Publishing, 2017)

Franklyn, R, Budd, T, Verrill R and Willoughby, M, *Legal Problem and Resolution Survey (LPRS) 2014–5* (Ministry of Justice, 2017)

Garth, B, *The Radical Promise of Legal Education* (Centre for Public Legal Education, Alberta, Canada, 1980)

Genn, H, *Paths to Justice: What people do and think about going to law* (Hart Publishing, 1999)

Gibbs, P, 'Defendants on Video – Conveyer Belt Justice or Revolution in Access' Paper given at the Access to Justice and Legal Services Conference, University College, London, June 2018

Gibson, C, *Dissolving Wedlock* (Routledge, 1994)

Giddings, J, *Promoting Justice through Clinical Legal Education* (Justice Press, Melbourne, 2013)

Gocker, JC, 'The Role of Volunteer Lawyers in Challenging Conditions of a Local Housing Crisis in Buffalo, NY' in R Granfield and L Mather (eds), *Private Lawyers and the Public Interest: The Evolving Role of Pro Bono in the Legal Profession* (New York, Oxford University Press, 2009) ch 11

Goriely, T, 'Rushcliffe Fifty Years On: The Changing Role of Civil Legal Aid Within the Welfare State' (1994) 21 *Journal of Law & Society* 545

Goriely, T, 'The Development of Criminal Legal Aid in England and Wales' in R Young and D Wall (eds), *Access to Criminal Justice: Legal Aid, Lawyers and the Defence of Liberty* (Blackstone, 1996) 412–44

Granfield, R and Mather, L (eds), *Private Lawyers and the Public Interest: The Evolving Role of Pro Bono in the Legal Profession* (New York, Oxford University Press, 2009)

Haden, J, 'Do Litigants in Person have an Unfair Advantage?' *Family Law Online* 3 February 2017: http://www.familylaw.co.uk/news_and_comment/do-litigants-in-person-have-an-unfair-advantage#.WcKQAf6Wxyt

Harvard Law School, Center on the Legal Profession, 'Addressing the Supply Problem: how medicine made space for physician assistants' *The Practice*, 4 July 2018: https://thepractice.law.harvard.edu/

Hilborne, N, 'Relate puts pioneering online divorce project on hold': https://www.legalfutures.co.uk/latest-news/relate-puts-pioneering-online-divorce-project-hold

Hitchings, E and Miles, J, 'Mediation, financial remedies, information provision and legal advice: the post-LASPO conundrum' (2016) 38 *Journal of Social Welfare and Family Law* 175

Hogg, E, Kendall, J and Breeze, B, 'Knitting together? the third sector and the state in England' (2015) *Sociologia e Politiche Sociali* 27

Honoré, T, 'The Future of law and the future of society: thoughts from a world conference' in A Erh-Soon Tay and E Kamenka (eds), *Law-Making in Australia* (Hodder & Stoughton Educational, 1980)

Hood, C, 'The New Public Management in the 1980s: Variations on a Theme' (1995) 20 *Accounting, Organizations and Society* 93

House of Commons, *Briefing Paper 03372* (March 2017)

House of Commons Justice Committee, *Impact of changes to civil legal aid under Part 1 of the Legal Aid, Sentencing and Punishment of Offenders Act 2012 Eighth Report of Session 2014–15 Report* (4 March 2015)

Hubeau, B and Terlouw, A, *Legal Aid in the Low Countries* (Intersentia, 2014)

Hunter, R, 'Inducing Demand for Family Mediation – before and after LASPO' (2017) 39 *Journal of Social Welfare and Family Law* 189.

Hyde, J, 'SRA keen to lift barriers to solicitors offering unbundling' *Law Society Gazette* 1 February 2017

Hyndman, N and Lapsley, I, 'New Public Management: The Story Continues' (2016) 32 *Financial Accounting and Management* 385

Ipsos Mori, *Analysis of the potential; effects of early legal advice/intervention* (November 2017)

Judicial Statistics 1993–4, Cm 2623

Judiciary of England and Wales, *The Judicial Working Group on Litigants in Person: Report* (July 2013)

Kaganas, F, 'Justifying the LASPO Act: authenticity, necessity, suitability, responsibility and autonomy' (2017) 39 *Journal of Social Welfare and Family Law* 168

Kirwan, S, '"Advice on the law buy legal advice not so much": weaving law and life into debt advice' in S Kirwan (ed), *Advising in austerity: Reflections on challenging times for advice agencies* (Bristol, Policy Press, 2016)

Kirwan, S, 'The UK Citizens Advice service and the plurality of actors and practices that shape "legal consciousness"' (2016) 48 *The Journal of Legal Pluralism and Unofficial Law* 461

Law Centres Network, *Funding for Law Centres* (25 November 2014)

Law Commission of Ontario, *Increasing Access to Family Justice through Comprehensive Entry Points and Inclusivity* (Toronto, February 2013)

Law Society and Legal Services Board, *Online survey of individuals' handling of legal issues in England and Wales 2015* (2016)

Law Society, *Pro Bono Charter*: http://www.lawsociety.org.uk/support-services/practice-management/pro-bono/pro-bono-charter/

Law Society, *Pro Bono Manual*: http://www.lawsociety.org.uk/support-services/practice-management/pro-bono/pro-bono-manual/

Law Society, *Pro Bono Protocol*: https://www.lawsociety.org.uk/Support-services/Practice-management/Pro-bono/The-pro-bono-protocol/

Law Society, *The Pro Bono Work of Solicitors* (2016): https://www.google.co.uk/search?q=Practising+Certificate+Holder+Survey+2015&oq=Practising+Certificate+Holder+Survey+2015&gs_l=psy-ab.3...327592.329587.0.329698.5.5.0.0.0.0.160.463.3j2.5.0....0...1.1.64.psy-ab.0.3.237...33i160k1.neZ3MPPgZdA

Law Society, 'Court duty scheme for private family clients' (Law Society, London 2017) available on the Law Society website: https://www.lawsociety.org.uk/support-services/advice/practice-notes/court-duty-scheme-for-private-law-family-clients/

LawWorks Clinics Network Report, April 2015–March 2016 (LawWorks, November 2016). https://www.lawworks.org.uk/solicitors-and-volunteers/resources/lawworks-clinics-network-report-april-2015-march-2016

Legal Action Group, *A Strategy for Justice* (LAG, 1992)

Legal Aid Board, *Annual Reports 1996/7*

Legal Aid Statistics England and Wales (December 2016)

Legal Services Commission, *Annual Report 2006/7*

Legal Services Consumer Panel, *Fee Charging McKenzie Friends* (April 2014): http://www.legalservicesconsumerpanel.org.uk/publications/research_and_reports/documents/2014%2004%2017%20MKF_Final.pdf

Lord Chancellor's Department, *Community Legal Services Consultation* (25 May 1999)

Lord Chief Justice of England and Wales, *Reforming the Courts Approach to McKenzie Friends, Consultation* (February 2016): https://www.judiciary.gov.uk/wp-content/uploads/2016/02/mf-consultation-paper-feb2016-1.pdf

Low Commission, *Tackling the Advice Deficit: A strategy for access to advice and legal support on social welfare law in England and Wales* (Legal Action Group, 2014)

Low Commission, *GETTING IT RIGHT IN SOCIAL WELFARE LAW: The Low Commission's follow-up report* (Legal Action Group, 2015)

Luban, D, *Lawyers and Justice: An Ethical Study* (Princeton University Press, 1988)

Maclean, M, 'Can one lawyer help two clients?' (2016) 46 *Family Law* 212

Maclean, M, 'Delivering family justice: new ways of working with lawyers in divorce and separation' in H Sommerlad, S Harris Short, S Vaughan, and R Young (eds), *The Futures of Legal Education and the Legal Profession* (Hart Publishing, 2015)

Maclean, M, Eekelaar, J and Bastard, B (eds), *Delivering Family Justice in the 21st Century* (Hart Publishing, 2015)

Maclean, M and Eekelaar, J, *The Parental Obligation: A study of parenthood across households* (Hart Publishing, 2007)

Maclean, M and Eekelaar, J, *Lawyers and Mediators: The Brave New World of Services for Separating Families* (Hart Publishing, 2016)

Maclean, S, 'Public Involvement in Private Problems: Legal aid and the family justice system' (2000) 22 *Journal of Social Welfare and Family Law* 145

Marshall, TH, *Sociology at the Crossroads and other Essays* (Routledge, 1963)

Mayo, M, Koessel, G, Scott, M and Slater, I, *Access to Justice for Disadvantaged Communities* (Policy Press, Bristol University, 2015)

McDermont, M and Kirk, E, 'Working in Law's Borderlands: Translation and the Work of an Advice Office' (2017) 7(7) *Oñati Socio-legal Series* [online] 1445: http://ssrn.com/abstract=3067359

Melville, A, 'Giving Hope to Fathers: Discursive constructions of families and family law by McKenzie Friends' (2017) 31 *International Journal of Law, Policy and the Family* 147

Menkel Meadow, C, 'Dispute resolution: Raising the Bar and Enlarging the Canon' (2004) 54 *Journal of Legal Education* 4

Ministry of Justice, *Proposals for the Reform of Legal Aid in England and Wales* (Cm 7967, November 2010)

Ministry of Justice with Department of Education and Welsh Government, *Family Justice Review, Final Report*, November 2011

Ministry of Justice, *Court Fees, Proposals for Reform* (December 2013)

Ministry of Justice, *Report of the Family Mediation Task Force* (2014)

Ministry of Justice and Legal Aid Agency, *Legal Aid Statistics in England and Wales, January to March 2015* (2015)

Ministry of Justice, *Court Statistics Quarterly April–June 2014* (2014)

Ministry of Justice, *Family Court Statistics Quarterly, England and Wales, Annual 2016, October to December 2016* (2017)

Ministry of Justice, *Family Court Statistics Quarterly, England and Wales, Annual 2016* (2016)

Ministry of Justice, *Family Court Statistics Quarterly, England and Wales, Annual 2016*

Ministry of Justice, *Family Court Statistics Quarterly, England and Wales, Annual 2016, October to December 2016* (2017)

Ministry of Justice, *The Findings from the Legal Problem and Resolution Survey (LPRS) Survey* 2014–5 (2017)

Ministry of Justice, *Legal Aid, Sentencing and Punishment of Offenders Act 2012: Post-Legislative Memorandum submitted to the Justice Select Committee*, (Cm 9486, October 2017)

Morgan, RI, 'The Introduction of Civil Legal Aid in England and ales, 1914–1949' (1994) 5 *Twentieth Century British History* 38

Munby, Sir James, *View from the President's Chambers (16) Children and vulnerable witnesses – where are we?* (19 January 2017): https://www.judiciary.gov.uk/wp-content/uploads/2014/08/view-from-the-president-of-family-division-16-jan-17.pdf (last accessed 5 June 2018)

Munby, Sir James, 'Because it is the right thing to do', Speech at the 6th Annual 'Voice of the child' FJYPB Conference in Manchester 24 July 2018, 3: https://www.judiciary.uk/wp-content/uploads/2018/07/pfd-speech-fjypb.pdf

National Audit Office, Ministry of Justice and Legal Aid Agency, *Implementing Reforms to Civil Legal Aid* (2014)

Nicolson, D, 'Legal Education, ethics and access to justice: forging warrriors for justice in a neo-liberal world' (2105) 22 *International Journal of the Legal Profession* 51

Office for National Statistics, *Statistical Bulletin, Divorces in England and Wales 2012* (February 2014)

Office for National Statistics, *Home Ownership and Renting in England and Wales (full story)* (19 April 2013)

Office for National Statistics, *Marriage in England and Wales 2014* (March 2017)

Patel, A and Mottram, C, *Civil Legal Advice mandatory gateway: Overarching research summary* (Ministry of Justice, 2014)

Paterson, A, 'Professionalism and the legal services market' (1996) 3 *International Journal of the Legal Profession* 137

Paterson, A, *Lawyers and the Public Good: Democracy in Action?* (Cambridge University Press, 2012); (2013) 35(1) *Journal of Social Welfare and Family Law, Special Issue*

Paterson, A, 'Does independence matter for Legal Aid Boards', Paper given at the Research Committee on Sociology of Law Working Group, Andorra (July 2018)

Perry, J, Williams, M, Sefton, T and Hadda, M, *Emergency Use Only: Understanding and reducing the use of food banks in the UK* (Child Poverty Action Group with the Church of England, OXFAM GB, and the Trussell Trust, London 2014)

Personal Support Unit, *Annual Report 2016/17*

Personal Support Unit, *Report and Financial Statement for year ended March 2017*: https://www.thepsu.org/media/1318/psu-annual-report-201617.pdf

Personal Support Unit, *Spot Survey Summary Report 2014–16*, May 2016: https://www.thepsu.org/media/1405/spot-survey-summary-report-2014-2016.pdf

Peters, S and Combrink, L, 'Customer Journey Research within the Legal Aid Reform', Paper given at the Access to Justice and Legal Services Conference, University College, London (June 2018)

Pleasence, P, Buck, A, Balmer, NJ, O'Grady, A and Genn, H, 'Multiple Justiciable Problems: Common Clusters and their Social and Demographic Indicators' (2004) 1(1) *Journal of Empirical Legal Studies* 301

Pleasence, P, Balmer, N, Patel, A and Denvir, C, *English and Welsh Civil and Social Justice Survey* (Legal Services Commission 2010)

Pleasence, P, Balmer, NJ, Patel, A, Cleary, A, Huskinson, T and Cotton, T, *Report of the 2006–9 English and Welsh Civil and Social Justice Survey* (Legal Services Commission and Ipsos Mori, 2011)

Pleasence, P, Balmer, N and Moorhead, R, *A Time of Change: Solicitors Firms in England and Wales* (Law Society, Legal Aid Board and Ministry of Justice, 2012)

Pleasence, P, Balmer, N and Sandefur, R, *Paths to Justice: a past, present and future roadmap* (Centre for Empirical Legal Studies, 2013)

Pleasance, P, Balmer, NJ and Denvir, C, *How people understand and interact with the Law* (Cambridge, PPSR, 2015)

Pruett, MK, Schepard, A, Cornett, L, Gerety, C and Kourlu, RL, 'Evaluating the University of Denver's Center for Separating and Divorcing Families: The First Out-of-Court Divorce Option' (2017) 55 *Family Court Review* 375

Pruett, MK, Schepard, A, Cornett, L, Gerety, C and Kourlu, RL, 'Law Students on Interdisciplinary Problem-Solving Teams: An Empirical Evaluation of Educational Outcomes at the University of Denver's Resource Center for Separating and Divorcing Families' (2018) 56 *Family Court Review* 100

Public Legal Education, *Developing Capable Citizens: The Role of the Public Legal Education, Report of the PLEAS Task Force* (July 2007): www.pleas.org.uk/uploads/PLEAS%20Task%20Force%20Report.pdf

Raad voor Rechtsbijstand, *Legal Aid in the Netherlands* (2015): http://www.rvr.org/binaries/content/assets/rvrorg/informatie-over-de-raad/brochure-legalaid_juni2013_webversie.pdf

Report of the Poor Persons Rules Committee (Second Lawrence Committee) (Cmd 2358, 1925)

Rhode, DL, *In the Interests of Justice: Reforming the Legal Profession* (Oxford University Press, 2000)

Riboldi, M, '#FundEqualJustice – increasing public funds for legal assistance', Paper given at the Access to Justice and Legal Services Conference, University College, London (June 2018)

Ryder, Mr Justice, *Judicial Proposals for the Modernisation of Family Justice* (The Judiciary, London, 2012)

Rushcliffe Report, *Report of the Committee on Legal Aid and Advice* 1945 (Cmd 6641, 1945)

Sandbach, J and Gregor, M, 'Hearing the Client's Voice in Pro Bono – What helps and What gets in the Way?', Paper given at the Access to Justice and Legal Services Conference, University College, London (June 2018)

Sandefur, RL, 'Lawyers' Pro Bono Service and Market-Reliant Legal Aid' in R Granfield and L Mather (eds), *Private Lawyers and the Public Interest: The Evolving Role of Pro Bono in the Legal Profession* (New York, Oxford University Press, 2009) ch 5

Sandefur, R, 'Lawyers pro bono service and American-Style Civil Legal Assistance' (2007) 41 *Law and Society Review* 79

Scott-Samuel, A, Bambra, C, Collins, C, Hunter, DJ, McCartney, G and Smith, K, 'Neoliberalism in Health Care: the Impact of Thatcherism on Health and Wellbeing in Britain' (2014) 44 *International Journal of Health Services* 53

Sefton, M, Moorhead, R, Sidaway, J and Fox, L, 'Unbundled and Pro Bono advice for litigants in person: a study for the Cabinet Office' (Office for Civil Society Transition Fund, 2011)

Sherr, A, Moorhead, R and Paterson, A, 'Transition Criteria: Back to the Future' *Legal Action*, April 1993

Sherr, A, Moorhead, R and Paterson, A, *Lawyers: The Quality Agenda vol. 1 Assessing and developing competence and quality in legal aid; the report of the Birmingham Franchising Pilot* (HMSO, 1994)

Singer, JB, 'Bargaining in the Shadow of the Best-Interests Standard: the Close Connection between Substance and Process in resolving Divorce-related Parenting Disputes' (2014) 77 *Law and Contemporary Problems* 177

Smith, L, Hitchings, E and Sefton, M, *A study of fee charging McKenzie Friends and their work in private law family cases*, Cardiff University and Bristol University for the Bar Council, 2017

Smith, R, 'The decline and fall (and potential resurgence) of the Rechtwijzer': http://www.legalvoice.org.uk/decline-fall-potential-resurgence-rechtwijzer/ (last accessed 31 May 2018).

Smith, T and Cape, E, 'The rise and decline of criminal legal aid in England and Wales' in A Flynn and J Hodgson (eds), *Access to Justice and Legal Aid: Comparative Perspectives on Unmet Legal Need* (Hart Publishing, 2017)

Solicitors' Regulation Authority, *Handbook 2011*

Solicitors' Regulation Authority, *A New Route to Qualification: The Solicitors Qualifying Examination (SQE)* (October 2016)

Solicitors Regulation Authority, *Looking to the future: better information, more choice: post consultation position* (14 June 2018)

Sommerlad, H, 'Access to Justice in Hard Times and the Deconstruction of Democratic Citizenship' in M Maclean, J Eekelaar and B Bastard (eds), *Delivering Family Justice in the 21st Century* (Hart Publishing, 2015)

Spolander, G, Engelbrecht, L, Martin, L, Strydom, M, Perovova, I, Marjanen, P, Toni, P, Sicora, A and Adaikalam, F, 'The implications of neoliberalism for social work: Reflections from a six-country research collaboration' (2014) 57 *International Social Work* 301

Stowe, M, 'One couple: one lawyer?' (2017) 47 *Family Law* 737

Streeck, W, 'Markets and Peoples: Democratic Capitalism and European Integration' (2012) 73 *New Left Review* 63

The Lord Chancellor, the Lord Chief Justice and the Senior President of Tribunals, *Transforming Our Justice System* (Ministry of Justice, September 2016)

Trebilcock, M, Duggan, A and Sossin, L (eds), *Middle Income Access to Justice* (Toronto: University of Toronto Press, 2012)

Trinder, L, 'Losing the particulars? Digital divorce and the potential for harm reduction' (2017) 47 *Family Law* 17

Trinder, L, Hunter, R, Miles, J, Moorehead, R, Smith, L, Sefton, M, Hinchley, V and Bader, K, *Litigants in person in private family law cases*, Ministry of Justice Analytical Series (2014)

Tyler, T, 'The influence of citizen experiences on trust and confidence in the courts', Paper given at the Conference on the Future of Justice, University College, London (May 2018)

Walters, M, 'McKenzie Friend "jailed for deceit in family court"' *Law Society Gazette* 17 October 2016: https://www.lawgazette.co.uk/law/mckenzie-friend-jailed-for-deceit-in-family-court/5058352.article

Walters, M, 'New alarm over role of McKenzie advisers' *Law Society Gazette* 3 October 2016: https://www.lawgazette.co.uk/news/new-alarm-over-role-of-mckenzie-advisers/5058028.article

Walters, M, 'McKenzie friend entrepreneur backtracks on student portal' *Law Society Gazette* 28 March 2017: https://www.lawgazette.co.uk/law/mckenzie-friend-entrepreneur-backtracks-on-student-portal/5060442.article

Walters, M, '"No such thing as a quasi-solicitor": judge slaps down paid McKenzie' *Law Society Gazette* 28 June 2017: https://www.lawgazette.co.uk/law/no-such-thing-as-a-quasi-solicitor-judge-slaps-down-paid-mckenzie/5061767.article

Walters, M, '"McKenzie students" have a role to play – but only under supervision – says professor' *Law Society Gazette* 1 August 2017: https://www.lawgazette.co.uk/law/mckenzie-students-have-a-role-but-only-under-supervision-says-professor/5062211.article

Wildblood, S, Goldingham, CW and Evans, J, 'The way we are: accessing the court after LASPO' (2014) 44 *Family Law* 1597

Wilmot-Smith, F, *Just Justice* (Harvard University Press, 2019)

Wintersteiger, L, 'Legal Exclusion in a post-LASPO era', in L Foster, A Brinon, C Deeming and T Haux (eds), *In Defence of Welfare 2* (Policy Press, Bristol, 2015) 68

Wintersteiger, L, *Legal Needs, Legal Capability and the Role of Public Legal Education, A Report for Law for life: the Foundation for Public Legal Education* (2016)

Wintersteiger, L and Mulqueen, T, 'Decentering law through PLE' (2017) 7(7) *Onati socio-legal series* 1557: http://ssrn.com/abstract=3058991

Work and Pension Committee 14th Report: *Child Maintenance Service* (HC 587) (2 May 2017)

Zorza, R, 'Towards the best practice in complex self represented cases' (2012) 51 (1) *Judges Journal* 36

INDEX

Note: For multi-authored works, only the first author is indexed